TREATISE

—

THE LONDON DIARIES

BUSINESS AND MANAGEMENT PERSPECTIVES

DR. GURINDER SINGH

DR. SANJEEV BANSAL   DR. ANUPAMA RAJESH

PRATEEK MANGAL   NIRAV SAHNI

PARTRIDGE

To order additional copies of this book, contact
Partridge India
000 800 10062 62
orders.india@partridgepublishing.com

www.partridgepublishing.com/india

TREATISE

—

THE LONDON DIARIES

CONTENTS

FOREWORD

THE LAND OF A MILLION DREAMS
AND BROKEN HEARTS

"London" - the very name of this iconic capital of both United Kingdom and London evokes strong emotions and associations - wanderlust, fashion shopping, a plush lifestyle, land of the "rich and famous", architecture dating hundreds of years, rainy days, tea-time - the list is endless.

Thousands of students, professionals and immigrants aspire every day, every year to study, work or live in the city they feel will "magically" change their lives for the better. They will live in classic architecture, wear fashionable clothes, and rub shoulders with billionaires, celebrities and even royalty.

The dream does have its challgenges though - The cost of living, dingy one room apartments being shared by several people and located in far-off suburbs, cultural differences and resultant inability to integrate with the English Society; and of course the tremendous work pressure and associated stress breaks many a heart and the will to continue living there.

Fear and disrespect of all kinds of foreigners and immigrants and even "hate crimes" are on the rise across the world. London is no different. The fear may be of losing jobs, on religious grounds or purely racial. This leads to increasing ghettoization of the city where the people want to live in areas where there is a majority of "their kind of people" - which then defeats the very purpose of being a Global Citizen or worker.

The wonders and joys of living in a multi-cultural, multi ethnic international city like London abound. Of course, there are several caveats and there is no "one size fits all" scenario. Hard work, sincerity. tenacity, flexibility are mantras for success anywhere. This book "Treatise - London Diaries" is a compendium of scholarly articles, experiences, view- points, research reports and even some historical accounts all with a perspective to London and United Kingdom and is intended for a holistic reading experience

Happy Reading!!

Anupama

Prof. (Dr.) Anupama Rajesh
Professor, Amity Business School

FOREWORD

It is a privilege to be asked to write an introduction to Treatise - The London Diaries which contains writings from renowned authors from the United Kingdom and India. It contains some reflections and experiences shared by students of Amity University Uttar Pradesh as well as analysis of some key sectors.

The case method in all its many approaches transforms learning in Business Schools. Through class discussion it combines the impact of storytelling with rigorous academic practice and theory. It encourages the application and testing of theory, the questioning of accepted practice, and dialogue between business practitioners and academics.

Students gain experience of real-life decision-making within class-based discussions – this is the essence of the case method. This type of learning also allows students to develop a wide range of vital practical skills essential to their future business careers.

It is part of The Case Centre's role to champion creativity, innovation and original thinking in case teaching and writing and to support its growth in schools and territories around the world. We are pleased to extend that support to the academic editors and student authors of this collection.

The editors of this collection have given their students an invaluable additional opportunity to research and write research cases across key areas of business. Students gain so much from overseas study. I am pleased that this book allows them to share with you the research analysis, and interviews they conducted in the course of their visit to London.

Richard McCracken
Director, The Case Centre
www.thecasecentre.org

Opening Chapter

AUTHOR BIO

Prof. (Dr.) Gurinder Singh
Group Vice Chancellor, Amity Universities

Prof. (Dr.) Gurinder Singh, Group Vice Chancellor - Amity Universities, Director General, Amity Group of Institutions and Vice Chairman, Global Foundation for Learning Excellence & Director General Amity International Business School, has an extensive experience of more than 21 years in Institutional Building, Teaching, Consultancy, Research & Industry.

A renowned scholar & academician in the area of International Business, he holds a prestigious Doctorate in the area along with a Post Graduate degree from Indian Institute of Foreign Trade where he illustriously topped with 7 merits.

He holds the distinction of being the youngest Founder Pro Vice Chancellor of Amity University for two terms, the Founder Director General of Amity International Business School and the Founder CEO of Association of International Business School, London. He has been instrumental in establishing various Amity campuses abroad including at London, USA, Singapore, Mauritius & other parts of the world.

To understand the dynamics of Industry, Dr. Singh went on a sabbatical to Industry for one and half years and spearheaded the indigenous and international strategic operations of a renowned Industrial group with a business strength of INR 200 billion in the capacity of Chief Executive Officer.

He has spoken at various international forums which includes prestigious Million Dollar Round Table Conference, at Harvard Business School, Thunderbird Business School, NYU, University of Leeds, Loughbrough Business School, Coventry Business School, Rennes Business School, Essex University, UK, University of Berkeley, California State University, USA, NUS, Singapore, and many more.

He has received more than 25 International and National awards and has graced a host of talk shows on various TV Channels.

He is a mesmerizing orator and has the rare ability of touching the human soul.

He is internationally recognized as a known Professor in the area of Management and is known in the field of academics as an institution builder, a writer, professor, distinguished academician, a top class trainer, International Business Expert & the Champion of the Hearts of Students.

Opening Chapter

Prof. (Dr.) Gurinder Singh
Group Vice Chancellor, Amity Universities

It has been said that in the earlier times the "Sun never sets…" in The United Kingdom, as for many centuries, large portions of the World were under its direct or indirect control. London had been the centre of world power for several hundred years. Hence the English influence is still felt in many countries of the world such as Australia, Africa, India and many more.

The British have been discredited or credited – depending on the perspective of the Historians but nevertheless contribution of the English to both the economic and cultural evolution of the world has been note-worthy, and been significant to its development. "English – the universal language of business", has been a uniting medium and is probably its biggest gift to the world.

London being one of the most cosmopolitan metropolitan of the world sees the confluence of almost all nationalities, races and religions. It thus sees an amalgamation of all kinds of view-points and ideologies. High on Intellectual Capital, The United Kingdom fosters innovation and research which has already helped millions of people. Capability of United Kingdom's educational institutions to stay relevant with the times is remarkable. Their ability to match educational and research outcomes to the requirements of contemporary industry has made it, one of the most preferred locations for hundreds of students across the world for pursuing higher education as well as research.

London's ability to adapt with the times is also evident from the way it emerged from its recession in the 1950s to turning the London City into an industrial centre and then to a service based economy presently. Today, 9 out of 10 jobs in London are in the service industry, especially in the Banking and Insurance sector. London's support to Indian industries, including Bollywood has been commendable; several Bollywood films have been shot here over the years in picturesque locales like Borough Market, Westminster Palace, London eye etc. London continues to thrive and attract people with talent and potential to make use of endless opportunities and make a better life for themselves.

Amity University has come a long way from its single campus in Noida, India in the mid 90's to several campuses across the World. Our aim has always been to create an educational environment at par with International Standards which can help students of our country prepare for challenges faced by the society and the World, both today as well as in future. Initiatives to help students apply their theoretical knowledge to practical scenarios are being implemented in all our degree courses.

At Amity, we strive to create an environment of achievement by constantly guiding and mentoring our students and motivating them to excel. We believe that no matter what the academic achievement is one can still be a "champion" if the value system is in place. Despite any kind of hardships an individual can rise to echelons of the Society with constant support and motivation. The role of a teacher is to understand the strength of the student and then give him confidence that this strength can help him/ her do well in life. And if they are able to do that, then positions, money, satisfaction, will keep on coming automatically. Life is full of challenges and we at Amity are ever committed to teach our students how to overcome those challenges and win.

It has been a challenging as well as an exciting time for us. Amity might be the only Asian University to have campuses across major cities of the world, and setting up of each campus had its own set of challenges. As part of our International exposure initiative, we have just launched an Internship Abroad Program where we give our students a fantastic opportunity to either work abroad or complete a semester of their program abroad. This will definitely help students get exposure to life across the globe and help them understand the various international perspectives in solving challenges.

I take pride in Amity University's ability to encourage youngsters towards Innovation and Entrepreneurship, and it has always motivated me to liaison with renowned academicians of the United Kingdom to create international opportunities. My objective is simple: not only should students innovate but should also be motivated to discover life outside traditional streams. We have a special focus on research which is all about understanding the mindset of targeted testing audience.

London Diaries is another initiative to enable students to understand the positives and challenges of life in UK, in terms of Scientific, Commercial and Domestic perspective. Like everything in life, living/ residing/working abroad has its own set of challenges and difficulties Students will get an enjoyable exposure to understand this through the articles of our various co-authors of this book.

I am happy to be a part of this initiative of "London Diaries" which intends to inspire students through cases on London by various authors and students.

Happy Reading!

Prof.(Dr.) Gurinder Singh
Group Vice Chancellor, Amity Universities
&
Vice Chairman, Global Foundation for Learning & Excellence

Changing Paradigms of Study Abroad

AUTHOR BIO
Prof. (Dr.) Sanjeev Bansal

Dean - Faculty of Management Studies & Director, Amity Business School, Amity University Uttar Pradesh

Prof. (Dr.) Sanjeev Bansal is Dean FMS & Director of Amity Business School, Amity University Uttar Pradesh. Under his leadership ABS has scaled heights and has been ranked in the top ten Business Schools of India in four consecutive years in succession. An admired academician, he is Ph.D and D.Litt, his doctoral work is an exemplary study in the area of Decision Sciences from Delhi. In an acclaimed career span of about 28 years in teaching, research and consultancy, he has been invited to be a part of several prestigious academic / professional bodies and in his advisory capacity, has steered them to success.

He is an avid researcher and has more than 150 research papers in prestigious journals to his credit. He has authored 27 books and has guided 17 research scholars to produce works of immense educational impact.

Apart from his areas of specialization, he also likes to explore and research the vistas of spirituality, management and quality of work life. During his distinguished career he has had many accomplishments and is hailed as an institution builder, a loved teacher and an ardent researcher.

Changing Paradigms of Study Abroad

Prof. (Dr.) Sanjeev Bansal

Dean - Faculty of Management Studies & Director, Amity Business School, Amity University Uttar Pradesh

INTRODUCTION

Education is the process of facilitating learning or the acquisition of knowledge, skills, values, beliefs and habits. The four challenges faced per the British Council of India Report on Status of Indian Education are - supply-demand gap, low quality of teaching and learning, constraints on research capacity and innovation and uneven growth and access to opportunity. Key challenges facing the system include quality assurance, credit transfer systems, movement between higher education and vocational skills streams and teacher training in higher education. There is an urgent need for systemic change in affiliated colleges to improve the quality of teaching and learning. Private businesses are waiting impatiently to enter the higher education market. The private sector will continue to grow, but 'for-profit' higher education is unlikely to be sanctioned soon.

Increasing internationalisation in research and teaching is strongly supported by the Indian Education sector and considered vital by Indian institutions in developing India's capacity in research and innovation, driving up India's institutional rankings and increasing the quality of teaching and learning. There is an eventual move towards international credit recognition to enable increased student mobility, although this process will have its own complexities. Institutions aiming for internationalisation look beyond sending students abroad; there is also strong demand for influx of international students and faculty to India. Many administrators and strategists feel that the restrictions on foreign faculty being hired in India needs to be lifted. Limited collaboration with industry is also an inhibiting factor. Indian institutions could engage with industry in the development of science parks, incubation centres and technology transfer units and there is interest in working with the United Kingdom on systemic support and institutional models in this area

Educationists in the private sector are frustrated with the lack of freedom they have under the affiliation system and have aspirations of becoming autonomous private institutions in their own right; some of the better funded institutions are looking to develop research capabilities, however they believe that strong industry links will attract international higher education partners interested in developing technology transfer. Digital learning technology and blended learning can also increase overseas collaborations. Some are planning to diversify as several of their markets are close to saturation.

Demand of courses for mature learners and for current students looking to enhance their employability, and develop entrepreneurial skills are creating new markets and new requirements for Higher Education Institutions. There is also a need to nurture the next generation of Indian researchers, through providing: early stage research facilitation experience and international networking;

Some of the possible notable areas of international engagement in consideration of these two broad areas of engagement, outlined are - Institutional collaborations in teaching and learning, Research collaboration, Enterprise education, entrepreneurship, links with industry, collaboration in pedagogies and design, establishing incubation centres and innovation units, Digital learning technologies, Blended learning and MOOCs have immense potential.

The 3 W's of SAP

The key moderating factors of Study Abroad Program (SAP) are prestige and quality of foreign education, the opportunity to gain practical experience overseas through internships and eventual employment. The potential for long-term residence and immigration after education certainly improves a destination country's attractiveness.

As the traditional Indian student market is primarily concerned with maximizing value and consider post-study working opportunities a key part of their return on investment, restrictive visa and immigration policies can significantly shift their preferred study destinations. Industry demand for science, technology, engineering and mathematics grads motivates a high proportion of pragmatic program choices – in the US, 36% of Indian students study engineering and 34.9% study mathematics and computer science.

Majority of Indian students abroad are in master's level programs or higher, as the nation's investments in higher education have yet to deliver graduate studies comparable to international competitors. An emerging segment of "highfliers" (academically successful with access to financial resources) are increasingly interested in bachelor's programs, life sciences and other alternative study options.

In such a large nation with diverse ethnicities, values and development, there is some variation in degree interest depending on the region. Surveys of secondary schools point out that, MBAs seem to be most popular in business hubs like Mumbai while bachelor's degrees are relatively more popular in the southern part of the country

Universities in the United Kingdom are, for the most part, collegiate universities, similar in structure to Delhi University. In this structure, a number of colleges responsible for the teaching process are affiliated to a single university, which is responsible for the award of degrees and other administrative duties. Colleges may enjoy varying degrees of autonomy. The exceptions are the so called red-brick universities, which were established in the Victorian era, and are largely engineering and technical institutions. Degrees normally take three years to complete. The tertiary education system here is significantly different from that in the rest of the UK. Degrees are normally four years long, with the students being able to take a wide variety of optional and external courses and change to a different degree after the first two years. The last two years, called 'honours year', is dedicated to the subject of the degree and the preparation of the dissertation.

The United States of America has the world's largest tertiary education system. It is unique in the world for its strong emphasis on a liberal arts education, with a large number of courses and universities requiring students to study a wide array of subjects before specialising in any single field. In addition to liberal arts colleges, there are also a number of research universities, which produce world-leading research. For their high-quality teaching and research, these universities are renowned the world over. At both liberal arts colleges and research universities, degrees are normally awarded after four years of studies.

Singapore is home to several high-quality universities, and is a popular destination for Indian students. In addition to the numerous public and private universities, a number of international universities have also established campuses in Singapore. Universities in Singapore, particularly the National University of Singapore, are well-known amongst international students for high standards of teaching, and courses in medicine and engineering are immensely popular.

Regulation of universities in Canada is the responsibility of the provinces, not the centre. As such, there is a great deal of variance in the governance of Canadian universities. Universities in Ontario, Quebec, and British Columbia are known for their extremely high standards of teaching across subjects, and are a popular choice for international students looking to study a wide array of subjects. Three-year degrees are the most common, but they are slowly being phased out in favour of 4-year degrees.

Some of the best universities in the world are found in Australia, with several being permanent mentions in the top 100 universities internationally, according to a number of rating systems. Australia's universities are extremely autonomous and self-regulating, with little governmental interference and may differ significantly with each other. It remains an attractive destination among students looking to obtain degrees in engineering. Courses are normally three years long, with exceptional candidates becoming eligible for four-year honours degrees.

Medical Education

With the National Eligibility cum Entrance Test (NEET) been made compulsory, several foreign university agents are using this as an opportunity to lure medical aspirants abroad, away from the highly competitive NEET. Education Consultants warn students to not fall prey to such messages or advertisements and research thoroughly before applying; though they observe that NEET by placing restrictions on the number of students accepted by every state may play a role in the increase in demand for these colleges abroad.

Every year, Indian parents spend nearly $500 million on over 300 medical colleges across the world — especially in China, Russia, Ukraine, the Philippines, Georgia and Nepal — for degrees which do not hold much value. From Ethiopia, Latvia, Mauritius and Bangladesh to Belize in Central America and Curacao in the Dutch Caribbean, everyone gets a share of this colossal national wastage of money. Last month, 6,948 Indian students reportedly appeared for the mandatory Foreign Medical Graduate Examination (FMGE) conducted twice a year by the National Board of Examination (NBE) for recognition of such degrees in India. Only 480 were successful. The rest face an uncertain future. Theoretically, they can keep appearing in the screening test for due recognition by the Medical Council of India (MCI), but very few make it.

At an estimated average spend of INR 2.5 - 3.0 million per student, the total annual loss on over 9,000 unsuccessful candidates is approximately INR 3 billion. The rules stipulate that any student aspiring to take admission in a foreign medical college should obtain an eligibility certificate from the MCI, granted against a minimum of 50 per cent marks in physics-chemistry-biology in class XII. Unofficial estimates suggest at least 10,000 students go abroad every year to study medicine. Barely 7 per cent are ultimately recognised by the MCI. The reasons are primarily economic. Most of the 'affected' students scored low marks in class XII, could not make it in the merit list for Indian colleges and found it cheaper to go Ukraine, China or Russia than pay INR 5 - 6 million capitation fees in private medical colleges back home.

Student Exchange

For every student who goes overseas to study, de facto India is financing the cost of faculty and infrastructure in the institutions abroad. That money could be better used to create more jobs and more facilities in India. Thus India has facilitated the formation of jobs overseas, and has failed to do so here. Closure of key Government departments has also led to downfall of Indian higher education. If the Indian government decides to allow foreign universities set up bases in India it would create an unequal play field in the present scenarios. A domestic university – with limits on fees, on payment to teachers, and curbs on capital spending will be unable to compete with foreign universities who would have free hand on all the three accounting heads. If a foreign university allowed into India pays more to faculty members than what the government permits aided institutes to pay, the best brains would flow to foreign universities within India. That will spell the downfall of all aided institutions.

Influx of international students has been constant over the past five years, though the out flux of Indian students is nearly ten times higher. Neighbouring countries such as Nepal are the largest suppliers of foreign students to India though their numbers are quite small. Reasons of this may include lack of a strategy to attract international students, even from neighbouring countries which are poorer and do not have established higher education systems. Proximity and relatively low costs of education even do act as catalysts.

For many countries such as USA, UK and Australia, immediate and measurable benefits from large numbers of international students are economic. International students contribute billions of dollars to these countries as many of them stay behind to work and live there and hence continue to contribute to the host country as skilled workers. Apart from direct and indirect economic benefits, foreign students bring social and cultural benefits to the host nation. Such benefits are hard to measure but widely-acknowledged as important for the host university and the immediate community.

Influx

Delhi University (DU) receives several thousand applications from international students. Some of the existing foreign students on campus tell us what makes DU the first preference for many aspirants abroad. A multicultural and peaceful atmosphere, wide range of courses and good job opportunities sums up why foreign students flock to Bengaluru colleges for higher studies. Over 5,000 students from various countries study in the city's different colleges and universities, making Bengaluru one of the most preferred cities to study in along with Hyderabad and Pune. Most of these students pursue BBA and BBM, while some pursue BCA as Bengaluru is the country's IT hub. Engineering and pharmacy come next while a good number of students also apply to visual arts programmes and law courses After management courses, students are more driven to opt for computer application courses in the Silicon City of India. Homely atmosphere and a healthy understanding between management and students are why some colleges are preferred over others. Mela James Lagos, general secretary of the Federation of International Students' Association, Bengaluru (FISAB) says that colleges which have a mutual understanding with international students tend to attract more of them every year. The Acharya Group of Institutions has over 900 foreign students from 60 countries including Nepal, Bhutan, Bangladesh, Sri Lanka,

Afghanistan, besides from the various African nations. Established in 1993 by Majed AA Sabha, an Indian citizen born in Palestine who did engineering from Bengaluru, Brindavan College has over 300 foreign students on its rolls, constituting 60% of all its students. Foreign students here are from a host of countries including Angola, Bahrain, Gambia, Germany, Namibia, and Mongolia.

To help students coming from non-English speaking countries, language coaching is imparted prior to the main courses. Christ University, which has over 600 students from 59 countries, has a specialized admission process in place for foreign students. Of these, 20% are pursuing different postgraduate programmes the university offers. "We have an active international students' office. We help them obtain residents' permits from the Foreigners' Regional Registration Office (FRRO) and in other formalities as well. Through a comprehensive orientation process, we make them aware and help them adjust to the university norms regarding discipline and academics," adds Prof J W Lobo, director of international students' office, Christ University.

Ailing Education System and the Road Ahead

Creating a few more schools or allowing hundreds of colleges and private universities to mushroom is not going to solve the crisis of education in India. And a crisis it is – we are in a country where people are spending their parent's life savings and borrowed money on education – and yet still not achieving education of international standards, and struggling to find employment of choice. Mind numbing competition and rote learning do not only crush the creativity and originality of millions of Indian students every year, it also sometimes drives brilliant students to commit suicide. People often see education as the means of climbing the social and economic ladder.

Indian education system is geared towards teaching and testing information at every level as opposed to inculcating skills. Information is largely forgotten after the semester exam is over. Still, year after year Indian students focus on rote learning. The best crammers are rewarded by the system. This is one of the fundamental flaws of our education system. Our education system rarely rewards true academics. Deviance is discouraged. Risk taking is mocked. Our testing and marking systems need to be built to recognize original contributions, in form of creativity, problem solving, valuable original research and innovation. If we could do this successfully Indian education system would have change overnight. Memorising is no learning; the biggest flaw in our education system is perhaps that it incentivizes memorizing above originality. For way too long teaching has become the sanctuary of the incompetent. Teaching jobs are until today widely regarded as safe, well-paying, risk-free and low-pressure jobs.

It is high time to encourage a breed of superstar teachers. The internet has created this possibility – the performance of a teacher now need not be restricted to a small classroom. Now the performance of a teacher can be opened up for the world to see. The better teacher will be more popular, and acquire more students. We need leaders, entrepreneurs in teaching positions, not salaried people trying to hold on to their mantle. India needs to embrace internet and technology if it has to teach all of its huge population, the majority of which is located in remote villages. Now that we have computers and internet, it makes sense to invest in technological infrastructure that will make access to knowledge easier than ever. Instead of focussing on out-dated models of brick and mortar colleges and universities, we need to create educational delivery mechanisms that can actually take the wealth of human knowledge to the masses. The tools for this dissemination will be cheap smartphones, tablets and computers with high speed internet connection. While all these are becoming more possible than ever before, there is lot of innovation yet to take place in this space. Our education system is still a colonial education system geared towards generating pen-pushers under the newly acquired skin of modernity. We may have the most number of engineering graduates in the world, but that certainly has not translated into much technological innovation here. Rather, we are busy running the call centres of the rest of the world – that is where our engineering skills end. The goal of our new education system should be to create entrepreneurs, innovators, artists, scientists, thinkers and writers who can establish the foundation of knowledge based economy rather than the low-quality service provider nation that we are turning into. Until today, an institute of higher education in India must be operating on a not-for profit basis. This is discouraging for entrepreneurs and innovators who could have worked in these spaces. On the other hand, many people are using education institutions to hide their unaccounted wealth, and often earning a hefty income from education business through clever book keeping and therefore bypassing the rule with respect to not earning profit. As a matter of fact, private equity companies have been investing in some education service provider companies which in turn provide services to not-for-profit educational institutions and earn enviable profits.

Sometimes these institutes are so costly that they are outside the reach of most Indian students. There is an urgent need for effective de-regulation of Indian education sector so that there is infusion of sufficient capital and those who provide or create extraordinary educational products or services are adequately rewarded. Our education system today encourages mediocrity – in students, in teachers, throughout the system. It is easy to survive as a mediocre student, or a mediocre teacher in an educational institution. No one shuts down a mediocre college or mediocre school. Hard work is always tough; the path to excellence is fraught with difficulties. Mediocrity is comfortable. Our education system will remain sub-par or mediocre until we make it clear that it is ok to be mediocre. If we want excellence, mediocrity cannot be tolerated. Mediocrity has to be discarded as an option. Life of those who are mediocre must be made difficult so that excellence flourishes. Assembly line education prepares assembly line workers; and the drift of economic world is away from assembly line production.

An educational institution is not just many more classrooms. If that were the case, Harvard would have opened 10,000 Harvard clones across the world. Education is a matter of culture and organic growth; of chemistry between students, teachers and the university administration. Premier educational institutions should be allowed the autonomy they deserve. Institutions should not fall prey to the temptation of having directors or teachers who follow a certain ideology.

Other changes that Indian colleges are making to get their students job ready:

1. Using demonstrative teaching methodology to show the applicability of the course content
2. Addition of value aided certification courses along with professional degrees.
3. Enhancing the industry-academic institution connection through Confederation of Indian industry (CII).
4. Introduction of multi entry and multi exit course curriculum
5. Development of sound entrepreneurship skills in the institution itself
6. Encouragement and nurturing of start-up companies
7. Introduction of "earn while you learn" concept

Impact of Technology

The introduction of ICT technology in classrooms in the last two decades has meant not just a change in the delivery of content, but introduction of the concept of remote, digital and virtual classrooms. "In the last 20 years, we were introduced to things like digital libraries and simulation technology to show dissection of animals, since the actual procedure is not allowed any longer. Technology has made delivery of content easier, and also introduced e-governance in institutes of higher education, from online admissions to fee payments and exams, making it a more transparent system. Earlier, due to manual admissions, only students from the neighbourhood area would apply for seats but in online admissions, we get students from across the country. For example, in our MSc Botany course, from 50 applications for 24 seats, we now receive 300 applications from across the country," said Rajendra Zunjarrao, principal of Modern College, Shivajinagar.

Technology has challenged traditional assumptions about learning, and the proliferation of MOOCs and vocational training programs has led to new choices for aspiring students. Education is undoubtedly becoming more global, with record numbers of students seeking to go abroad for further study. Technology has facilitated our ability to know about other educational options, travel with ease to study in different places, and even learn from distant places MOOCs - Massive open online courses.(online course aimed at unlimited participation and open access via the web) provide interactive user forums to support community interactions among students, professors, and teaching assistants

Incentives for the Industries

The Government of India is offering many scholarships for the engineering students belonging to minority communities for studying abroad and the concerned stakeholders should take full advantage of the same.

Mr. U. Sudhir Lodha in an interview said that the programme for the welfare of minorities provides scholarship for meritorious students for pursuing studies in overseas countries and this will promote educational advancement of the beneficiaries. The objective of the scheme is to award interest subsidy to meritorious students belonging to economically weaker sections of notified minority communities so as to provide them better opportunities for higher education abroad and enhance their employability. He said that study abroad scholarships up to 50 per cent on tuition fee was being offered exclusively for students from Tamil Nadu. Apart from international study, the scheme also takes care of job opportunities. He said that the scheme benefitted more than 500 students belonging to minority communities from South India last year. He said that the banks are well-prepared to sanction educational loans, provided the students submitted all the related documents to them.

The Indian government has reinstated the two-year study abroad admission criteria for expatriate students to engineering and technical colleges in India following a ruling by the Delhi High court on May 22, this year, much to the relief of protesting parents. The residential criteria for undergraduate (UG) admissions under DASA for Indian nationals shall be: "at least two years of education inclusive of 11th and 12th grade or equivalent in a foreign country during the last eight years and they must pass the qualifying examination from abroad". This rule has been made applicable only for 2017-2018 admissions and is likely to be implemented next year too. It may be recalled that on April 1, just one day before Indian expatriate students could apply for undergraduate engineering and technical courses in India, the Indian government had abruptly amended the DASA eligibility criteria to a minimum of five years' study abroad instead of the mandatory two years. This had affected many Indian expatriate students in the UAE and other GCC countries, especially in cases of students whose parents were on deputation for only two years abroad until 2016. The student is also required to take a Scholastic Aptitude Test (SAT). Parents of students seeking admission are upset about a few other things as there is a lot of confusion about the admission quota. Earlier, there was a separate quota for Children of Indians Working in the Gulf (CIWG). Their fees were also on a par with students in India. Students under the Non-Resident Indian (NRI) quota, which included all Indian students across the globe, were expected to pay $7,500 per year. Now the fees for CIWG and NRI have both been brought up to $8,000. But students studying in the Gulf are being asked to apply either through CIWG quota or NRI quota. Now there are only five per cent seats in the CIWG quota and 10 per cent in the NRI quota. When the fees have been brought on a par, why create this confusion in the minds of Gulf students?" he questioned.

CONCLUSION

Education is positioned very interestingly. While internationalization has potential to open up various opportunities, key systemic challenges remain. Technology is a great equalizer, and India has the ability to leapfrog and catch up with global standards. Private player participation should be handled carefully, but the Government of India should open up to opportunities. Education technology has the potential to completely upend the education system. Streamlining of processes and updating archaic rules should also be a priority for the Government.

*   *   *

Amity University Study Abroad Programme: Reflections

AUTHOR BIO

Professor Luke Minshall

Innovative and versatile Management Consultant with 20 years' experience in developing change initiatives and managing consulting operations. Luke specialises in designing, testing and leading people change initiatives across global organisations emphasising relationship management from business change awareness through to solution implementation. He is skilled at facilitating behaviour change, developing new learning methodologies, developing strategic leadership and embedding culture change. He operates as an interim executive or permanent employee depending on the nature of the client's needs. His early career with Royal Marines and Royal Artillery included operational leadership, general management, and development of high-performance sports teams and selection of talent.

Amity University Study Abroad Programme: Reflections

Professor Luke Minshall

Reflections

I have been teaching on the Amity Study Abroad program in London since 2010 covering topics of Entrepreneurship, Inter Cultural Behaviours in a Global Context and Psychology. I am proud to work with Amity University and have enjoyed teaching many bright, enthusiastic future leaders from India. I use a blended teaching approach that includes, engaging classroom activity, video case-studies, industry visits and team building activities. The purpose of this chapter is to provide insights into the teaching of entrepreneurship, culture and psychology and also to reflect on how different teaching approaches have accelerated learning with Amity students both in U.K. and India. These insights are based on over 2,000 students who have completed the Study Abroad programme and have been assessed through presentations, exams and interviews over the past seven years. I have also been very fortunate to have met many Amity teaching staff both in India and London.

When Amity students come to London, the mission is to provide a learning environment that will stimulate creativity in a totally new and different style to their home culture and norms of behaviour in India. It is always interesting during the first lectures, to observe how every student asks permission to enter the lecture hall. Sometimes, students may think they have not been given permission and so remain at the door until they feel able to come in: I cannot think of a more explicit example of showing respect to elders through these behaviours. However, by the time, students are in weeks 2 and 3, a new, interactive approach emerges which the students appreciate. This is often demonstrated by the way that students feel willing and able to ask open questions, propose ideas, challenge ideas and make presentations in a confident manner. What really matters is that they are able to open their minds and embrace totally different learning styles using innovation and creativity.

Students are with Amity in London for only five weeks so we have to move quickly introducing new ways of learning and teaching. Team Building plays a big part in enabling students to collaborate and share ideas during research activities as well as introduce an element of fun to teaching. One of the advantages of teaching students using a team based approach is that they are quickly able to test ideas against each other and begin to understand the power of the team in achieving a task. A powerful example of a team building activity that all students enjoy is building a paper tower to make a profit. In this team game, students complete two phases with three variables of height, time and materials presented in graphical form. During the first phase, the new teams have to form, brainstorm ideas and options so as to arrive at a plan that will achieve victory at building their tower – victory is demonstrated where the greatest profit is achieved.

Some of the Study Abroad groups have in excess of 50 students so up to 10 teams become possible. Imagine the excitement and noise during the second phase as teams realise they are not paying attention to the most important variable of time; instead focusing on height or materials and as a consequence are falling behind. This is a powerful learning moment as learning theory is visibly challenged against personalities, speed of reasoning and novel experiences. In this example, students visibly demonstrate how the 70:20:10 model for learning and development (created by McCall, Lombardo and Eichinger at the Centre for Creative Leadership in 1980) is successfully applied. The model suggests that only 10% of learning actually takes place during formal lessons and lectures but here this is extended so that the remaining 90% is achieved through time pressured real world scenarios involving plenty of brainstorming, generation of options and performance under time pressure. At the end of the Tower building activity, students review their performance with the task in parallel with their learning effectiveness using the 70:20:10 model – this forms part of their assessment and is delivered via a written report and team based presentation to the wider Study Abroad Group.

Students from Amity in India come from a range of different departments. One of the groups from the Psychology department conducted live research in London with interviews and behavioural observations. They were able to develop business plans based on their action research for potential on-line medical interventions such as therapeutic counselling. Business plans were presented and assessed by me and the Professor from Amity University Dr. Anupama Rajesh. Results of these student research activities were outstanding and were recommended for further development academically and in business – this was a proud moment for all the students and for me as well.

The learning during the Study Abroad Programme is enhanced by including a wide range of external visits. I have enjoyed taking my group to Bank of England Museum in the City of London and to the Building Centre in Bloomsbury. At the Bank of England, students have been able to see how the UK monetary system came into effect over 300 years ago. They particularly enjoy testing out interactive games that reveal how inflation, credit and economic stability are created and managed. A favourite part of this visit is where students are able to pick up a real bar of gold and get a 'hands on' understanding of how important gold has been, and still is a vital part monetary stability. During this visit, they are presented with a simple question: How can we enable productive yet stable economies that are of real benefit to the entire global population? Toward the end of the visit students attend a 30-minute presentation where they learn about business start-up, credit, inflation, financial fraud and cyber-crime. The final part is completion of a short assessment which they reference in their Study Abroad report.

Visiting The Building Centre in Bloomsbury near to the lecture halls gives students the opportunity to appreciate the scale and history of London over the past 2,000 years by examining a scale model of London. Here they get a helicopter view of the river Thames and all the main features of London such as The City, The Olympic Stadium on Stratford and the four Royal parks. Students are always amazed when they discover that the model has been mostly create using 3D printing. They receive a presentation where they see a 3D printing in operation and consider a wide variety of applications of this new technology such as medical, food, building and art. Many students have taken up offers to be photographed using a 3D camera and then have a scale model of themselves produced using the 3D printer – these are commonly known as "Mini Me's".

During 2016, I visited India and was invited to deliver a guest lecture at the Amity University campus in Noida. This was a fantastic opportunity for me to see first-hand how keen students are to experience learning through the Study Abroad Programme.

During my visit, I was shown around the Noida campus by Dr. Ajit Mittal and enjoyed a very friendly lunch in the main canteen. It was excellent to witness the collaborative style and behaviour in all areas at Amity University in Noida. As part of my trip to India, I was also welcomed in Jaipur by one of my Study Abroad students Shauryavardhan Rathore. This was a wonderful experience and a chance to hear and see how the learning from London has translated into success back in India. What all this has shown me is that the impact on students from a cultural learning perspective is extremely high and sets many aspiring students from India up for for great success once they return from London.

I was presented with the Amity University tie and plaque after my lecture in July 2016.

Active Learning: A 'Meta-Film' Approach

AUTHOR BIO

Dr. Anthony Basiel

Anthony is an eLearning innovation thought-leader with almost twenty years of experience in UK Higher Education as a Sr. Postgraduate Programme Leader, eLearning Consultant, UK/EC Project Manager & bid writer. As an Adobe International Education Leader he has instructional design & learning technology expertise. He has written eLearning research proposals for UK and EC funding in relation to his academic role at Middlesex University for Work Based Learning.

His major skill sets include web design, e-learning pedagogy, Human Computer Interaction (HCI), New Media learning design, webinar and web video conferencing.

He has been recognised by Adobe as a specialist in Web Communication - Adobe Certified Associate (2010).

Dr. Mike Howarth

Intelligent, fast video production, crafted with care for business and education, based on an action-packed practical career in education radio, multimedia and video, and grounded in academic experience. 5 years as a consultant to lecturer training at University College London, helping academics to teach and to present their research effectively through video, and teaching academic dissertation support at Middlesex University, using student smartphone video interaction for deeper learning, enhanced writing and efficient research. Visiting lecturer at online learning organisations; Glion, Oxford Courses. Application of video for local social issues and community projects, including volunteer work developing business skills for school students. More detail at MHMVR.com

Active Learning: A 'Meta-Film' Approach

Dr. Anthony Basiel
Dr. Mike Howarth

The Course Context

The Amity University Film Production course in London 2017, provided the opportunity to research and develop curriculum innovation design for the 3 Continent Programme (3C). Our aim was to introduce active learning using a 'meta-film' approach over the eleven-week course. The pedagogy found the learners generating the content of the curriculum through an applied assessment design in the form of a set of tasks. First, a project proposal research report and presentation was completed in week four by film consultant teams. The result of the research was a short video presented by each team and the process justified in a final written report.

The 'meta-film' approach is defined as a style of film-making which presents the film as a story about film production. The 'meta-film' approach in an education situation means that students do not just talk about video techniques, but employ them in the learning process. A student-as-camera-person model captured the learning events using the techniques discussed in the sessions. Our applied learning design intends to have the students use a learn-by-doing approach.

The implementation of this innovative curriculum design was through the use of guest speakers, professional practitioners sharing lessons learnt from the real world, grounded the sessions to provide practical advice for the student consultant teams doing research in producing their assessment films/videos. Dr. Mike Howarth[1], a former BBC Radio Producer, agreed to do a guest lecture. Merely standing in front of the class with PowerPoint slides was not his style. He mixed action with explanation to provide the students with a truly engaging experience.

A real-life example of the London commercial film industry was also provided, besides the classroom experience. Amplified Robot (Steve Dann, 2017)[2] an augmented/virtual reality production company in London – UK, invited the students to their offices to see demos of their projects, meet the project managers and production teams and get an overview of the organisation from the CEO, Steve Dann himself!

The course deliverables were: videos; recordings of presentations & interview testimonials; written reports both paper and electronic, with a long term function

---

[1] (Howarth, n.d.)

[2] http://www.amplifieDr.obot.co.uk/

as e-Learning resources and eMarketing media. The academic strategy intends to develop an archive or digital library of the video resources as well as a collection of sample reports for the next generation of film production students. Additionally, these video interviews and final film products can be used with a social media campaign to promote awareness and increase involvement of the 3C Programme.

Epistemology of an Active Applied Learning Design

Epistemology is defined as the way we perceive knowledge as mediated through a media, according to Basiel (2007). McLuhan (1967) goes further to suggest that the media is the message. For this course, the knowledge gained was seen as a process and not as a product.

As Visiting Professor for the Amity London Film Production course; I looked at this learning opportunity as a 'bottom-up' approach, that is a learner-generated content (Web 2.0) process[3]. The starting proposition was that the students would be composed of teams acting as a Film Production Consulting Company. The Module Learning Outcomes included 'hard skills' (e.g. film storyboarding) as well as 'soft skills' (e.g. project and team management) which would be realised in two stages:

1. Film / Video Project Proposal – Team Presentation and Individual Reports
2. Final Film / Video Production – Team Presentation and Individual Reports

Team Building

The first stage was to form teams and identify team Project Managers. To help the team members identify their personal strengths and weaknesses they undertook a colour psychometric test[4]. Then the talent management exercise was followed by a self-selecting team exercise. The established groups set about writing team charters[5]. These documents encouraged weekly meetings that addressed milestones set out on a Gantt chart[6]. I was emailed weekly progress updates from the project team managers. The aim was to monitor threats and take a prevention approach to critical incidents[7].

---

[3] (content, n.d.)

[4] (Psychometrics, n.d.) https://general-psychology.knoji.com/which-color-personality-are-you-red-blue-green-or-yellow/

[5] (Charter, n.d.)

[6] (Chart, n.d.)

[7] (Incident, n.d.)

Film Production Class Curriculum

We started each session with the 'one-minute essay'[8] as a reflective and analysis exercise. Students were given only one minute to write, using film and business vocabulary to identify one new bit of knowledge or understanding they have acquired since the last class. The essay was discussed with a colleague next to them for review, and finally shared with the class. But, the information had to be presented with supporting evidence and that required a reference or real-world illustration is needed. For example, the student may say they learned how to muffle wind noise by putting tissue around the microphone. But the statement should start, 'According to [name the source of the information], by using a Deadcat (term for the microphone windscreen) over the microphone the quality of the sound will be better for the recording.' The exercise helps the student to write in a clear, concise fashion with supporting references. Another form of exercise required students to review current news events each week. My goal was to get the students to research current literature, not just to provide evidence to support their design decisions, but link current breakthroughs in technology to current issues and to regulations.

The teams were encouraged to do primary research as well as desk research, so we also reviewed the ethical issues and guidelines[9] to ensure that proper protocols were used for interviews and surveys.

Corporate Visits and Guest Speakers

Along with a trip to a local London Augmented Reality production company, Augmented Robot[2], we had several guest speakers. The British Library Business and IP Centre[10] was kind enough to send Nigel Spencer who did an engaging presentation about commercial research. Another guest speaker also participated as an expert for the assessment panel. Dr. Mike Howarth[1], a former BBC producer, provided a hands-on opportunity for the film students to apply their theoretical knowledge in class activities. This knowledge and skills was then applied to the final film/video production assessment and presentation. In the next section of this chapter, Mike provides details and samples of student videos from the Amity 3C film production workshops.

Session 1: How to film a Story

---

[8] (Essay, n.d.)

[9] (BERA, n.d.)

[10] (Library, n.d.)

My first session on the course followed a presentation by students of their initial video production proposals. I had a chance to understand their ideas and react to the practicalities of filming their subjects. I was impressed, but it was the detail that concerned me: the 'how'. How to make their tasks easier and effective and therefore more satisfying, by using professional tricks of the trade. There seem to be various assumptions about the way media is recorded such as passively recording what is happening, instead of actively organising events in a natural way. Also, to help students understand and respond to the magic that happens as the camera and the production team engage in a 'dance of ideas' as events on location unfold.

I did not want to spend time criticising the student's proposal ideas or to talk at them for an hour. I wanted to practice what I preach - get in the action, and be there. So I thought it would be a good idea to give the talk but also video the process at the same time. Students filmed me and I filmed them. My smartphone was plugged into the digital projector too. The lecture became an event, a live cinema event. They could see the result of the filming method 'live' as it was taking place. The results can be seen on the website. Look at the video results and then read on as I describe first the background objectives, then in more detail, the process.

It is my thinking that film production is too important to leave to the filmmakers as an educational experience. They are concerned quite rightly with the end product: high production values, expensive gadgetry, making big money and general media hype. There is potential for the Amity Film 3C Production Course to be a deeper learning experience. A shift of 'focus' to hands-on activity, brevity and clarity in writing and speaking for camera - the craft of storytelling is the gateway to good communication skills, language and social interaction skills in an international context. The key is to make full use of the smartphone. Take its popularity: video blogging, the video selfie and the superficiality of "anyone can do it", and show ways to keep the fun and immediacy of using the smart phone but for greater engagement, - and turn it into professional tool for personal self-confidence and development.

I used the session to apply in practice lessons learnt as a radio broadcaster, with recent video journalist training and in my teaching. In a sequence common to video news gathering: shoot from the front where the action is, collect video components to edit together quickly and easily later. Keep everything simple; the essentials of film storytelling, show not tell, short, few words, a strong visual message. The students made the story of the session: students arrive though the door, the tutor greets them, close up of the tutor gives the essential opening message - three sentences of the main themes, cutaways to students after 10 seconds. Over the shoulder of the tutor allows a choice of relevant cuts to key student questions or to a voice-over of computer slides. Students work away by themselves as the lecturer gives a summary or in-depth interview close to camera. A few well-chosen words of conclusion from the tutor, students clapping. It is acceptable to reshoot the entrance of the students - to make sure they gather at the front of the class not huddle at the back and retake a more enthusiastic clapping at the end!

The assumption is that video media work is to be a watcher. How many lecturers are filmed from the back of the room. The camera needs to be at the front right by the action. The lecturer must be fully lit with a video light, and not in the shadow of the digital projector light.

The message: get out there and get filming. Physical. Hands on. Nothing happens unless you make it happen (*see Appendix*).

Session 2: How to Film a Location Visit

A chance to be part of the action came a few weeks later. Everyone finds it difficult to participate and, at the same time, be on the ceiling looking down watching events unfold. Students had an opportunity to manage and cope with both on this location visit. And not just any visit, but to a cutting edge 3D digital start-up company. Basiel's special contact with Director of Amplified Robot Steve Dann is a coup. Very few people have such an opportunity to turn up in such a large group for such a long time and film as well.

The irony of the visit is that the students are looking at a technology that the process could threatens film making as they know it! The company is exploring 360° video, immersive methods to capture the reality of places and events. Six tiny GoPro cameras in a spherical rig are pioneering used for applications in Virtual Reality movies and education, for entertainment and training. The task - they still have to tell the story without being overwhelmed by the experience.

The first task of a film crew is to get there and be on time. It is not an easy job to keep the smart camera steady, capture the exchange of ideas, the map reading and minding the traffic and busy pavements and even walk backwards. They managed it and soon fifteen people were listening to the briefing by Steve.

I make sure the students are recording the correct elements and notice they are filming everything but not make sure there is the variety of camera angles. One also has to contend with noise, and so many people in a confined space. It is important to take people aside to be interviewed in the quietness of a corridor.

After two hours it is time to leave. I have a brief moment to point out that a news crew could only have time to be in the building for a much shorter time. What were the key phrases to use from the briefing? What were the key shots, and the quotes? They all agreed the student wearing the VR helmet watching an operation shrieking "It's awful. But I like it!" was essential. Was there a good ending? Silence. So we recorded some quotes outside. It wasn't until we crossed Oxford Street we saw the giant advertisement hoardings for immersive VR helmets and filmed the new

Samsung phone and headset kit for sale. That was the real end visual. We had been to the Dream factory behind the street where the Dream was becoming a reality.

Just when I thought I was ahead of the game some new technology has come along. Even as I pause for a break and read the paper, page 8 in Times 2 supplement 18th April 2017 I read… *Thanks to virtual reality all your world is the stage*; a long article about experiencing being actors on stage by wearing VR headsets and interacting with a live person at The National Theatre. It's back to the Drawing board. I console myself that whatever the new technologies students will still need the same skills of storytelling, brevity and clarity, and also gain a real life pleasure of doing and making it.

The Final Session: Assessment

Students gathered to show their final projects. Ten minutes each. What an experience for me! The brilliant stills photography. The impact of humour and the power of music to support images. The presentations were recorded. Students were now filming the audience reactions, questions and staff responses to their own work. I thought that I could go a step further and give impact to the presentations and set students on course for their next continental visit with a final hands-on recording session.

A video journalist would be expected to walk into any event, such as this final assessment, and collect usable footage to tell the story. How would the task be achieved in a few minutes, in a crowded room and student's experience? Students were given the challenge. They were keen to get away and celebrate the end of the course, so set to the task at great speed. The boring method is to set up the camera and plonk each student in the seat one after another. No way! Encourage people to make statements - not answer to an off-screen question. The objective is to make the interviews visually interesting too, so each new interview needs to be set up with a new background. I was being filmed so a performance was called for. The inner voice of my tutor - 'This is how we do it at the BBC". I began to make suggestions. "No shots right angle to the wall". "No backs against the wall". "Use the on-camera light to expose for the view outside the window". "Use the video screen behind the interviewee to strip in the student's project video". "We need depth": So the camera is jammed in the corridor with the interviewee in the door frame to give a wide shot of the whole room behind. Finally we need a good ending. Do a two-person interview. What was the most important event of your visit? Students jumped into action. No messing. No uncertainty. Job well done! (*see Appendix*).

Footnote: Why the Enthusiasm for this Course?

Looking back in time, perhaps it makes some sense that a civil engineering background should lead to a career as a BBC Education producer of geography and nature broadcasts. I was brought up fascinated by places and things; outdoors, on big construction sites and with my father's cameras to record and publicise our business.

And so no surprise that after chance meeting hitch-hiking to college with climber and photographer Denis Kemp, I was soon in Peru, Iran, and Tanzania. But Denis, who was also a Kodak education officer, said, "You must do something useful on your travels" - and that was to make teaching resources. These expeditions and a teaching degree, lead to a lucky break at the BBC.

So still no surprise years later that as soon as Skip asked me to help at Amity I saw a chance to pass on the message; "You must do something useful on your travels" - but with a difference to match the times. When I started, the cameras & recording equipment were expensive, heavy and complicated. I made BBC broadcasts with young people helping with the technology, but they could not make broadcast standard material by themselves on their own.

Now a smartphone fits in the palm of the hand, does all the tasks of a full production crew, and students can now learn to, and make their own programmes. More important - that difference to match the times - students can now experience the power of education through Hands-On Learning. "Learning by Doing", Skip's 'meta film' approach is a real practical possibility in education whatever the subject, not an abstract subject. Instead of sitting behind a desk in a classroom the smartphone is a tool for learning about a new country, to meet people, experience the world for themselves and in safety. And have a record of their experience.

London welcomes visitors and specially welcomes students. There are limitations. Permits are issued for professional productions and for cameras on a tripod. Surveillance is total, but discrete and tolerant. One Amity student reported he was stopped by a policeman, but had an interesting chat about what his university project and then given a friendly goodbye hug!

The terrible attack at the Houses of Parliament, at the time students experienced the national response, and witnessed the quality and values of life in the UK. I read a quote recently, "In London everyone is different and that means anyone can fit in" and with a camera in your hand nothing could be truer for the 3C Programme students. The evidence is in their Country Reports –action study report of their own choice submitting evidence of their own research.

A few weeks after the course finished we were still being given positive feedback:

'Hello, Hi Anthony it's Hardik here. Hope you are doing amazing. We all miss you and your classes.
Yours, Hardik D'

Teaching methods with video are discussed in more detail in Teach like a Video Journalist Thinks. (See below)

CONCLUSION

The curriculum innovations applied in this course are:

1. Student-generated content
2. Action research projects
3. Team building and talent management development
4. One-minute essays
5. Current event reviews
6. London company visits
7. Guest speakers
8. 'Meta-film' workshops

These engaging learning interventions gave ownership of the knowledge building experience to the Amity 3C students. To be able to freely go out to the streets of London to create their final films was to experience a successful meta-film learning design in practice.

*   *   *

APPENDIX

See videos at http://www.mhmvr.co.uk/site/amity.html

REFERENCES

Anthony 'Skip' Basiel, D., 2007. eLearning Blog. [Online]
Available at: https://drive.google.com/file/d/0B5KEPSFKjo5OeWxIeGhYdWZO
    MzA/view BERA, n.d. [Online]
Available at: https://www.bera.ac.uk/ Charter, T., n.d. [Online]
Available at: https://redbooth.com/blog/7-components-of-an-actionable-team-charter
    Chart, G., n.d. [Online]
Available   at: https://www.officetimeline.com/timeline-template/gantt-chart-
    download content, W. 2. L.-g., n.d. [Online]
Available at: http://itdl.org/Journal/Oct_07/article02.htm Essay, D. A. B. -. O. M.,
    n.d. [Online]
Available at: https://youtu.be/sIivMlFE0FM Howarth, D. M., n.d. [Online] Available
    at: http://www.mhmvr.co.uk/

Howarth, M. S., 2017. Teaching Like a Video Journalist Thinks. Internet Learning, [Online]. Vol 5, No 1 Fall 2016/ Winter 2017, 47-67. Available at: http://www. ipsonet.org/publications/open-access/internet-learning/volume-5-number-1-fall-2016-winter-2017 [Accessed 20 July 2017]

Howarth, M. S. (2016, September) Dissertation tutoring with video. Poster. Exhibited at the annual Learning and Teaching Conference. Middlesex University, London. 594 cm x 841cm, 23" x 33".

Howarth, M. S. (2014). Metaphor and neuroscience: a message to online learning. In: Sutton, B., Basiel, A. (Eds). Teaching and Learning Online 2nd Edition. (pp.176- 189). NewYork & London: Routledge.

Incident, C., n.d. [Online]

Available at: https://www.app.college.police.uk/app-content/critical-incident-management/types-of-critical-incident/

Library, B., n.d. [Online]

Available at: https://www.bl.uk/business-and-ip-centre

McLuhan, M., 1967. [Online]

Available at: https://en.wikipedia.org/wiki/The_Medium_Is_the_Massage

Psychometrics, C., n.d. [Online]

Available at: www.colorcode.com/free_personality_test/

Steve Dann, 2017. Amplified Robot. [Online]

Available at: http://www.amplifiedrobot.co.uk/

Those Who Can Teach: The Power of Experiential Learning

AUTHOR BIO

Dr. Audrey Tang
Development Coach | Writer | TV Psychologist
CLICK Arts & Training Consultancy, UK
audrey@clickproductions.co.uk
Twitter/Instagram: @draudreyt
Website: www.draudreyt.com

Audrey is a Chartered Psychologist (CPsychol), and the author of "Be A Great Manager – Now" (Pub Pearson, 2016, Book of the Month in WH Smith Travel Stores July 2016). She is a CPD Accredited speaker and trainer, as well as a qualified FIRO-B and NLP Practitioner. She practices as a Development Coach and Training Consultant with her training consultancy CLICK Training and delivering keynotes on emotional agility and leadership at National and International conferences.

Audrey is also the resident psychologist on The Chrissy B Show (Sky 203), the only UK TV show dedicated to Mental Health and Wellbeing.

Audrey's doctorate is from Brunel University Business School (focusing on the training and emotional support of customer-facing professionals). During her research she lectured on Brunel's Business Undergraduate and Management courses, and subsequently trained as a Learning and Development Coach within the NHS. Prior to Training and Coaching, she was a secondary school drama teacher and Head of Psychology (QTS), later progressing to Programme Manager for vocational qualifications in Supporting Teaching and Learning, and Childcare, Learning and Development within Further Education.

Those Who Can Teach: The Power of Experiential Learning

Dr. Audrey Tang
Development Coach | Writer | TV Psychologist
CLICK Arts & Training Consultancy, UK
audrey@clickproductions.co.uk

ABSTRACT

Many new employees feel "well trained but unprepared" (Kress-Shull, 2000) commonly because their training has been largely classroom/powerpoint driven. The same judgment is often made by those who employ them. While many customer/client-facing professionals undergo a high level of training, nothing quite prepares them for performing the skills outside the classroom. Experiential learning is one of the most pure and basic forms of learning (Kolb, 1984), and when used within training it develops creative thinking, self-confidence, and self-reflection. Practice of skills in a safe environment enables delegates to reflect on their performance and understand that they have a) been through it once before should they face it again, and b) experience to draw from. This will enable greater confidence when performing the skill at a later date (Boal, 1979). On an action research basis, learners were given the opportunity to participate in experiential learning sessions to develop employability skills (alongside those run by the careers department of the university). From the feedback received, learners felt an interactive approach to be most helpful in developing not only their skills but their confidence as well.

Index Terms: Experiential learning, Employee training

INTRODUCTION

The University of Kent conducted a number of surveys on the skills that recent graduates needed within the professional world and found that the top three most sought after skills in graduates were "Verbal communication, Teamwork and Commercial Awareness" (University of Kent, 2015). However, the media continually prints stories of how this is not the case in the current recently graduated workforce.

"Approximately 788,000 students graduated at the end of academic year 2012/13…[and] data suggests that in excess of half-million (512,000) graduates were not properly prepared for work." (Weinstein, 2014). In particular, graduates lacked "...business, soft and technical, and hard skills..." including team working, communications, and commercial and customer understanding (Weinstein, 2014).

However, while he recommends that institutes of higher education focus on these skills, what is sometimes lacking is the knowledge of how to go about it effectively.

BACKGROUND

The advent of social media has made us more aware of what is going on but ever more passive. We are outraged, upset or elated by what we see, but rather than engage directly with the issue we choose instead to "share" it (assuming we even do that). This makes us feel as if we have done something, but the reality is, we have really only conversed superficially, and done little to affect it.

Oliver Sachs (2015) wrote a moving reflection published by the New York Times, after learning he had terminal cancer, through which he concludes: "Above all, I have been a sentient being, a thinking animal, on this beautiful planet, and that in itself has been an enormous privilege and adventure."

As such, students are lucky to be in a position to impact on those around us, yet have somehow learned not to do so. They prefer to engage in "Buzzfeed quizzes" (Grandiono, 2014) because we find enjoyment and community in mock personality tests – while not looking for anything deep or life changing. Yet, they are not necessarily happy where they are.

The Mental Health Foundation (2015) predict that "1 in 4 people will suffer some sort of mental health problem (commonly anxiety or depression) within the course of a year", that depression will affect 20% of young people, and self-harm statistics are one of the highest in Europe "400 per 100,000 population)".

A classic school of thought with regards to depression and anxiety is that both can be due to a "perceived lack of control" (Rotter, 1966). Such behaviour is reinforced every day through a student's interactions with social media. With so many things happening in the world, few of which they can do little about directly, why should a passive approach to live not bud?

Throughout school, learning has historically been passive, the teacher speaks, the pupils listen. With the introduction of more interactivity, many teachers chose to stick to what they knew rather than embrace new skills, and now, the changes in the curriculum and focus on targets means that even those who engaged in experiential learning can no longer do as much because of the amount of material learners need to take in, and the amount of testing that needs to be done.

"I have A-level students who cannot do a practical Science experiment because we've not had the chance to teach them – we have to just lecture at them in order to get the information in so they can be tested...again!" (Head of Biology)

Recent research keeps impressing that active learning is the best method not only for understanding the material, but also for holistic education (eg. Naoui-Kaur, 2015; Aydin, 2015). Unfortunately, the same research also revealed that although this was known "theoretically", few trainers and teachers of the samples studied were comfortable engaging with it beyond an icebreaker or a flipchart activity, which in turn did not engage the learners.

This leaves a "Catch 22" situation. People who use experiential techniques might be doing it wrong, which is putting both teachers and learners off using them. When it is done well, the evidence is also significant.

Smith et al (2007) ran a programme for Kent Constabulary where actors played the role of the public and staff was videotaped and able to reflect on their performance, and airlines and hospitals are now introducing this sort of dynamic methodology (e.g. Bentley (2006); Lagnado, (2011)).

METHODOLOGY

Taking an action research approach, students were engaged in a 12-week experiential learning employability programme "#LIFESKILLS" (passive learning programmes were also available within the Careers Centre), participants were asked to reflect on their learning after each session and again after the 12 weeks ended. Unfortunately only four students completed the course in full, others attended only some of the sessions.

The feedback was analysed using grounded theory methodology (Glaser & Strauss, 1967). Grounded Theory differs from standard qualitative investigation because, although it utilises questionnaires, observations, case study, interview and other qualitative methods of data gathering, it does not seek to verify already established theories, but rather subjects the data gathered to rigorous inferential and deductive analyses, finally generating a "Formal Theory". Its purpose is not to "...eek out small gains of knowledge from existing theories...[but to]...explore new areas that are not yet covered." (Glaser & Strauss, 1967). The result is that a landscape is shaped by the data which may offer new starting points for further research based on an authentic representation of 'what's out there now'. Data was coded for general themes, sub themes and then specific themes.

RESULTS

These are the testimonials from three of the students who completed the programme:

"Today I feel so great and I did not want these unique twelve sessions to end. The journey of the Masterclasses has been so knowledgeable and I have learnt a lot...I would surely recommend these to Business students even if you just go for ones you can, it will add a lot more to your degree. These are life learning skills and best experience under these Professionals."

"This program is indeed the most practical and self-starter skill enhancement program, combining physical and psychological aspects of training. When you have a great teacher you become a great learner and practical application of the knowledge acquired becomes part of your business life."

"I want to thank you for the wonderful sessions – I kept coming back only because it was worth it."

However other testimonials from individual workshops were also collected:
Managing Change workshop:

"The course is not only about career or professional management, but also involved a lot of self-improving, which can be useful for a lifetime."

"I got to network with Business Management students who evaluate situations in a different manner."

Communications workshop:

"It has made me realise a few things in my own behaviour and I hope to change them for the better in future."

"It helped me gain a deeper understanding to my communications."

"The way we do exercises to portray our behaviour and then get an explanation rather than just the trainer talking...it makes me realise a lot about myself and it is easier to remember after the funny and interactive exercises."

Applying Grounded Theory analysis, the majority of the positive comments highlighted specifically the interactive nature of the sessions, the next popular theme was the trainer.

DISCUSSION AND RECOMMENDATIONS

It is important to note that the sessions were voluntary and not all students attended the entire programme which may askew results to the positive. Further, the programme was delivered to an average age of 25 years which again may affect results.

Therefore, while the outcomes may be generalizable, to an extent, to university students (albeit from undergraduate to PhD), they may not apply to training the workforce at large.

However if a university wishes to incorporate a kinaesthetic approach to learning (applicable to employability and indeed a variety of topics), the remainder of this paper gives you some ideas for its incorporation into their own classrooms:

Create Curiosity

The engaging learning environment is as important for the training room as it is a classroom (Burnham and Baker, 2010). Bright pictures, or even blank flip charts on the walls, a question already put up, training toys on the desk and music can all contribute to stimulating learner curiosity.

However, learning is also a frightening experience (for children as well as for adults, Wlodkowski, 2008) so having the agenda up somewhere may put nervous minds at ease.

Choose the right icebreaker

An icebreaker for a group that does not know each other needs to get them speaking, but not be too personal (McGrath and Crawford, 2008 – please do read their article for a list of awful icebreakers to avoid!) Further it should enable your delegates to learn each other's names and start talking without them feeling bored… the icebreaker where you introduce each other is an absolute no-no in a group of more than 10!

Energizing moments

An energizer is not an ice-breaker. The Energizer is a good way to get your delegates focused when they come back from a break and usually involved moving around. A quiz based on what has been learned in the earlier section can also work – as long as you give your delegates buzzers, or something (ideally noisy) to "buzz in" with their answer – otherwise, it's just a test!!

Every interactive training technique can be re-applied (with a twist)

Question and Answer sessions can be enhanced by getting all questions written on post-its and placed on a wall, then asking other delegates to pick them up and answer them. Simple quizzes can be made more interesting by getting the delegates to write the answer but guess the question (again using the buzzers). Flip chart work can be developed by having some answers written in a brainstorm then passing the chart around each group to add.

Training for organisations can also include delegates identifying the problem and generating their own solutions – as well as a "call to action" to ensure the momentum continues outside the classroom.

If you have the luxury of actors – don't just "role play"

Use the "forum". This is a technique developed by Augusto Boal (1989) where the actor plays one of the characters in a problem scenario and the delegate "performs" as s/he would when faced with the situation. It is possible for the facilitator to stop and start the action, and get suggestions from the floor as to how the delegate should proceed. The technique allows the delegate to practice and reflect on their skills in a safe environment, and they leave the session armed with new ideas, and the knowledge that they've done it once, they can do it again!

These are just some of the ideas which make teaching more interactive. The ones mentioned above are extremely easy and require little more preparation than you would already do. The most important thing is to make the forum a meaningful place to practice skills. This means scenarios have to be based on the experiences of the learners or on true case studies which allow the delegates to "perform" within the situation and discuss it afterwards.

CONCLUSION

Experiential learning is not just about making the learning experience more "enjoyable", it is about engaging your delegates to care about the issue and empowering them (because you have stimulated their creativity) to find their own solutions. One does not need a background in theatre; the roots of experiential learning are based firmly in pedagogy, with a little imagination.

*   *   *

REFERENCES

Aydin, O (2015), Pre-service Teachers' View About the Creative Drama used as a method in Primary Schools, Paper presented at the International Conference for Academic Disciplines, Las Vegas, USA, March 2015

Bentley, R (2006) Using the Actor Factor – Drama based training, Personnel Today, http://www.personneltoday.com/hr/using-the-actor-factor-drama-based-training/ (retrieved Sept 2015)

Boal, A., (1979) Theatre of the Oppressed, Pluto Press

Burnham, L. and Baker, B (2010) NVQ/SVQ Supporting Teaching and Learning in Schools, Level 3, Pearson Education Ltd, Heinnmann

Glaser BG, Strauss A. (1967) Discovery of Grounded Theory. Strategies for Qualitative Research. Sociology Press (3)

Grandioni, D (2014) Buzzfeed quizzes – how do the work? The Huffington Post http://www.huffingtonpost.com/2014/02/20/buzzfeed-quiz-how-do-they-work_n_4810992.html (retrieved Sept 2015)

Kolb, D.A., (1984) On Experiential Learning, Prentice Hall

Kress-Shull, M (2000) Well trained by unprepared. One rehabilitation counsellor's journey. Journal of applied Rehabilitation Counselling, 31, 11-13

Lagnado, L (2011) These troupers take dramatic role at the hospital. The Wall Street Journal, http://www.wsj.com/articles/SB10001424053111904007304576498941542648146 (retrieved Sept 2015)

McGrath, J. and Crawford, S (2008) 10 Worst Corporate Icebreakers, How Stuff Works, http://money.howstuffworks.com/business-communications/worst-ice-breaker.html (retrieved Oct 2015)

Mental Health Foundation website (2015) http://www.mentalhealth.org.uk/help-information/mental-health-statistics/ (retrieved Sept 2015)

Naoui-Kaur, A (2015), The Flipped Classroom and Foreign Language Teaching. Does it Work? Paper presented at the International Conference for Academic Disciplines, Las Vegas, USA, March 2015

Rotter, J.B (1966), Generalised expectancies of internal versus external control of reinforcements, Psychological Monographs 80 (609)

Sachs, O (2015) My Own Life, New York Times http://mobile.nytimes.com/2015/02/19/opinion/oliver-sacks-on-learning-he-has-terminal-cancer.html?referrer=&_r=0 (retrieved Sept 2015)

Smith, S.L., Colquohan, R., Cornelius, N., Elliot, M., & Mistry, A., (2007) Making a Drama out of a crisis: Performative learning in the police service, Reynolds, M., Vince, R. (2007) Experiential Learning and Management Education, Oxford

University of Kent (2015), What are the Top Ten Skills that Employers Want? University of Kent website: http://www.kent.ac.uk/careers/sk/top-ten-skills.htm (retrieved Oct 2015)

Weinstein, G (2014), Work-Ready Graduates, Training Journal, https://www.trainingjournal.com/articles/feature/work-ready-graduates (retrieved Oct 2015)

Wlodkowski, R.J (2008), Enhancing Adult Motivation to Learn, Jossey-Bass, a Wiley Imprint

The Bearable Likeness of Experience: Why Experiential Learning is Powerful

Dr. Audrey Tang
Development Coach | Writer | TV Psychologist
CLICK Arts & Training Consultancy, UK
audrey@clickproductions.co.uk

Many new employees feel "well trained but unprepared" (Kress-Shull, 2000) commonly because their training has been largely classroom/powerpoint driven. The same judgment is often made by those who employ them. While many customer/client-facing professionals undergo a high level of training, nothing quite prepares them for performing the skills outside the classroom. Experiential learning is one of the most pure and basic forms of learning (Kolb, 1984), and when used within training it develops creative thinking, self-confidence, and self-reflection. Practice of skills in a safe environment enables learners to reflect on their performance and understand that they have a) been through it once before should they face it again, and b) experience to draw from. This will enable greater confidence when performing the skill at a later date (Boal, 1979).

...and that's the science bit.

I have been delivering this message at conferences for the last three years. The importance of experience has been underpinning my teaching for the last 10 – it's why I lock corporate teams in my Escape Room as the key element of one of my teambuilding workshops, and use actors in my other sessions. My book on Management focuses on practical application as much as it does academia. Finally, this year, I managed to get a paper published in the Journal of Management and Applied Science.

You can teach messages as much as you like. You can even practice skills in a classroom, but until you deepen the context to heighten its realism, the moment you are faced with the real situation and the adrenaline gets pumping, those carefully practised skills out of context are all but forgotten.

To Illustrate

I have the pleasure of being one of the Chrissy B Show's resident experts and yesterday her program was on self-defence. As I am usually asked to give a commentary, one of the key things I had prepared was the importance of context. Learning self-defence in a school hall is not the same as practicing it in a dark alley.

Before I could get there, the phenomenal team from the Combat Academy were already on it.

"Unless you practice in context, it is extremely hard to apply the skills."

"The brain scrolls through a series or responses, and if it cannot find anything it freezes. By giving some training in context, the brain has something it can draw from to help react."

(The Combat Academy HQ Team on The Chrissy B Show, Sky 203)

Experiential learning is not going to prepare you for every eventuality; however it allows you to have a starting point from which to respond. It empowers you to make a start, and enables your own experiences to help you get it to the endpoint. However, you also need to have an endpoint.

"It is not about 'winning'; it is about not losing...and being able to achieve whatever your objective is". (The Combat Academy)

In any situation contextual experience will give you a start, and you also need to know where to end.

What is your goal?

Are you looking to close a deal? Are you looking for a settlement? Are you just wanting to get someone out of your office?

The start and the finish are the most important - experiential learning gives you the start, experience will give you the finish.

To return to the Combat Academy example - if you are being attacked, having some training will give you a headstart on response (rather than freezing, or relying on instinct), however, the very fact that you have undergone the training forces you to consider the outcome - of which there are many. This is the same of any training.

By considering a situation we can at least think about the options. By undergoing training, we are offered options we may not have thought of, and by experiencing that training within a context that offers a little more realism than the classroom - our brain is already off the starting block. Not only does it know it has some sort of response, but that it has also successfully performed it at some point. Our will can then take it to the end.

Although perhaps less dynamic than Self Defence, within my management training we often use the "forum". This is a technique developed by Augusto Boal (1989) where the actor plays one of the characters in a problem scenario and the delegate "performs" as s/he would when faced with the situation. It is possible for the facilitator to stop and start the action, and get suggestions from the floor as to how the delegate should proceed. The technique allows the delegate to practice and reflect on their skills in a safe environment, and they leave the session armed with new ideas, and the knowledge that they've done it once, they can do it again!

One of my "Customer Service" sessions where delegates work with professional actors

However, even if there is no time for "rehearsal" in this way - at the very least reflect on the experience you have had.

Even without training, reflection makes actions meaningful, and offers much needed time to think and adapt them for the future.

Simple reflective questions to ask:

- What did I notice...?
- When did it happen?
- Why did that happen?
- How did I react?
- How can I use that information positively?

(Kolb, 1984)

These can be asked anytime, anywhere.

When I talk about experiential learning it is not just about making the learning experience more "enjoyable"! Experiential learning engages your delegates in the situation, motivates them to care or at least to think about the issue and empowers them to respond and to find their own solutions.

It bridges that gap between theory and practice. It is experience...just a little safer (the first time round).

For more about the Combat Academy, please visit: http://www.combat-academy.co.uk/

and watch: https://www.youtube.com/watch?v=F0oN86om8uw

For more about Experiential Learning in management, please visit www.draudreyt.com.

All sessions are CPD accredited.

*   *   *

Coaching Emotion: The Use of Coaching as a Management Technique to Support the Emotional Labour of New Teachers

Dr. Audrey Tang
Development Coach | Writer | TV Psychologist
CLICK Arts & Training Consultancy, UK
audrey@clickproductions.co.uk

ABSTRACT

An emotional labour job role requires the "physical and bodily display of emotion" (Hochschild 1983) whether harnessed to convey discipline or sympathy; supressed to show compassion and understanding; or simple politeness in the face of a hostile client and as such, emotional support is essential. Tang (2012) conducted semi-structured interviews with 44 emotional labourers (mainly teachers) over three years using the Critical Incident Technique (Flanagan, 1954) and analysed them using Glaser & Strauss' (1967) Grounded Theory methodology, and found that a significant contributor to burnout or leaving the profession was a lack of emotional support from managers. Issues included micro-management, support for the client (student) over the staff member, a lack of acknowledgement of role demands (overloading the worker outside the "9-5"), and no place to fully relax (e.g. an uninterrupted staff room (described by Goffman (1956) as a "backstage area"). One recommendation made was to support the professional emotional labourer through coaching – something which has so far proved successful for the emotional labourers (healthcare staff) within some UK National Health Service Trusts. Coaching (whether external or provided by the organisation) enables the staff member space and time to reflect on their actions and explore the choices available to them thus valuing their input while furthering their development. The effect of coaching as a management tool within the teaching profession is considered in this study. A case study of two teachers (one new to teaching and one with experience who had become disillusioned with the profession was conducted using an action research approach. Both participants were given a series of 6 coaching sessions (one every two weeks) conducted by the researcher, and self-reports on their feelings were taken before and after the sessions as well as reports from three nominated people who were close to the participants. In both cases the participants reported feelings of calm and an ability to better deal with their respective work situations) following the sessions (reiterated by their nominated "observers" who noted this change in behaviour), and while, due to the limitations of such a small sample it is hard to generalise the results, there is a clear indication that coaching has a positive effect on both wellbeing and performance[11].

Keywords: *Coaching, Emotional Labour, Management*

INTRODUCTION

"It is increasingly recognised that good coaching skills are an essential and integral part of effective leadership and positive workplace cultures." (Ellinger et al 2011, cited in Grant & Hartley, 2014).

The use of coaching as a management tool to support staff is slowly gathering momentum (cf. Institute of Employment (2008), NHS Leadership and Development (2010)). As a structured means of empowering another person in their actions, "Coaching" has entered the business world as a style of management and as an external means of executive development.

Derived from the original transportation term "coach", personal coaching is the act of bringing someone from one place to another, helping them to "move forward or to create change" (Starr, 2011).

Coaching happens through a "structured conversation" – the structure of which is held and shaped by the Coach (although the topics are generated by the coachee) – which enables the coachee the time and space to focus on their circumstances, explore the issues they may be experiencing, and generate their own solutions. The outcome of the coaching conversation usually includes the coachee's own ability to think, learn and act progressing, empowering them to make better choices in future.

Coaching is not:

- Giving advice.
- An excuse to do nothing/avoid taking responsibility!!
- A substitute for line management (especially if there are performance issues.

Rather, it can be (trained) and implemented in the following ways:

1.   Executive Coaching – External coaching
      • Referral from Line Manager/Self-referral (Line manager aware).
      • Or Private Clients.

---

[11] *Unfortunately the original school had to drop out due to unforeseeable circumstances. However, the research continued with a different school, also with a teacher new to the profession. In both cases, the teacher had come from an industry background. In both cases, the teacher was in their first year of teaching. The only difference was that in the second school, the teacher was not undergoing the "Graduate Teacher Programme".*

- A series of 4 – 6 sessions is arranged over a period of 3 – 6 months.
- In a referral case a review with the line manager after 3 and 6 sessions, in Private Client case, the review occurs privately.

2.   Management Training – "In House" coaches
   - Training leaders and managers via an ICF recognized course.

(NHS Leadership Academy, 2014)

The results of coaching programmes within organisations have been positive: "Coaching is the most effective talent management activity used by organizations." (CIPD, 2009); and "Coaching improved self-confidence, communication, interpersonal skills, work performance and relationships." (ICF, 2009). However, it has not yet been applied to the teaching profession.

Teaching, like nursing, is a "customer facing", "emotional labour" profession. As with other such professions, part of the role is the suppression of one's personal emotions and desires to suit the demands and expectations of the job. With coaching being a management tool that encourages empowered thinking, it would seem a positive means of acknowledging the "performance" while encouraging the staff member's personal development.

Emotional Labour and Teaching

Emotional labour was defined by Arlie Russell Hochschild in 1983 as a socially constructed behaviour where a service worker manages his or her "feeling to create a publically observable facial and bodily display – This kind of labour calls for a coordination of mind and feeling, and it sometimes draws on a source of self that we honour as deep and integral to our individuality." (Hochschild, 2003:7). For Hochschild, emotional labour was constructed as the outward display of emotion that fits organisational norms. Sometimes, she proposed, those 'norms' are defined by display rules that performers of emotional labour might share (eg. A nurse is supposed to present as an approachable and sympathetic person; or "feeling rules" by Hochschild, (2003) within the context of everyday life. For example a bride is supposed to feel happy on her wedding day (Hochschild, 2003:60)).

One of Hochschild's strongest claims is that emotional labour causes emotional strain for workers who perform it, because an organisation's display rules may be at variance with one's true feelings, for example, an educational behavioural unit demanding that the staff "…be warm and loving toward a child who kicks, screams, and insults you – a child whose problem is unlovability…" (Hochschild, 2003:52). In addition, this organisational demand may weigh heavy on top of the ordinary, everyday strain of obeying the taken-for-granted "feeling rules" that already govern our everyday behaviour, for example, that same staff member being expected to feel grateful because her colleagues remembered her birthday (Hochschild, 2003:83), as "Managing feeling is an art fundamental to civilised living." (Hochschild, 2003:21). However, for Hochschild, the demand from the organisation is greater than that from private life, "In private life," Hochschild warns, "we are free to question the going rate of exchange and free to negotiate a new one. If we are not satisfied, we can leave...But in the public world of work, it is often part of the individual's job to accept uneven exchanges, to be treated with disrespect of anger by a client, all the while closeting into fantasy the anger one would like to respond with." (Hochschild, 2003:86)

Hargreaves (1998, 2000) finds that not only do teachers need to manage their emotional displays to deal with the issues arising within the classroom (such as a sick pupil, forgotten homework, a poor work ethic) but actually use them to deliver an engaging lesson. This finding that emotions enhance teaching delivery is supported by Naring et al (2011).

For Hargreaves, "Good teaching is charged with positive emotion. It is not just a matter of knowing one's subject, being efficient, having the correct competencies, or learning all the right techniques. Good teachers are not just well-oiled machines. They are emotional, passionate beings who connect with their students and fill their work and their classes with pleasure, creativity, challenge and joy." (Hargreaves, 1998:835).

However, teaching is also a profession where its workers feel undervalued. Tang (2012) investigated the perceptions of support teachers felt they received and found that this was an area that was severely lacking.

Emotional labourers often complain of having to meet "targets" imposed by the management which they felt, fore mostly, were impossible to meet (e.g. Bolton, 2000, Bolton & Boyd 2002). This furthered the resentment of the management whom professional emotional labourers perceived to misunderstand the job. Such responses were related to targets being easily measurable "key performance indicators". Researchers in the field of teaching have found that recently there has been a shift towards a more target-orientated educational measure of success (e.g. Barrett, 2003) rather than the less quantifiable, personal development of well-rounded individuals.

What was noticeable within the interviews that Tang (2012) conducted with the participant teachers is that they felt that the targets are reinforced by the management who are then perceived as a source of strain rather than support. Perhaps a reason for this resentment is that within the teaching profession at least, the Headteacher is themselves a teacher, who perhaps is perceived by the emotional labourers as knowing what it is like. Therefore seeing "one of their own" seemingly turn against them, can result in resentment. Two respondents did mention a source of stress was when a colleague they formerly enjoyed working with got promoted and suddenly behaved "...like the Senior Leadership Team, rather than a teacher." The application of coaching as a management method opens up a more equal dialogue between

Headteacher and staff and the bridging of this gap may encourage a better working relationship as well as promote performance as not only do both parties listen, but they may also learn.

Display rule demands were also a source of strain, and were interpreted by the professional emotional labourer as another example of the management's lack of support, and were again demonstrative a perceived misunderstanding from the management of the job the labourer was doing. "I think there are a lot of things we do because we're told to – because it needs to be done in a certain way – the Head's way...not because it's best for the Students. Even the way we have to write the Title and Aim, and yeah it'll help. But traffic lighting their aim at the end of the lesson – not necessarily the best thing to do –or at least there are other ways of doing it that you might like...there are certain ways you have to do things." (Teacher)

Another thing noticeable within the teaching profession, which requires some support yet may be overlooked through normal "management" strategies is the emotional connection between teacher and pupil.

Tang (2012) found that many teachers experienced a variety of emotional labour struggles with their service recipients. This may be because the very nature of their position means that they are personally offering the service that is required (e.g. Hargreaves, 1998 – teachers). Unlike the shop assistant who may work the till for the customer to purchase the item they require, the teacher, doctor or lawyer is themselves also the service that the recipient requires. The teacher needs to impart knowledge, the doctor needs to heal, and the lawyer needs to stand up in court. As such to impart their service, the professional emotional labourer needs the co-operation of the service recipient, and striving to build a relationship is a known part of the job.

"some of these children, you see more of them than their parents do and have more of an impact than their parents in developing their character than some of their closest relatives, and I had been with them for all five years, I still see them down at the gym now, and that's nice. We go out, do the pub quiz – that sort of thing." (Teacher)

Although there were clashes and difficulties, and unpleasant behaviours reported by the emotional labourers, the vignettes emphasised very pleasant and heart-warming, positive outcomes and a continuance of the relationship after the service had ended. It is unclear whether this is common across all professional emotional labour relationships of whether this was specific to this sample, but 20 sources reported a continuation of the relationship with at least some service recipients after the service relationship had come to an end.

It is not clear whether the emotional labourer is driven to do this, as Bolton (2000) suggests, because they are caring people who merely wish to care, nor is it clear that the resulting continuation of a relationship is because of an attachment need as Riley (2010) suggests. It might be because of something individual to each labourer; it might also be because if one is to be forced into a long-term relationship with a recipient – as is the case with many of the professional emotional labour jobs, it is best to try and get along where you can. However, there was also a "longing" identified on the part of some professional labourers:

"There is no nicer feeling than being the sole person that person needs. I should have been a wet nurse" (Teaching Assistant)

"...I feel sorry for them. I grew up without a father myself, and I sort of want to be a father figure to them..." (Teacher)

"It's like because she doesn't see her own child anymore, she's trying to save souls. She has these little projects and those students never get punished – they can do ANYTHING!" (Teacher)

As identified above, there is often an "ongoing" relationship between the professional emotional labourer and the recipient, in comparison to the fleeting interaction of the occupational emotional labourer. If some teachers are in pursuit of an emotionally "corrective" experience (Riley, 2010) they may transfer the emotion of that relationship to their recipient into something beyond the professional. In applying Bowlby's (1969) attachment theory principles to service work (Popper 2005; Riley 2010), if the service worker has an emotional need and the organisation is unable to provide a secure environment, he or she may be "seduced" by the needs of the recipient. This is made worse if there is a grey area around what constitutes a 'professional relationship' e.g. Ofsted suggests that male teachers become "father figures" for male students (2008) and this is imposed at the micro level of display rules. For teacher and pupil, repercussions of an ill-defined emotional relationship have a potential to be detrimental to both parties' emotional wellbeing, and potentially the career of the professional emotional labourer, and this is definitely an area that requires further consideration, and is something that a coaching relationship could better explore.

METHOD

The single (or in this case, double) case study approach is used along with an action research methodology.

Due to the nature of coaching it was important to take a case approach with each participant in order to be able to fully understand its effect, and as coaching will result in change for the participant which is in turn analysed within the research, an "action research" methodology is also incorporated.

Action research is a methodology commonly used in healthcare (eg. Lingard et al., 2008; Whitehead et al., 2003) which involves empowering research participants as they engage with their situations and generate solutions to the issues they are facing (Meyer, 2000). It enables a reflection on practice as well as the implementation of change. As the very nature of coaching seeks to empower, reflect and move the participant forward in generating their own solutions, it is the most appropriate methodology in this study.

Case history – AW

- AW worked for many years as a regional manager for a nursery group. Following the birth of her children she changed professions, becoming an assessor which brought her into her current job. Due to a recent restructure (in August 2013) she was given additional responsibilities which included teaching.
- For the first year she was not given any support in this, despite having to teach one programme alone, and cover others, in her second year she was given a mentor.
- She met with her mentor on a relatively regular basis but he was off sick intermittently, so these meetings deteriorated. No other support was given.

Case history – VS

- VS, a teacher of over 10 years had just left her last job and wanted to leave the teaching profession due to her experiences at her last rganization.
- VS had been signed off sick for a period of 1 month prior to leaving during which time she had been the subject of a disciplinary investigation (for what she had not been told, and in any event – one which had not occurred.)

Both participants consented to 6 face-to-face coaching sessions at their homes lasting 1 hour long on subjects directed by them.

After each session they were given action points and at the start of the next session these would be reviewed.

The following was used to evaluate the success of the coaching regime:

- Participant self-reports.
- A transcript of the coaching sessions.
- Feedback from **others about the participants.**

RESULTS

After each of the sessions, both AW and VS reported a marked difference in their thinking. AW had a new feeling of "calm". She felt that she had had "thinking space" which she used positively rather than "stewing". VS said that she felt she "… understood her anger better" over her experiences – finding that it related to the behaviour of one person rather than the organisation as a whole.

After the second session, both also reported finding a better method of dealing with others – AW with some of her colleagues at work; and VS with her interactions in general.

By the fourth session, a change in AW and VS was commented on by others. AW colleagues noted that she was "smiling more", and VS's friends said that they noticed she was so much "calmer in her demeanour and approach to life".

At the end of the 6 sessions, both AW and VS reported a development of coping strategies and a clearer direction for their future: AW said she was "…in a position to enjoy the present, while looking to the future." At the point coaching started she felt she could have "walked out" because she felt she was failing and then jumped into the "next best thing" to pay the bills. She now "…understood what [she] wanted and what was right for [her] career progression". VS said she had developed productive coping strategies including "…writing things down so [she] wouldn't catastrophize them when trying to remember them"

Further, it was clear that both AW and VS had reached a positive place in their working lives as well as in their own personal development: AW's teaching was complimented during the course of the sessions and she was offered more BUT while she "…was flattered" she said that she didn't want to take that on as she knew teaching itself, as much as she enjoyed it, was not right for her. She said this enhanced awareness was "…due to the coaching". By the final session VS had applied for and achieved a new role within teaching which she was very excited about.

DISCUSSION

Specifically, the following was noted:

• For both participants coaching generated positive outcomes in terms of their personal journey.

Both participants reported feeling emotionally healthier within themselves, and for AW this was noted in her demeanour at work. This in turn could have had an effect on the students. While this was not requested within this study, this is something that could be considered in future research – although one my question if it is appropriate to explain to students their teacher's mentoring/support process.

- Both participants reported that coaching gave them "support" but maintained their freedom to make their own decisions – it was more "…like having a sounding board" in sessions, and enabled them to "…reflect calmly" outside them.

This echoes the findings in Grant & Hartley's (2014) study where leaders who were appropriately trained were able to apply coaching skills in the cases they identified it was correct to do so, but delegate or use other skills in others. This is significant because coaching is still somewhat misunderstood in the workplace (ICF, 2009).

- Both participants (and those that knew them) reported a positive change in demeanour.

As discussed above, this may have positive effects for the student within their classes, but the benefits of coaching include the transference of the change to the coachee's personal lives as well as within the work setting.

When done properly the value of coaching is clear – and this is likely to transcend all organisational fields. This is because the focus of coaching is to enable someone to move forward in their thinking which has a positive impact on their decisions, choices and actions. (Specifically related to emotional labour professions, an emotionally healthy professional can only benefit their clients/customers/patients/students! (Hochschild, 1989)

LIMITATIONS

Despite the reported positive outcomes, there are limitations to this study.

- It is possible that without coaching, participants may well have come to the same conclusions anyway.
- Researcher and the coach was the same person, so it is possible that participants may have wished to give socially desirable responses, or responses that would "please" the researcher/coach.
- There is also no way of controlling for external variables which may have resulted in the outcome (other than the coaching).

- The data is self-reported, and no objective performance measures were used.
- Further, a single case would also be hard to generalize even within the teaching profession.

There are many limitations with the single case and action research approach. With regards to single cases – the first is that, without a control it is possible that without coaching, AW and VS may well have come to the same conclusions anyway. There is no means of comparison. Further, a single case would also be hard to generalise even within the teaching profession.

The biases within self-reporting have been widely explored to the point where it is not seen as the most reliable technique for business research (Stewart & Eliza, 2002), however, due to the long-term and fundamental nature of coaching, it is difficult to find a method that is more suitable. Self-reporting is the methodology of choice for Grant & Hartley (2014)'s study on the efficacy of Coaching within Leadership.

Within this action research context, the research also ended when the sessions ended. There was no follow-up planned which may mean that although positive change was reported during the sessions, both participants may have returned to their old behaviours. There is a follow-up planned for each participant, but this is due to take place after this paper has been completed. Further, because the researcher and the coach were the same person, it is possible that AW may have wished to give socially desirable responses, or responses that would "please" the researcher/coach. There is also no way of controlling for external variables which may have resulted in the outcome (other than the coaching). The data is self-reported, and, while reflections were sought from colleagues and friends of the participants, these were not quantifiably objective measures of performance. Additionally, cause and effect is also hard to confirm – for example, AW was complimented on her teaching during the course of the coaching, as well as in her observation, and in turn offered more teaching responsibility – but this is may have been due solely to AW's natural aptitude and ability for the skill.

However, as Hargreaves (1998) says, the teacher uses emotion within their job role, and if they cannot, or it is compromised this may impact on the students, not to mention the teacher themselves, and therefore a method that brings about a positive emotion in the service professional must be entertained.

CONCLUSION

However, despite the limitations, there is one clear benefit of coaching on an emotional labour profession – especially teaching, and that is the effect on the demeanour of the emotional labourer.

A development of this research would be to work with Headteachers or mentors who may be trained to use coaching as a management tool and reflect on their experiences with the skills as well as on the performance of those they support. This will have the benefit of further investigation into the value of coaching, but also impart the coaching skills themselves to managers in the correct manner. The bigger problem perhaps, is the term "coaching" is still misunderstood (and misapplied) which can, at best lead to poor delivery – at worst can damage an intervention that has huge positive potential

*   *   *

REFERENCES

Barrett, R., (2003) Vocational Business: Training, Developing and Motivating People, Business & Economics, Nelson Thomas

Bolton, S.C., & Boyd, C., (2003) Trolley Dolly of Skilled Emotion Manager. Moving on from Hochschild's Managed Heart, Work Employment & Society, 17 (2), 289-308

Bolton, S.C., (2000) Emotion here, emotion there, emotional organisations everywhere, Critical Perspectives on Accounting, 11, 2, 155-171. Cited in Kinman, G (2008). Emotional labour and wellbeing in the front line: does mode of delivery matter? (Unpublished)

Bolton, S.C., (2000) Who cares? Offering Emotion work as a "gift" in the nursing labour process, Journal of Advanced Nursing, 32 (3), 580-586

Bolton, S.C., (2005), Emotion Management in the Workplace, Palgrave MacMillan

Bowlby, J., (1969) Attachment and loss: Vol. I: Attachment, New York: Basic Books

Brouwers, A., and Tomic, W., (2000) A Longitudinal Study of Teachers' perceived self-efficacy in the classroom, Teaching and Teacher Education 16, 239 – 253

Bullpugh, R.V., Gitlin, A.D., (1994) Challenging Teacher Education as Training: four propositions, Journal of Education for Teaching, 20 (1), 67-81

CIPD research 2009 cited in Starr, J (2011), The Coaching Manual, Pearson

Ellinger, A.D., Ellinger, A.E., Bachrach, D.G., Wang, Y.L., Bas, A. (2011) Organizational investments in social capital, managerial coaching, and employee work-related performance, Management Learning 42 (1), 67 – 85 cited in Grant, A.M., & Hartley, M. (2014) Exploring the impact of participation in a Leader as Coach programme using the Personal Case Study Approach, The Coaching Psychologist, Vol 10(2), December 2014

Flanagan, J., (1954) The Critical Incident Technique, Psychological Bulletin, 51 (4) July, 327-358

Gibson, H., & Patrick, H., (2008) Putting words in their mouths: The role of teaching assistants and the spectre of scripted pedagogy, Journal of Early Childhood Literacy, 8(1), 25-41

Glaser, B.G., and Strauss, A.L. (1967) The Discovery of Grounded Theory: Strategies for Qualitative Research, Chicago, Aldine.

Goffman, E., (1959) The Presentation of Self in Everyday Life, Doubleday Anchor (1959)

Grant, A.M., & Hartley, M. (2014) Exploring the impact of participation in a Leader as Coach programme using the Personal Case Study Approach, The Coaching Psychologist, Vol 10(2), December 2014

Hargreaves, A., (1998), The Emotional Practice of Teaching, Teaching and Teacher Education, 14 (8), 835-854

Hargreaves, A., (2000), Mixed Emotions: teachers' perceptions of their interactions with students, Teaching and Teacher Education, 16, 811-826

Hochschild, A.R., (1983) The Managed Heart, University of California Press

Hochschild, A.R., (1983) The Managed Heart, University of California Press

Hochschild, A.R., (2003) The Managed Heart (reprinted), University of California Press

ICF research 2009 cited in Starr, J (2011), The Coaching Manual, Pearson

Institute of Employment Research, (2008) cited in Viney, D. (2012), Embedding a Coaching Culture in the NHS, NHS Leadership Academy, 2014

Larson, H. A., (2008), Emotional Labor: The Pink Collar Duties of Teaching, Currents in Teaching and Learning, 1 (1), 45-56

Linghard, L., Mathieu, A., Levinson, W., (2008) Grounded Theory, Mixed Methods, and Action Research, British Medical Journal 337(2008): 567-567

Meyer, J., (2000) Using Qualitative Methods in Health Related Action Research, British Medical Journal, 320, 178-181

Morss, K. & Murray, R., (2007) Teaching In Higher Education, Sage Publications CA

Naring, G., Briet, M., & Brouwers, A., (2006) Beyond Demand-Control: Emotional labour and symptoms of burnout in teachers, Work and Stress, Oct-Dec 20(4), 303-315

NHS Leadership Academy (2014) Website article

http://www.leadershipacademy.nhs.uk/resources/coaching-register/ (accessed 2014)

OECD statistics (2005), http://stats.oecd.org/ (accessed July 2014)

Ofsted cited by Clark, L. (2008) Teachers need to act like father figures for white working class boys says Ofsted The Daily Mail http://www.dailymail.

co.uk/news/article-1037327/Teachers-act-father-figures-white-working-class-boys-says-Ofsted.html (accessed 2012)

Pineau, E.L. (1994). Teaching is performance: Reconceptualizing a problematic metaphor. American Educational Research Journal, 31, 3-25

Popper, M., (2005) Leaders Who Transform Society: What drives Them and Why We are Attracted, Greenwood Press

Riley, P., (in production). Attachment theory and the student-teacher relationship, London: Routledge (chapters kindly sent for use in thesis from the author)

Starr, J (2011), The Coaching Manual, Pearson

Stewart, I., Elisa, J., (2002), Understanding self-report bias in organisational behaviour research, Journal of Business and Psychology, Vol 17(2) Winter

Strati, A., (2007) Aesthetics in Teaching Organisational Studies, Reynolds, M., Vince, R.

(2007) Experiential Learning and Management Education, Oxford Press

Tang, A. (2012), Love's Labours Redressed: Reframing Emotional Labour as an Interactive Process Within Service Work, Doctoral Thesis, BURA.Brunel.ac.uk (accessed July 2014)

Whitehead, D. (2003), Evaluating Health Promotion: a model for nursing practice, Journal of Advanced Nursing 41 (5), 490-498

Wldokowski, R.J., (2008) Enhancing Adult Motivation to Learn: A comprehensive Guide for Teaching All Adults 3rd Edition, Jossey-Bass, A Wiley Imprint

A Model of Soft Skills for Trainers

Dr. Audrey Tang
Development Coach | Writer | TV Psychologist
CLICK Arts & Training Consultancy, UK
audrey@clickproductions.co.uk

The UK workforce is largely tertiary - much of what we have to offer is customer/client-facing on a service basis. This means that huge numbers of workers engage in emotional labour (Hochschild, 1983) - the management of their emotions to elicit appropriate responses within a professional interaction. To exemplify this, a teacher not only needs to have the skills and knowledge to impart their subject, but also be compassionate to a child who is going through troubles at home. A nurse not only needs to know how to take blood, but be supportive of a patient frightened over a diagnosis. Along with the hard skills, emotional agility is a central part of the job itself.

As hard skills may be judged through not only examination, but by many professions' own standards as well as within the job interview, a minimum standard is more objectively defined. This is less true of soft skills and this is the area offering the greatest amount of variation. As such, a lot of external (i.e. non field-specific) training is directed in this regard.

Yet that variation remains.

I propose that this is often down to what is needed firstly being misunderstood, and secondly, conducted inappropriately.

I offer a representation to address the former:

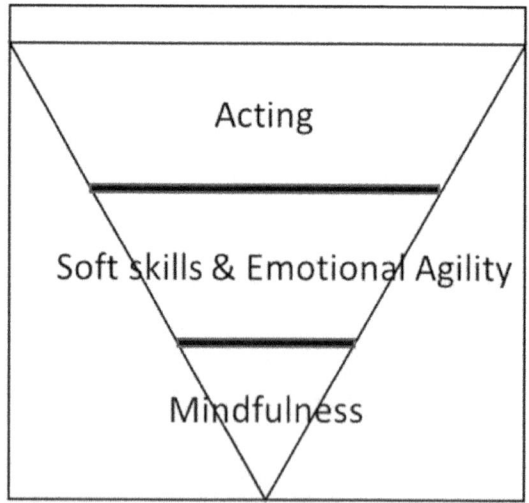

The first level is "Acting."

The performance of soft skills without the need for authenticity. Many people are able to "act" 'being nice' - hence the triangle being inverted. Even the most naturally indifferent people (for whatever reason) are able to present the mask of politeness for a short time if required (Goffman, 1956).

It is this which is often 'taught' through scripting (Smith et al 2007, Daly et al 2009).

In-house support can often comprise scripting, for example, giving the worker a patter of statements to read while on the phone. Sometimes required behaviours can be posted around the organisation eg "Smile, you're on the Asda stage."

While this can be helpful as a new employee gets used to the job, it is often perceived by the client or customer as inauthentic, and may be recognised as such by the 'actor'. Further, the mask cannot be held up for long and the actor almost always needs time to relax and recharge after a 'performance' (Tang 2012).

This also has the added problem of underappreciating the skills a naturally bubbly and emotionally agile person may already bring by curtailing them.

Nonetheless, "acting" can be taught - and there are also cases where it can be very convincing - there are many teachers who would not want children of their own who behave with ease in a nurturing manner to their charges.

The next level is that of authentic soft skills. Fewer people are able to engage with these in comparison to the top level, but still many do – especially in caring or service-facing professions. Arlie Hochschild's seminal 1983 book "The Managed Heart" called this "emotional labour". These skills can also be learnt to some degree – and is often the focus of training sessions.

Worryingly however, some of those sessions are thought possible to take place online only, or are conducted "lecture-style".

Especially when working with people not naturally used to demonstrating these skills, they must be practised in context (or at in least simulated context) in order for them to become authentic and natural. When training, due to time pressures or inexperience of instilling this particular type of personal skill in delivery, has not been delivered in a meaningful manner it can lead to some people feeling "well trained but unprepared" in a job which demands emotional agility (Kress-Shull 2000).

This is why I favour an immersive, experiential approach utilising a number of different resources (actors*, "escape rooms", even things like aerobics and ballroom dancing) to elicit performance followed by a meaningful reflection.

*[*I should add that I know "actors" can be utilised poorly which has generated much suspicion of this approach in training sessions as top level executives fear being placed back into "GCSE drama" - this is not what I do...there is a huge difference between applied theatrical practice, and "teaching drama".]*

For example, in the session, delegates worked through a case study and had to account for their decisions (and their consequences) within a "press conference". The reporters and people who may have been affected by their choices were played by actors.

This taught not only the importance of making managerial decisions that could be justified, as well as offering practice in the skills of managing difficult conversations (the subject of an earlier workshop) but also embedded confidence and the knowledge that they were able to respond appropriately when put on the spot.

At the very deepest level of emotional agility or soft skills practice comes mindfulness. Fewer still are practised at this depth. At this level, the soft skills demonstrated are the most natural choices of the person engaging in them, and they are delivered without emotional scars or burnout to the performer. With the open mind and self-awareness required to take such action, comes the ability to know one's own limitations and to practice similar compassion and kindness as self-care.

Implications from research have indicated that emotional support provided for the emotional labourer has been found to mediate the negative effects of service work (Verbeke, 1997). This can come in the form of management support, appropriate training or coaching (for both managers in this regard, and staff), as well as positive colleague relationships within the workplace termed "communities of coping" (Korcynski, 2005).

However, another positive contribution is the practice of mindfulness.

At this level, the soft skills demonstrated are the most natural choices of the person engaging in them, and they are delivered without emotional scars or burnout to the performer. With the open mind and self-awareness required to take such action, comes the ability to know one's own limitations and to practice similar compassion and kindness as self-care.

The Guardian suggests that the (even lower) take-up of Mindfulness training is due to suspicion of this "cult-like" practice, or a "snack sized" approach such as "lunchtime wellbeing sessions" now appearing in some companies and institutions which left one researcher "profoundly depressed" (The Guardian, 2015).

Yet, when done meaningfully, research is positive. Aetna, one of the leading organisations to include mindfulness in their day-to-day working, found that "…on average, stress levels dropped by 28%". But too often I still see a number of places approach mindfulness and wellbeing as a series of links to "MIND" on their website. This is not enough.

As trainers the very core of our work is to instil transformational change. That first transformation is often needed in our own understanding and approach. We are not providing a means of ticking a box, we have the opportunity to positively influence organisations, and more importantly, the people who work there.

*   *   *

REFERENCES

Daly, A., Grove, S.J., Dorsch, M.J., Fisk, R.P. (2009) "The impact of improvisation training on service employees in a European airline: a case study", European Journal of Marketing, 43 (3/4), 459 - 472

Goffman, E., (1959) The Presentation of Self in Everyday Life, Doubleday Anchor (1959)

Hochschild, A.R., (1983) The Managed Heart, University of California Press

Korczynski, M. (2005) The Point of Selling: Capitalism, Consumption and Contradictions, Organization 12(1): 69–88

Kress-Shull, M (2000) Well trained by unprepared. One rehabilitation counsellor's journey. Journal of applied Rehabilitation Counselling, 31, 11-13

Smith, S.L., Colquohan, R., Cornelius, N., Elliot, M., & Mistry, A., (2007) Making a drama out of a crisis: Performative learning in the police service, Reynolds, M., Vince, R. (2007) Experiential Learning and Management Education, Oxford

Tang A (2012) Love's Labours Redressed PhD Thesis presented at Brunel University London

Verbeke, W., (1997) cited in Hennig-Thurau, T., Groth, M., Paul, M., & Gremler, D.D., (2006) Are All Smiles Created Equal? How Emotional Contagion and Emotional Labor Affect Service Relationships, Journal of Marketing, 70 (July), 58-73

Hard Facts About Soft Skills

Dr. Audrey Tang
Development Coach | Writer | TV Psychologist
CLICK Arts & Training Consultancy, UK
audrey@clickproductions.co.uk

The world is changing – in some ways for the better but there are difficulties. One thing that many people have to appreciate now is that there are few "jobs for life". This also means that there may be fewer "set friendships" or communities. If an average project lasts around 2 years, people – families – can be moving around a lot and we need to be able to make new friends, fit into new places. These skills are important in a social context.

As humans we cannot help but affect one another – when we are let out in traffic we are more likely to let someone else out. As such skills that mean we are a good person to have around and be around are likely to attract the same.

We will always need people – admittedly some may need more than others – but we do need some form of living contact. By always bringing some value to the table, we are more likely to share in the fruits of a very abundant meal – and be better for it.

But it goes deeper than that.

Historically "soft skills" have been referred to as "presentation skills" or "networking skills" – skills of communication, but they also include the following core strengths, or values:

1. Reliability: People can be ambitious, or talented, but to work well in any environment they need to be reliable. If you can be counted on then you will more often be counted in. There will otherwise come a time when a sparkling personality will not be enough to merit inclusion if there has been too much flakiness.
2. Striving for excellence rather than perfection: I read this one in Forbes – and love this point. If you can barely be "perfect" to your standards, the likelihood of being "perfect" to anyone else's is far less. Also "perfection" looks only at the outcome. Striving for excellence focuses on the whole process. Being reliable, being conscientious, and doing a good job at the end.
3. Courage: This can be to start something new, to leave something old, to do something different, or to act in the way you believe in. Too often we bind ourselves by what others may think. If we are unhappy we need to take the time to think about why, what the options are, and who or what

is in the way. More often than not, the answer is we are the barrier. We are the saboteur – if we can find the courage to break through, we will find a way to deal with the outcome.

Of course you don't have to make any changes - you've got this far just fine after all.

But if you do want to become a little more flexible then there's one more strength you need.

4. You have to get real: Change is more effective if its foundation is where you know you are NOT where you think, or hope you are. It can be scary looking, but a little work now, and the rewards are abundant. Also, they will be genuine.

* * *

The More Rejections, The Higher You Can Climb: Lessons From A Published, Entrepreneur, Bond Girl

Dr. Audrey Tang
Development Coach | Writer | TV Psychologist
CLICK Arts & Training Consultancy, UK
audrey@clickproductions.co.uk

I have been so privileged to be asked to contribute to this wonderful book "The London Diaries". It was my utmost pleasure to meet Dr. Anupama Rajesh and work with the students on the Amity University Uttar Pradesh Summer Abroad Programme. Dr. Rajesh invited me to offer some of my teaching philosophies which I have done, and to conclude offer a short insight into my own life. I conclude with this.

Like most, I post my achievements on Facebook. In response, it's always lovely to get the "Congratulations!", "You're amazing", "Inspirational" comments... I mean that's the only reason you post - for "likes" right?

Of course I don't mean to belittle the lovely things my supportive friends and family write. I am extremely grateful. To have people who celebrate your success unconditionally is probably the real measure of achievement. However, there is always one comment which is written rhetorically, which probably deserves a longer response than a "thumbs up", and that is "I don't know how you do it!"

The simple answer - hard work and perseverance as you learn and climb, and learn and climb the pile of rejections.

In fact, the real subtitle of this post is: Lessons from a right-place-right-time, souped-up teacher, acting failure...but you won't read that would you!?

"Be a Great Manager Now"

I am delighted that my book "Be a Great Manager Now" is not only published, but (at the time of writing this) sits at "Business Book of the Month" in WH Smith Travel stores, and you can pick it up at Amazon. It took a year to complete the manuscript, a further three months to tweak, and a lot of support from the excellent editors at Pearson.

But the writing wasn't the hard part.

My academic background has always been writing based. I loved to read as a child - and still do, and I had written and was teaching a practical management programme which complemented the chapters.

Getting the platform was the struggle.

Lesson 1

Match, Pace, Lead - a simple NLP technique - sometimes you need to learn how something is done and do it, before you can change it.

For a long time during my PhD I could see a broad gap between theory and recommendation, and being of practical (rather than theoretical) persuasion, wanted to build a bridge. This wasn't particularly acceptable in academic circles (as demonstrated when I had major corrections at my first viva, and what should have been 3 years, turned into 5 with two changes in my supervision team and numerous re-writes). Thanks to some excellent mentoring from the wonderful academics at Brunel Business School, I learned to express myself in the manner worthy of a doctorate and received my piece of paper in July 2013.

I promptly returned my focus to teaching (practical applications of theory), and the next time I walked through the doors of Brunel University it was to deliver my programme on Practical Business which, while grounded in theory, focused on action.

The niche was there, and I thought I could fill it - and I did as a teacher, but not as an academic. Journals weren't interested...so I wondered if publishers would be.

Lesson 2

If you believe you have something to say, and can say it better than someone else - persevere.

The usual advice is a matter of statistics - send out enough CVs, one will land in the correct in-tray.

However, from Lesson 1, it's not enough to send out a "great idea for a book" - it needs to be done in the format that, agents and publishers will accept (if they even accept unsolicited submissions).

Another learning curve ensued - do it as an editor would want it. Send it to the right people, and don't annoy them! ...and be prepared for a number of rejections:

"Great idea - not for us."

"It would be a good book, but we aren't taking submissions in that field anymore."

Or the less positive:

"Sorry, we don't do that sort of thing." (when they do!!)

"We wouldn't be able to sell it."

and...

No response at all.

My proposal went through over 30 redrafts, and finally I got a very interesting email... "...we are developing a new series... and I think you would be the right person."

Lesson 3

Be adaptable. It wasn't the exact book I wanted to write, but it was the style I wished to write it in, and you don't turn down Pearson!

Again, I learned what was required of me...to shorten my sentences, to 'speak' more directly, to precis like there was no second paragraph.

I learned to think more about my audience and their needs, to target but also to encompass where possible, to stop being precious - constructive criticism is only ever to help improve.

By the time "Be A Great Manager" hit the shelves, I'd also received notification that one of my conference papers (on the importance of a practical approach to training) had been accepted into the "International Journal of Management and Applied Science". A Journal that was in its infancy...but still "Management and Applied Science"!. I'd honed my academic writing, but academia was making changes too.

"CLICK Training" and "A Great Escape"

I'd found my vocation when I became a teacher in 2004, and until 2014 I remained within the system as a classroom teacher, Head of Department and then Programme Manager. In 2014, with a PhD which revealed the darker side of teaching - the lack of support from some managements, the expenditure of emotion extra to the practical skills, the dissolution felt by staff – I'd also become tired. I liked teaching, but I didn't want to teach at a school. I wanted - and still do - a lectureship at a University. But, if you read part 1 of this blog, I'm not your conventional academic.

Lesson 4

Create a network and use it.

In 2014 - after regular monthly rejections since attaining my PhD in 2013; to get an administrative post at a University, let alone a research assistant position...

let's not even think about "lecturer" I decided I needed to take matters into my own hands. If my experience wasn't good enough as it stood, it needed to improve. I went "self-employed" and pitched myself as a course designer to my alma mater - and managed to get a 0 hours contract to deliver a programme. This probably had more to do with happily doing extra teaching and workshops while a PhD Student. The staff had got to know me.

Lesson 5

If you build it they will... only come if they want to.

My first programme was a success with the students and it was their requests that led to the next. Like everything, if the attendees didn't see a benefit, why attend? This is particularly significant to a class that was voluntary attendance only, and extra-curricular... not only that, but in the evening!

Of course, there were a couple of incentives provided by the Business School, but it was also important that the content (developed in line with Business School needs) was relevant, and well delivered. This meant engaging ideas, ensuring development, responding to evaluations, and if outsourcing any element (I work with actors for some elements of skills practice) making sure those sourced are high quality (*Indeed, I am very thankful to my wonderful actors Alex Coles, Paul Brennecke, David Sanderson, Ashley Alymann and Heather Carr*).

Thanks to the attention to detail demanded of me from Brunel's Business Life Programme (session plans, powerpoint slides, course evaluations, student feedback), I was able to apply for CPD accreditation in 2015 which I was given, and in turn for 2015 - 16 we were offering CPD hours to the attendees as well!

Lesson 6

Seize Opportunities - but know the limits of your capability.

While continuing with the conference circuit (despite not having a University post), I came across an activity called an "Escape Room" in the May of 2015. In basis, you're locked in a room for an hour and you solve puzzles to get out (a bit like a cerebral Crystal Maze). That is, I was in Oslo speaking at a conference, and in my "down time" was looking for something to do. So "hooked" was I on the concept after my first time that I continued playing them and by July had managed to hook most of my friends, and in December had the chance to licence a game from Pfeffermind GmbH, Berlin.

This would involve formally creating a company, licensing business premises and making sure if I built it, people would want to come.

I'm not going to go into the ensuing struggle of learning how to create a good website, getting people to work (for free) because you don't have all the skills you need - and with a fledgling company - no money to pay for them, teething troubles as the directors learn to collaborate, and the fear that "Tripadvisor" strikes into the heart of any small business...but there's a lot of work, a lot of utter terror, and I'm still learning!

However, while I also learned that while I could get better at some elements (branding, marketing, developing a booking system etc.), there were others that I should hand over to the professionals (accounts, physical construction, game design etc.).

I also found a new outlet for my Training Company - corporate teams loved the "teambuilding" element of the activity, but what about offering them a CPD accredited training session too?

But, about a month ago, I realised that while getting the business off the ground was fun, I'd begun to lose track of my goal. Yes, I was doing a little more training. Yes, I was making enough to survive. And yes, my book looks quite nice in reception - and I am extremely grateful to my neighbours, identifi Global, and The National Museum of Computing for spreading the word about the escape room when we opened, and sponsoring my Book Launch when I published.

But I was caring more about a 5* TripAdvisor review as a Gamesmaster - often out of my control - than developing myself towards that lectureship.

I realised it was time to follow my own advice - start focusing on my management role (and arguably my age) rather than doing a job which really, a school leaver could excel and develop in.

Hiring that excellent school leaver was where my experience paid off, and A Great Escape, while still a fantastic place for me to meet wonderful new players, is now in the capable hands of a superb young lady for whom a Gamesmaster/Team Leader role is straightforward, and offers great potential for professional and personal development in these early stages of her career path.

As of December 2016, to reach a wider market, A Great Escape "ENIGMA" joined The Panic Room family where it is enjoying continued success in its new location.

Bond Girl?

If you don't blink during the "Nine Eyes" meeting in Tokyo, in Spectre, you'll see me next to the "Head of China"...Yes, looking like I'm trying to check my phone under the table...but they gave me a laptop to type on...honest!

Lesson 7

Never be too proud.

The reality of this story is simple - I was part of an Extras agency. They needed a Chinese girl of my description, my face fitted.

But why was I part of that agency in the first place? I needed money.

I'd given up my dreams of stardom at 23 when I dropped out of the "Miss Saigon School" and went back to Uni to do my Masters. I'd danced since I was 3, then gone to Sylvia Young, taken my LAMDA examinations - and made it to the last 4 of Miss Saigon and the last 6 of Starlight Express...and that was about as far as my acting career was ever going to take me.

I don't have the talent of the triple threat, and I didn't have the discipline nor drive to work at it. While the young lad in front of me has since finished countless, professional tours most recently Panto with Katie Price, my days of the 6am cattle calls at Pineapple were, thankfully, over. I got my Masters, became a teacher - and that's where this whole piece started.

But I carried on with am dram - after all, if the professionals weren't going to cast me, I may as well cast myself...and since the completion of my Masters, I have produced, directed and been in a lot of shows, and worked with other amazing, talented people for whom acting is just a hobby. (Even learned a song on the saxophone for the last one!!)

But Spectre?

Working at Brunel was "0 hours", and at best, variable. While I was lucky to be invited back to teach the following year, between May and September I had no income - but I didn't want to get a full time job which would jeopardise the opportunity to keep developing my training.

Two agencies were looking for Chinese extras. I signed up - ended up (due to Brunel commitments) not being available for the show that they needed Chinese extras for - but I remained on their books.

I did the 6am starts, the dragging along your whole wardrobe selection, the endless walking across roads for different camera angles...and I got paid. Being reliable, and having experience in acting, I was soon given more work and eventually was put forward for Spectre. It's not glamourous. It's regimented, you are certainly not allowed to talk to the main stars - after all it's their professional working environment, and the reality is – you're probably not going to be plucked out for stardom!! (...my arm, the back of my head, my profile [insert unrecognisable body part here] has however now been in Eastenders, Holby, Hoff the Record, Flowers among others and may even show up in Dr. Strange!). You are discussed, prodded and poked (and made to wear Spanx even for a seated role!). You are selected - and de-selected, you work shifts is over 10 hours, and you don't (usually) say a single word.

But I loved every second of it. I could pay my bills while I wasn't teaching. In the "rest" time, I could read, or develop my training courses, I met fascinating people, I learned new jargon "Reset to ones", "rest", "rolling..." and hell yes you can see my face in Spectre!!

Lesson 8

Every experience is a learning experience you can use.

Because of the confidence that being on a set had given me, I saw no reason not to apply for the position when I noticed that the Chrissy B Show (Sky203) urgently needed a psychologist. Although I was working specifically as a business trainer and coach, my first degree was psychology, it was in psychology I was Head of Department, and my PhD was Business Psychology - and being a member of the BPS, I thought, well why not? I was invited in.

Being in a studio was no different to being on set, in fact it was more intimate. Also the production team is so welcoming and helpful with Chrissy herself being so down to earth you can see why empowerment, inspiration and wellbeing is the foundation of the programme.

I'm not a star, I'm not even an actress - but I am delighted to be one of Chrissy's resident experts, and to have had the opportunity to develop my profile and confidence within her team.

Lesson 9

Remember those who helped along the way.

And if you don't need to remember them because they are still in your life - be very very grateful.

It is not easy to know who to trust, whose advice is meant to assist you - rather than a hidden agenda, and most importantly of all, you are only as good as people think you are...and I mean inner-good.

If you behave with integrity, you will keep those around you who have integrity.

My close ones have seen me through a divorce, an enforced rebranding of "CLICK" in 2011, and the numerous failures to reach this point in my life - all my bad choices that came to bite me. But it's not just about appreciating their value, and acknowledging that they cared enough to give you a hand when you needed it - but remembering you can sometimes help them too...and you should look for those chances to do it.

It's more than just reciprocity – it's about maintenance of positive relationships. You need them more than anything!

So where are we now?

Lesson 10

Keep pursuing your goals

I'm a CPD accredited speaker now too, so if you did want me to speak at your event, just Drop me a line: audrey@clickproductions.co.uk

But, I'm still not quite there yet...that coveted University lectureship (department of Business/Business School), at which the climb has been aimed - still eludes me.

I've got the academic certification, the publications (book and journal), and a decent media profile. I can teach, I can lecture, I can mentor and mark...and I'm available now, especially since CLICK Training can run itself, as can A Great Escape.

I'm potentially willing to move if the Northamptonshire and surrounding area yields no success...(and my goodness, I'd love to teach in LA - spoke at a conference in Riverside two years ago).

So - if this post inspires you to work hard, and go for it - great!!

...if it gets me tenure - even better! ;)

Otherwise, it's best foot forward and let's keep going!

*   *   *

Verrier Elwin and the Gonds

AUTHOR BIO

Raj Mangal PCS (Retd.)

Raj Mangal has been a senior Provincial Civil Services (PCS) Officer of Uttar Pradesh. He has served the Government of Uttar Pradesh for about 37 years under different capacities. Some notable positions are Deputy Director – Mandi Parishad (Gorakhpur & Varanasi Division), Additional Commissioner (Moradabad Division), Municipal Commissioner (Gorakhpur), Additional District Magistrate (Kannauj & Gautam Buddh Nagar), Chief Development Officer (Shahjahanpur), Regional Deputy Director (Census), General Manager in Cooperative Sugar factories, Managing Director (UP Small Industries Corporation), Managing Director (UP Handloom Corporation), Managing Director (UPICA), Regional Food Controller (Varanasi Division), Special Secretary (Dept.'s of Madhyamik Siksha and PWD for all of Uttar Pradesh) among others.

He did his M.Sc. (Statistics) from University of Allahabad. He has a profound interest in literature, Indian history and culture. Post his retirement he is working for the welfare of tribal people of Uttar Pradesh and is the president of an NGO Sarv Adivasi Samaj, Uttar Pradesh. He is also the working president of PCS Retired Officers Welfare Association. Furthermore, he is a scholar of 'Land Laws' in Uttar Pradesh and also has keen interest in Indian Constitution.

Verrier Elwin and the Gonds

Raj Mangal PCS (Retd.)

Verrier Elwin (1902-1964), a renowned self-trained anthropologist, ethnologist and tribal activist, worked amongst the tribal people of India throughout his life. He was born on 29th August 1902 in Dover, England. When he was a student at Oxford, he developed keen interest in Indian Civilization and philosophy. In his early days he was a devout Christian and dreamed of becoming a missionary. His quest for mystic religious knowledge brought him to India in 1927. Here, he joined a Christian Service Society in Pune and worked to spread the gospel but soon was attracted to Mahatma Gandhi. He met Gandhi Ji and started to develop interest in the Freedom Movement of India. Gandhi Ji was greatly impressed by Elwin's participation in the movement. In 1930, Gandhi Ji told Elwin that he looked up on him as his own son. Elwin also met other prominent leaders of the times such as Sardar Vallabh Bhai Patel and Pt. Jawahar Lal Nehru and discoursed about the freedom movement. He also travelled with Sardar Patel across India and closely observed the sufferings of colonized India. All these activities of Elwin irked the Church superiors and British Government.

On advice of Sardar Patel, he with one *Shamrao Hivale*, an adept and selfless volunteer came to Central India to study and work among the *Gond* Tribe. The Gonds are a simplistic tribe relying mainly on nature and agriculture for their survival. They believe in nature being the almighty and the provider. Though the Gonds had a societal structure in their habitation but due to their naive ways they did not document their history. Ancient *Gondi* folklore passed on through generations is a treasure of unexplored knowledge. Legend has it that *Pahandi Pari Kupar Lingo* along with *Kali Kankali Mai* was the founder of the Gondi way of life; he did this in the era of *Shambhu - Shek* (first mentions of *Shiva - Parvati*). There were eighty eight generation of Shambhu – Shek; written literature prominently mentions *Shambhu – Mula*, followed by *Shambh - Gaura* and lastly *Shambhu - Parvati*. Pari Kupar Lingo laid the rules and regulations for formation of Gond Society. The '*Gotra*' system based on the names of different trees and animals was initially created by him; there are 750 gotras in Gondi cultutre. Pari Kupar Lingo was a visionary much ahead of his times, establishing the '*Ghotul*' System, with the support of Kali Kankali Mai and *Raitad Jango* (his sister). In the Ghotul System, large huts were made away from the settlements; for the education and interaction of young men and women. Historians have placed this system somewhere around 6000 B.C. It is only logical to interpret that since Gondi culture predates all other civilizations in Central India; it would be a source of inspiration in setting up of their respective societies for them.

Before we go further, let us have a bird's eye view of the contemporary and historical status of the Gond Tribe. Gond are one of the largest tribes in India by number, according to the 2011 Census of India, there are 12.7 million Gonds; largely concentrated in Central India. Traditionally they have been tilling land, producing food crops and raising livestock as a means of livelihood. They are spread out in Madhya Pradesh, Chattisgarh, Jharkhand, Orrisa, Uttar Pradesh, Maharashtra, Andhra Pradesh, Bihar, Assam and West Bengal.

It is pertinent to mention that Muslim writers of Mughal Era; narrate a rise in the status of Gonds after the 14ᵗʰ century. *Abu'l Fazl* also mentions the Gonds in *Ain-i-Akbari*, in the times of Akbar. Gonds ruled in four kingdoms namely *Garh Mandala, Deogarh, Chanda,* and *Kherla* in central India between 16ᵗʰ and 18ᵗʰ century A.D. Though migration in search of livelihood or out of sheer venture is a common phenomenon in ancient human beings but Gonds faced a forced migration in late 16ᵗʰ century; when *Subedar Asaf Khan* leading Mughal ruler *Akbar's* battalions, defeated Gond queen *'Rani Durgavati'* of Garh Mandala in 1564. Hundreds of Gond people were hanged on trees and several thousand were taken as slaves. A large number of Gonds left their original inhabitation in Garh Mandala, a kingdom of *Gondwana*. Still a large population of Gonds resides in Bastar (erstwhile part of Gondwana).

Gond people speak *'Gondi'* language which is closely related to Dravidian family of languages. Dr. Moti Raven Kangali, a famous scholar of Gondi language and culture relates it to Indus Valley Civilization also. However, at present about half of the Gond population speaks Gondi language while the rest converse in other Indo-Aryan language including Hindi. Noted historian V. Smith had said that centuries ago Gonds migrated from Central India to different parts of the country in search of livelihood; this is one of the main reasons they do not have any specific profession. Similarly, David G. Mandelbaum (an understudy of Verrier Elwin) in his book "Society in India (1975)" in Chapter 31 writes that – in 17ᵗʰ century this tribe (Gond) had entered the Hindu Society as domestic helps and they started to become a part of the *Jati* (Caste) System. He further pens – contrasting example of the movement from tribal to Jati society are from the two divisions of Gond people. The Raj Gonds have moved into high Jati ranks, The Hill Maria Gonds have tried to reject Jati engagement yet they have become involved in them.

In a comparable study an eminent social scientist Dr. Kailash Nath Sharma in his book "Indian Society, Culture and Problems (1952)" has said "In ancient times this caste (Gond) had two divisions – Raj Gond and Dhur Gond. Those who live in plains and have good economic status and call themselves Khatriya are called Raj Gond. The others who live in jungle and hills and whose cultural status is very low are called Dhur Gond. These two adjectives of Gonds are now eliminated." He further adds, "These people have no specific occupation, they are dependent on agriculture."

Regions with significant populations of Gonds are as follows:

State	Population
Madhya Pradesh	5,093,124
Chhattisgarh	4,298,404
Maharashtra	1,618,090
Odisha	888,581
Uttar Pradesh	569,035
Andhra Pradesh (old)	304,537
Bihar	256,738
Karnataka	158,243
Jharkhand	53,676
West Bengal	13,535
Gujarat	2,965

*Census of India, 2011

It is relevant to mention that Gonds have constantly been the inhabitants of present Eastern Uttar Pradesh. Sir H. M. Elliot, in his book 'Memoirs on the History, Folklore and Distribution of the races of the North-Western Provinces of India' has said – The Gonds an indigenous tribe are found almost exclusively in Gorakhpur, Banaras and Mirzapur. There are also a few in Allahabad and a few scattered throughout the Jhansi Division."*

*The book was revised and rearranged by John Beams MRAS in January, 1869. Please see Volume I, page 289.

*   *   *

Coming back to Elwin; the service agenda of Elwin was not liked by Church superiors, undeterred by the impositions Elvin later gave up being a missionary. Overwhelmed by the desire of serving the tribal people he pierced into thick forested area along with his dedicated companion Shamrao and reached village *Karanjia* of a Gond tribe, deep in the thicket. Here he made an Ashram and started a School and a Dispensary. Though he started leading a simple life like a tribal to understand them; at the same time he worked to eliminate superstitions and ignorance from the minds of the tribal folk. Initially, the tribe was apprehensive towards Elwin and looked upon him with suspicion but slowly they realized that this man was extremely kind towards them. As time passed, villagers and tribal people from distant places and thick forests came to the ashram and started availing the education and medical facilities there.

By this lifestyle of serving tribal Gond people, the then Christian authorities were further angered but Elwin was so influenced by the tribal culture; he vigorously professed that tribal Gonds and their culture were far superior than that of so called civilized societies. They had persistent human values like – affirmable life style, sense of enjoyment, unity, gender equality, hospitality etc. it was ironical that all this was not widespread in the country. By his consistent effort, Elwin brought into limelight an almost geographically isolated; and generally overlooked tribal people. To increase the reach of his efforts, he established another Ashram at Chitrakoot with the help of Shamrao. As long as he was being involved with tribal villagers his role as a clergyman was gradually decreasing. Lastly he gave up his membership from Church of England in 1931.

Elwin's inclination towards the tribal people made him convert from Christianity to Hinduism and he later also married a Raj Gond tribal girl named *Kosi* at *Raythwar* in Madhya Pradesh, in April 1940. It was an exemplary yet underrated incident in the history books; this marriage was solemnized in the times when the rest of the world was still reeling under the catastrophic consequences of color discrimination. Elwin and Kosi had a son *Jawahar Singh*. However, the marriage did not last; Elwin took an ex parte divorce in 1949. He wrote in autobiography, "I cannot even now look back on this period of my life without a deep sense of pain and failure". Subsequently, he married another girl of Pradhan Gond tribe named *Lila* of the village *Patangarh* and moved to Shillong with her in the early 1950s. They had three sons, Wasant, Nakul and Ashok.

Due to his dedication towards tribals and their culture Elwin had already become an authoritative figure. Upon the formation of Anthropological Survey of India in 1945, Elwin was appointed as its Deputy Director. Post-independence he chose to become an Indian citizen. In 1953, he was appointed as an Advisor for Tribal Affairs to the administration of India's North East Frontier Area (NEFA) now Arunachal Pradesh, with its' headquarter at Shillong. Swayed by his authority over the subject, Pandit Nehru, the then Prime Minister, appointed Verrier Elwin as a consultant to reform and improve living conditions of tribals in India. While serving at this position he received the honor of D.Sc. from Oxford University and Padma Bhushan award was conferred upon him by the Government of India in 1961.

In the late 1950's, Home Minister G.B. Pant had said "It has been the great work of Dr. Elwin to raise the status of tribal people in public opinion all over India. He has shown us that they are not just backward people but have an art and culture of their own, and so has influenced the policy of the whole country."

Leading a life of service to tribals and India, Elwin breathed his last on 22nd February 1964 due to a heart attack in Delhi.

The words of David G. Mandelbaum aptly summarize – "He (Verrier Elwin) was an Englishman of high talent who deliberately chose to become an Indian

Citizen. His life story tells how happily he lived in India, in remote tribal villages, how blessed his marriage to a tribal girl was (after an unfortunate previous marriage), and the joy he took in his children."

*   *   *

REFERENCES

Census of India, 1931. Vol. XVIII: United Provinces of Agra and Oudh. Part II: Imperial and Provincial Tables; Census of India, 1931; Turner, A C
Census of India, 2011
https://en.wikipedia.org/wiki/Verrier_Elwin
https://en.wikipedia.org/wiki/Gondwana_(India)
https://en.wikipedia.org/wiki/The_History_of_India,as_Told_by_Its_Own_Historians
https://en.wikipedia.org/wiki/Gondi_people
http://www.historyfiles.co.uk/KingListsFarEast/IndiaGondwana.htm
http://www.wiki30.com/wa?s=Kahar

BIBLIOGRAPHY

Ek Gond Gaon Me Jeewan (2007), Verrier Elwin
Indian Society, Culture and Problems (1952), Dr. Kailash Nath Sharma
Memoirs on the History, Folklore and Distribution of the races of the North-Western Provinces of India (1869), H. M. Elliot
Society in India (1975), David G. Mandelbaum
The Gonds – Genesis, History and Culture (2013), Anuradha Paul

Oppression of Indigo Farmers: Emergence of Gandhi

Raj Mangal PCS (Retd.)

In the 19th and early 20th century '*Neel*' or Indigo was an important chemical for textile industry for production of blue dye. Cultivation of indigo crop was prevalent in Bengal, Bihar and Eastern Uttar Pradesh. Indigo planters, nearly all British, and other local landlords known as '*Zamindars*' were also British loyalists they usually exploited the local peasants by forcing them to grow indigo on their lands instead of necessary food crops like paddy, maize etc.

In Bihar there was a *Teen Kathia* system, in which peasants or *ryots* (tenant farmers) were forced to cultivate three *Kattha* (a unit of land measurement) of indigo out of every twenty kattha (in one Bigha). They were offered small payments to be adjusted against final payment at the time of delivery of the produce. Once the farmers accepted the offer, it was like a ruse. Innocent farmers were cheated of the weight and value of the produce. Indigo is a very unforgiving crop to cultivate, there is extensive labor with little or no returns for the farmers; unlike the planters who made a lot of money selling the crop to the chemical industry.

Owing to the low returns for the crop, confrontation grew between landlords, and peasants and farmers. Outcome of such confrontations was outburst of anger among peasants. In 1859, this anger exploded in form of a revolt in Bengal called '*nil-bidroh*'; this was led by two brothers Digamber Biswas and Bishnu Biswas. The Bengali intelligentsia played an important role by supporting the organization of mass meetings and expressing sentiments of the commons through newspapers. Similar was the situation in Bihar and Eastern U.P., A British civil servant after his return in 1948 wrote that 'not a chest of indigo reached England without being stained with human blood'.

Mohandas Gandhi had returned from South Africa in 1915 and established Sabarmati Ashram in Gujarat. On advice of Gopal Krishna Gokhale, whom Gandhi considered as his guru; he travelled throughout the country to understand the plight of Indians, especially the villagers. He had visited Calcutta (now Kolkata), Shanti Niketan, Kanpur, Rishikesh, and Rangoon; however, Bihar and eastern U.P. were untouched.

Raj Kumar Shukla, a representative of indigo farmers from *Champaran* (Bihar) and Lakhan Pratap Singh from *Ratasia Kothi* (Deoria, Eastern U.P.) another dynamic leader of the indigo growers; along with their supporters met Gandhi Ji at the 31st Session of Congress in December 1916 at Lucknow. They requested Gandhi Ji to come and witness the miseries of peasants and ryots, and atrocities done by '*Neelahas*' (Indigo Planters). Gandhi Ji agreed but a date was not set; unrelenting, Raj Kumar Shukla and Lakhan Pratap Singh followed Gandhi Ji up to Bombay (now Mumbai).

Listening to accounts of their agonizing plight Gandhi Ji assured them that he will come after visiting Calcutta. It is pertinent to mention that these leaders had also requested Lokmanya Tilak earlier to visit the indigo growing regions but he could not agree due to health reasons. Another point needs to be cited in this context – Raj Kumar Shukla and Lakhan Pratap Singh were working for this cause, with the blessings of Dr. Rajendra Prasad – then a prominent lawyer, who later on went to become the first President of independent India.

Later Gandhi Ji went to Calcutta, and then to Patna in April, 1917 where he stayed at the residence of Dr. Rajendra Prasad. At the time of Gandhi Ji's arrival, Dr. Prasad was out of station and his father Mahadev Sahai, a scholar of both Sanskrit and Persian languages; had hosted Gandhi Ji. On April 15th, Gandhi Ji arrived at *Motihari* Station (a town of Champaran) where he was welcomed by thousands of peasants and growers along with Raj Kumar Shukla and Lakhan Pratap Singh. Other popular leaders present were Braj Kishore Prasad, Anugrah Narayan Sinha, Ramnavmi Prasad and Shambhu Sharan Verma.

The adjoining regions of Eastern Uttar Pradesh and Bihar had four prominent indigo processing factories at *Ratasia Kothi, Chakia Kothi, Jagdishpur Kothi,* and *Shahpur Kothi* with their headquarter at Ratasia Kothi; *'Tommy Saheb'* was the then chief of these factories. Remains of these factories are still present narrating the stories of their oppressed past. The last Chief of these four kothis was known as *'Kent Shaheb'* in the peasant class. Lakhan Pratap Singh was fighting for the common cause of indigo farmers against chiefs of these kothis.

On the second day of stay at Motihari, Gandhi Ji visited *Jasaulipatti* Village where a tenant-farmer had been beaten and his property destroyed by the *'Neelaha Saheb'* (Indigo Planters). By then, Dr. Rajendra Prasad, Mazhar-ul-Haq, Mahadeo Desai, Narhari Parekh and J. B. Kriplani had joined Gandhi Ji and started collection of testimonies of various atrocities against farmer-peasants.

Gandhi Ji was then on the continuous watch of the district administration, and was considered a danger to law and order of the district. Subsequently, he was served a notice giving an ultimatum to leave the district by the Deputy Commissioner (equivalent to the rank of District Magistrate). Gandhi Ji defied the order and replied to the administration that he was unable to leave the district but if it so pleases the authorities, he shall submit to the order by suffering the penalty for Civil Disobedience.

This was a turning point in this phase of history, when he used the term 'Civil Disobedience' or passive resistance, which later became *'Satyagrah'* in the Rowlette Act agitation. On April 18th, 1917 Gandhi Ji was sure that he would be sent to jail. News of his possible arrest spread like wild fire. Thousands of peasants assembled outside the court. Observing the near explosive situation, the district administration told Gandhi Ji that if he promised to leave the district and not return, his pending case would be withdrawn. Gandhi refused and replied, "Not to speak of this time alone, I shall make Champaran my home even after my return from jail." Quivered by the massive support of the people of Champaran and Gandhi Ji's stand, the administration decided to withdraw the case to avoid any possible breach of peace. Gandhi Ji had admitted that "the country thus had its first object lesson in civil disobedience."

Concerned by the huge support of people of Champaran and possible unrest, the British Government appointed a committee of enquiry. Gandhi Ji was also a member of this committee. Gandhi Ji submitted over eight thousand testimonies of atrocities against farmer-peasants already collected. On report of this committee, the 'Teen Kathia' system was abolished.

As it is already mentioned this first Civil Disobedience or passive resistance proved to be a turning point. Gandhi Ji had later said that when he arrived no one knew him (despite his successful reputation in South Africa) and the Congress Party was practically unknown to the masses at Champaran and other adjoining regions at that time. As told by his biographer DG Tendulkar "The real significance of the Champaran Movement was that Gandhi Ji forged a weapon by which India could be made free."

Authors Note: This above article is based on the memoirs of Sri Baleshwar Nath, a retired Block Development Officer and noted scholar of regional history of Eastern Uttar Pradesh, who has also witnessed the freedom struggle of India in person; and Dr. Tej Pratap Singh, a prominent educationist and Great Grandson of Sri Lakhan Pratap Singh.

*   *   *

REFERENCES

https://academy.gktoday.in/article/indigo-revolt-1856-57/
https://en.wikipedia.org/wiki/Champaran_Satyagraha
http://www.hindustantimes.com/india-news/remembering-the-first-satyagraha-100-years-of-champaran/story-myCg143UxOQJYuxlSrAqEJ.html
http://www.historydiscussion.net/history-of-india/peasant-and-tribal-movements-in-india-during-independence/664
http://indiansaga.com/history/mutiny_farmers.html
https://www.revolvy.com/main/index.php?s=Indigo%20revolt
http://www.yourarticlelibrary.com/sociology/summary-of-champaran-bihar-movement-1917-18/31984

BIBLIOGRAPHY

A Brief History of Modern India, by Rajiv Ahir IPS

Impact of Brexit on India-EU
Free Trade Agreement

AUTHOR BIO

Nirav Sahni

Nirav, a 2018 graduate of McGill University (undergraduate business school) is an author of several management publications. His first book titled *'Compendium: Management Cases from Emerging Markets'* was published in 2016. Additionally in 2017, he co-authored a Deloitte thought leadership publication on the TMT sector. His research paper on FDI in India won the 2016 Renvoi International Case Competition and was subsequently published in a book titled the same. Nirav also holds to his name a case study on the co-operative sector published by the Case Centre, UK.

While at McGill, Nirav served on the Dean's advisory council for freshman engagement, was appointed a Teaching Assistant for the Entrepreneurship and Innovation course and ran a radio podcast show with Prof. Karl Moore (Top 50 Management thinkers of the World) called 'The CEO Series' having interviewed leaders that include- Justin Trudeau (Canadian Prime Minister), Muhammad Yunus (Nobel Prize Winner), Narayana Murthy (Infosys Chairman) and George Daley (Dean of Harvard). In 2017, he completed a 6 month project with McKinsey in their Montreal office and was recalled the subsequent year as mentor for the same program. For corporate experience, Nirav has worked at Deloitte for 3 consecutive summers across their strategy consulting, corporate finance and analytics teams. Prior to McGill, Nirav took courses in Financial Statistics and Economics at Harvard University and was ranked amongst the top 5% of his class and recommended by his professors. An avid learner with a keen interest in emerging markets, he has attended, been invited to and organized conferences at Harvard Business School and Columbia Business School and was also offered admission to IIT Delhi as a visiting student.

Impact of Brexit on India-EU Free Trade Agreement

Nirav Sahni

INTRODUCTION

The Free Trade Agreement

The United Kingdom and the European Union (EU) have been very prominent and important trading partners of India and its economy. Value of this trade relationship has grown significantly from over 28.6 billion euros in 2003, to 72.5 billion euros in 2014, and over 34.7 billion euros invested in India from the EU and Britain. The rising importance and growth of India on the global map and its contribution to the world economy led to the initiation of negotiations of a Free Trade Agreement (FTA) in 2007 between the EU (including United Kingdom) and India. Till date most of India's trade agreements and partnerships had been confined within Asia and other neighboring countries of the subcontinent. This phenomenon has been same for the EU with other geographically adjacent nations. FTA was vital and unique for India as till date most of its trade agreements were with emerging countries with similar developmental standards. There was a considerable difference between these two economic units as United Kingdom was economically more developed than India at the point when the negotiations started. Thus, the economic synergies that would possibly arise from this FTA has been highlighted and deliberated. While negotiations are underway, the nations are very optimistic reach mutual consensus.

Brexit

In 2016, the United Kingdom decided to exit the European Union which led to direct effects on this trade agreement. Even though, Brexit is not officially expected to be completely initiated and transited till 2019, the start of the legalities and the rising volatility has had an effect on the markets and foreign exchange rates. While, these effects may not be ever-lasting and be caused only due to uncertainty, the real point of issue is the validity of the agreement without the United Kingdom a member of it. Technically, all existing international deals of the EU as an entity will exclude the United Kingdom. The Brexit movement will have the UK file a separate charter of their own as an individual member of the WTO leading to trade costs and opportunity costs.

Impact on India

Considering the current situation, trade agreement between the European Union and India that was initiated in 2007 will have a different economic impact that was originally forecasted and expected, given the departure of Britain from the Union. The severity of the change of impact is fluctuating by the day but is expected to be major as UK contributed up to 22% of total exports from the EU to India alone. Thus, European Union and India need to alter the policies and points of referendum leading to increased trade and enhance output. It becomes imperative therefor to understand the revised impact and benefits of the trade agreement to India post the exit of UK from the EU.

History of the India-EU FTA

Since 1970, Europe, Britain and India have shared very progressive diplomatic relations. The partnership being one of the first India fostered at the advent of liberalization. Relations have mainly been trade related and the dependence was rather mutual and equal in the 90's. However, as time progressed, EU and Britain became more important for India than India for them as a strategic trade partner. This has been one of the main reasons for Free Trade Agreement not yet fully reaching a consensus. It has often been argued that the structural composition of EU with so many countries as a part of it made it a challenge for India to be more influential to them; given the uneven distribution of exports to member nations. Main sectors of trade have been dairy, textiles, beverages and automobiles but stringent import regulations and restrictions along with high import duties have never let the agreement be very lucrative on the other side. The separation of UK from EU poses an opportunity for increased trade and GDP as in India the tariff structure will now be revised. Whenever the economic impact of an FTA is analyzed, one of the first metrics or variables that is negotiated and looked upon is the import tariff. While there are other factors as well such as domestic production, trade volume and gain, reduction in import prices is believed to have a major impact on the welfare of both the Indian and the British economy. Tariffs are a very sensitive variable because it directly and majorly affects the trade behavior of a country. Given the high interconnection of countries today, the effect is directly reflected upon the world economy. The trade relations between the two parties have evolved significantly over time and so has their importance on the rest of the world.

Trade Structure

Foremost element and data set to assess when proposing and evaluating a Free Trade Agreement is the importance of the trade partners to each other. Higher interdependence results in more trade volume which subsequently means lower costs. Trade structure and patterns between India and the EU have been shifting but on a macro level, EU has always been one of the largest partners. Both in imports and exports, EU (with UK) have represented over 12% in both the segments which is relatively significant. Trade volume on the other side has been taking a downfall and seeing a downward trend which makes the new trade structure between the potential deal between India and the UK very essential to have a strong presence in the European domain. China and the USA at the moment are the dominant trade partners not only for the UK but a majority of the nations.

Current trade composition between the two partners that over 90% of the concentration comes from industrial products. Reliance on a single commodity is what leads to an imbalance in importance. Agricultural products have been an important as well but not at a very high concentrated level as industrial products.

Impact

A Free Trade Agreement has a strong impact on both the trade partners and also on the countries excluded from the agreement. Trade diversification and policy leads to an altered approach towards countries outside the agreement. While, FTA gives India and EU and UK access to each other's markets, their export and import structures affect other nations which may have agreements with the EU and the UK. If the excluded countries of the agreement have very similar export behavior and trends as of the agreement, competition and pressure increases because the output and product is the same but preference and economies of scale result in higher competitive advantage. For instance, Nepal is heavily dependent on the Indian market with respect to exports and doesn't have strong partnerships with other nations. Thus, the competitive pressure is relatively lower. However, for other South Asian countries, competitive pressure is relatively higher from this agreement because of their similarity to the India-EU FTA.

European Union works under the principle of a single market where the flow of capital and goods within its member nations is not restricted. This results in increased efficiency and competition amongst the members as also expanding the market size. However, it does take away the individuality of nations to frame rules in accordance with their own domestic needs and economy which can harness their growth at times. Thus, with the exit of UK from the EU, Britain will face a loss in efficiency and higher costs that it earlier enjoyed compelling it to increase dependence on nations like India. The member nations of EU have been the largest trading partner of the UK and with that going away now the British economy is expected to take a toll. Thus Brexit will have severe impact on the two nations and even the rest of the world. It is not certain when and who will feel the impact as it also is contingent on the new policies implemented.

Post Brexit FTA

The scenario post the official completion of the Brexit in 2019 very heavily affects the economic situation of India and other partner nations. The negotiated terms of departure will result in the growth/de-growth of the relevant parties. It is likely that India's gain in welfare will reduce when UK is not a part of the EU because of formation of two new entities resulting in increased costs. Export behavior is going to be very similar when dealing with both the UK and the EU which as discussed above which would result in high competitive pressure. The overall gain from the India-EU FTA will be offset by departure of UK and the magnitude would depend on the tariff policy. There will be a downside for all three parties but common trade policy and already existing international trade deals of the EU would help them relatively stay stable. Quantifying the macroeconomic effects of this move is rather challenging given the high uncertainty and time lag. The direction in which the United Kingdom shapes its trade story would be given an actual and accurate picture of the benefits and consequences.

CONCLUSION

This chapter explores the existing Free Trade Agreement between India and the EU with the UK as a part of it, from a trade point of view. Implications of the current trade policy and the shift from it would be felt by not just the two or three concerned economies but other nations around the world as well. Britain's decision to leave EU is a historic move and one that is going to have several extended after-effects on the welfare, economic and social both. India's impact on this story is yet to be quantified precisely, rather any nation's story is yet to be quantified precisely which is the reason the world's eyes are on the UK and the policy it plans to implement. The most ideal way to move forward is to keep relations, agreements and negotiations with both the European Union and the United Kingdom in steady and stable shape.

*   *   *

Economic Impact of the British Rule: India-Pakistan Partition – Enemy Property Act Analysis

AUTHOR BIO

Vatsal Sahani

Vatsal Sahani is currently studying Economics at University of Pennsylvania and the Wharton School of Business. He did his schooling from Mayo College, Ajmer (India) and served as the College Captain of the Batch of 2018. He secured a perfect 10 CGPA in Class-X C.B.S.E. and was awarded a Special Medal for Excellence in Academics along with the Mayo College General Council Scholarship and Mahindra Search for Talent Scholarship for topping the batch for two consecutive years. He has cleared the Advance Placements Exams (AP) with Honors and secured a 35 on the standardised ACT test placing him in the 99th percentile globally. Vatsal holds a B1 DELF certification from the Ministry of France where he cleared all the levels with distinction.

He has represented and served as an ambassador of Mayo and India in over 11 countries including events such as World School Debates, Slovenia, Round Square International Conference in Singapore, World Sports Festival in Austria and the French Festival in Pakistan.

He is a certified Google Adwords, Google Search and Google Analytics specialist and Microsoft Office Specialist (MOS) Master who codes in C and C++. Additionally, he is a certified Stock Market / MCX Research and Technical Analyst and has work experience in the financial sector through his internship at Market Hub Stock Broking and in analytics at Vrentin Tech Pvt. Ltd.

Vatsal has attended the Brown University Leadership Institute in the United States and completed the program. In 2017, he completed a project with the Harvard University South Asia Institute with recommendation and was accepted into the Young Leaders for Active Citizenship (YLAC) cohort.

Economic Impact of the British Rule: India-Pakistan Partition – Enemy Property Act Analysis

ABSTRACT

On the basis of oral interviews and conversations with concerned stakeholders, this research paper seeks to scrutinize the legal rights and legislations pertaining to Enemy Properties in India and Pakistan, after the British India partition and after the Indo-Pak War of 1965 and 1971. The partition post the British rule led to mass migration due to which properties worth of USD 16 Billion had been taken over by the newly formed Indian government. The paper describes the methods the government has taken to settle the claims and take control over these enemy assets after the British India partition in 1947. It also discusses the situation of the people who lost their assets during the partition. Through a historical perspective, the research paper attempts to explain the various Enemy Property bills and acts introduced, passed and enacted in India, the various factors influencing the enactment and implementation. Partition has always been looked as a historical and political issue; the economic and humanitarian aspect has received scant attention. The chapter gives pointed suggestions which could help to resolve the problem and infers that being neighbours India and Pakistan should realize the significance of economic integration, geographical contiguity, shared cultures and reach a peaceful solution to their outstanding issues, including enemy property.

INTRODUCTION

The interest in studying partition stories emanated from my visit to Pakistan for the French International Festival, a literary French competition at Aitchison College, Lahore. Pursuing my passion for France, my interest to delve deeply into the subject of Partition grew. While serving as an Ambassador to the Harvard University South Asia Institute, I worked on the project "Looking Back, Informing the Future: 1947 Partition of British India". The paper is an outcome of the extensive interviews and 15 hours of conversations across Delhi which helped me to gain fruitful insights into the events, actions and individual stories and emotions that partition has created in minds of people who have migrated from Pakistan leaving aside their emotional ties and property rights. Furthering into the subject, I researched the Enemy Property

Act and interviewed the Superintendent, Office of the Custodian of Enemy Property of India adding an economic angle to the much debated partition. During the interview, I was informed that after 1965 Indo-Pak War the government took over the properties which were left behind by the people who went to Pakistan and also the Government paid 25% claim to the refugees as well. She also informed that the Government has amended the Enemy Property Act 1968 recently on 14th March 2017 to curb the illegal transfer of enemy properties. She also emphasised that every war derails the financial progress of the country ten years back and it also adversely affected the revenue collection of the country. As per the Superintendent the misuse and misappropriation of the land has been done at large scale by the people after the partition.

The Partition of British India into India and Pakistan in 1947, instead of solving problems between the two nations marked the beginning of internecine conflict spanning across various issues. Even after almost seven decades, the two countries are grappling with these problems. The issue of Enemy Property rights and entitlement is one such area which has not received the required academic as well as scholastic attention. It is to fill this critical gap that this paper seeks to explore the dynamics of Enemy Property Acts and rights as evolved and altered in India. For attaining this research objective, the paper is organized into four parts. The first part traces the Enemy Property Rights in India and Pakistan following the Partition and particularly after the 1965 war. In the second section, the paper looks at the manner in which the issues of enemy property have become a point of recurrent discord between the Executive and the Judiciary in India. The next part touches upon the humanitarian dimension of this issue. In the fourth part, the enemy property is located in the economic perspective whereby lesser economic integration has acted as an abiding hindrance in making the Indo-Pak relations better. The final section suggests the potential areas which can offer ray of hope in ties between the two South Asian neighbours and thereby could address the issue of enemy property.

Historical Context: Britain in India

It is a widely recognized fact that when states go to war, they tend to seize the properties in their countries of the citizens and corporations of the enemy country. This happened during the First and the Second World wars when both the United States and the United Kingdom seized properties of German corporations and citizens. Properties that are seized under these circumstances are referred to as 'alien properties' or 'enemy properties'. The underlying rationale behind seizing these properties is to prevent the enemy country from taking advantage of its assets in the other country during times of war. India too seized properties belonging to Pakistani citizens when it was at war with Pakistan. As the Defense of India Acts were temporary laws that ceased to operate once the wars ended, the need for a well-established law on enemy property was felt.

When war broke out between India and Pakistan in 1965 and 1971, the Indian government designated certain properties belonging to citizens of these as "enemy properties. During the outbreak of wars between India and Pakistan in 1965 and 1971, Indian government took over the properties of citizens of Pakistan in India under the defense of Indian Acts. The properties included land, buildings, shares held in companies, gold and jewelry of the citizens of enemy countries. These Acts defined an 'enemy' as a country that committed an act of aggression against India, and its citizens. The responsibility of the administration of enemy properties was handed over to the Custodian of Enemy Property, an office under the central government.

Following the Indo-Pak War of 1965, Tashkent Agreement was signed in 1966, which inter alia included a clause, which said that the two countries would discuss the return of the property and assets taken over by either side in connection with the conflict. Clause VIII of the Tashkent Declaration read as follows:

"The Prime Minister of India and the President of Pakistan have agreed that the sides will continue the discussion of questions relating to the problems of refugees and evictions/illegal immigrations. They also agreed that both sides will create conditions which will prevent the exodus of people. They further agreed to discuss the return of the property and assets taken over by either side in connection with the conflict."

However, the Pakistani Government unilaterally sold or otherwise disposed off all the enemy properties and assets, movable and immovable, of Indian nationals, firms, companies etc. in their country in the year 1971 itself. While in India, the enemy properties still continue to vest in Custodian of Enemy Property for India (CEPI).[12]

It was against this background that the Government of India enacted the Enemy Property Act in 1968 to administer the enemy property seized during the wars. This law laid down the powers of the custodian of Enemy Property for management and preservation of the enemy properties. According to the act, "enemy property" could include properties of persons who are believed to be a citizen of a state classified as an enemy state by to the Indian government.[13] The Enemy Property Act as amended in 1977 provides for the continued vesting of enemy property vested in the CEPI under the Defense of India Rules, 1962, and the Defense of India Rules, 1971 and

[12] Report of the Select Committee on Enemy Property (Amendment and Validation) Bill 2016, Rajya Sabha, Parliament of India, pp.2 Available Online at http://rajyasabha.nic.in/rsnew/bill/enemy_property_bill_2016.pdf

[13] Pandit, Aishwarya, 'What the new Enemy Act says about Indian Citizenry', The Caravan, Available Online at http://www.caravanmagazine.in/vantage/new-enemy-property -bill-says- indian-citizenry

the matters connected therewith.[14] The Government of India through the CEPI is in possession of enemy properties, both movable as well as immovable, spread across many States in the country. As per figure provided by the Ministry of Home Affairs, the immovable properties are valued at more than INR one trillion, while the valuation of movable property is more than INR 30 billion. Till date, about 9,500 enemy properties have been identified. A majority of them belong to Pakistani citizens from the time of the wars, and are valued at INR 1.04 Trillion.[15] Pakistan enacted similar laws to take over properties and assets of Indian citizens and companies in Pakistan during the wars. Unlike India, it sold off these properties in 1971.

The Enemy Property Act bestowed enemy citizens certain rights with respect to their properties vested in the Custodian. Nonetheless, the ambiguity in their rights and the powers of the Custodian to administer these properties resulted in disputes being raised before the courts. Some of these disputes related to Indian citizens challenging whether they could inherit enemy properties belonging to their ancestors who were nationals of enemy countries. The Supreme Court settled some of these questions in 2005 when it ruled that the Custodian of Enemy Property was administering the property as a trustee, and the enemy continued to be its owner.[16] Therefore, on the death of the enemy, the enemy property should be inherited by their legal heirs.

In 2010, the Indian Government issued an Ordinance[17] to expand the powers of the Custodian regarding enemy property. It sought to permanently vest enemy property in the Custodian even in case of the enemy's death or a change in his nationality. However, the Ordinance lapsed. The issue of enemy property attracted legislative interest again in 2016 when five more Ordinances were issued on the subject. These Ordinances went a step further and vested ownership rights over enemy property in the Custodian. This effectively negated the Supreme Court decision of 2005, and made the central government the owner of enemy property. While the first four Ordinances lapsed, the last Ordinance, issued in December 2016, has been replaced by the law passed by Parliament. The Bill passed by Parliament makes the Custodian the owner of enemy property retrospectively from 1968. The new law creates a situation where an Indian citizen who has legally bought and developed

---

[14] Report of the Select Committee on Enemy Property (Amendment and Validation) Bill 2016, Rajya Sabha, Parliament of India pp.2. Available Online at http://rajyasabha.nic.in/rsnew/bill/enemy_property_bill_2016.pdf

[15] Chaturvedi, A and Chiksu Roy, 'Enemy Property: what it is, how the new law changes its status', The Indian Express, 17 March 2017 Available Online: http://indianexpress.com/article/explained/enemy-property-what-it-is-how-the-new-law-changes- its-status-4572372/

[16] Why the Enemy Property Ordinance needed Parliaments Reconsideration, The Wire, 26 December 2016. Available online at https://thewire.in/89572/pranab-mukherjee-enemy-property- ordinance/

[17] Ordinances are temporary laws which can be issued by the President (under Article 123) when both the Houses of Parliament are not in session.

an enemy property after 1968, will be divested of his rights in the property.[18] This situation could be challenged in court as a violation of Article 14, which guarantees the right to equality and protects people from arbitrary actions of the government. Further, following the passage of the Bill, judicial recourse on enemy property disputes will only be available before High Courts and the Supreme Court, limiting the options available to people whose property rights have been affected.

The parallels between the enemy property act and the evacuee property act are worth considering. The Evacuee Property Act which was passed in 1950 stated that a person whose place of residence was in any state in India, who departed on account of communal disturbances in 1947, may be declared to be an evacuee. It also included a person whom the state government or an authorized officer on behalf of the state government had declared to be an evacuee. The Evacuee Property Act barred the individual from selling or managing the property once it was declared to be evacuee— even though they might not have left for Pakistan.

At the behest of the central government, the government in many states introduced a new category—"intending evacuee." This classification was even more arbitrary. North India—especially Uttar Pradesh, Punjab, and Delhi—witnessed riots in this period, and attacks on Muslims were rampant.[19] In many states, evacuees were defined as people who had left their usual place of habitation. When the evacuee Act was extended to these places, in many cases, property of people who had left briefly or were hiding was seized. Only in some cases was the property returned. This issue with this act was also that, if an officer believed that a person had the intention of leaving for Pakistan, their property could be seized. The officer alone was the judge of whether a person wanted to leave or not, regardless of what the person wanted. However, parts of this act were repealed between 1953 and 1955 when it was understood that the migration issue was settled. The enemy property act, on the other hand, was passed in an entirely different circumstance after the 1965 war. A person became an enemy of the state, according to the act, if the state believed that they sympathized with Pakistan, or if their father or mother left for Pakistan, which was considered a proof of where their loyalty lay. It sent a much stronger message—the wording of the act makes clear that a person has no chance of getting their property back.

---

[18] Chaturvedi, A and Chiksu Roy, 'Enemy Property: what it is, how the new law changes its status', The Indian Express, 17 March 2017 Available Online: http://indianexpress.com/article/explained/enemy-property-what-it-is-how-the-new-law-changes- its-status-4572372/

[19] Pandit, Aishwarya, 'What the new Enemy Act says about Indian Citizenry', The Caravan, Available Online at http://www.caravanmagazine.in/vantage/new-enemy-property-bill-says-indian-citizenry

Altering the Enemy Property Acts in India: Tussle between the Executive and Judiciary

It is interesting to note that while Pakistan and Bangladesh resolved the issue of enemy property and disposed of enemy properties, India could not do anything since 1947 till date.[20] In 2013, 2,111 properties had been identified as "enemy." By 2015, their number rose to 14,759 - showing that the number of properties being declared "enemy" continues to rise even though we are not at war with our neighbors.[21]

During the initial stages of the functioning of the Custodian of Enemy Property for India, the judiciary supported the Government's action and upheld automatic vesting of enemy properties in the Custodian and restrained themselves from interfering in the orders passed by the Custodian. Of late, however, there have been various judgments by various courts that adversely affected the powers of the CEPI and the Government of India as provided under the Act.

Contesting claims and counter claims over ownership of these properties have been a recurrent feature in India. One such notable claim was the claim on the property of Raja Mehmudabad. A bench of the Supreme Court presided over by Justice Ashok Bhan had ruled in favor of the son of Raja Mehmudabad[22] who was the treasurer of the Muslim League and trusted lieutenant of the founder of Pakistan Mohammed Ali Jinnah. The key point that emerged out of the judgment has been summarized as follows:[23]

- On the death of an "Enemy", the property devolves in succession and ceases to be "Enemy Property" if the successor is a citizen of India.
- The Enemy subject has the power to sell the property by virtue of section 6 of the Act.

---

[20] Pandey, Onkareshwar and Manmohan Sharma (2015),'The Issue of Enemy Property and India's National Interest', Intervention Paper, India Policy Foundation, pp. 10 Available Online at http://www.indiapolicyfoundation.org/Encyc/2015/1/14/351_05_03_16_The_Issue_of_Enemy_Pr operty_and_Indias_National_Interest.pdf

[21] Pandit, Aishwarya, 'What the new Enemy Act says about Indian Citizenry', The Caravan, Available Online at http://www.caravanmagazine.in/vantage/new-enemy-property-bill-says- indian-citizenry

[22] Raja of Mehmudabad, an Indian citizen, owing vast properties mainly in Uttar Pradesh migrated to Pakistan along with his minor son soon after the partition of India. He ceased to be Indian citizen and had acquired the citizenship of Pakistan. However, his wife Kaneez Abidi remained in India

[23] Report of the Select Committee on Enemy Property (Amendment and Validation) Bill 2016, Rajya Sabha, Parliament of India. Available Online at http://rajyasabha.nic.in/rsnew/bill/enemy_property_bill_2016.pdf

- The Custodian has no right or title in the property and the Enemy continues to have the right, title and interest in the property.
- Natural legal heirs and successors, who are "citizens of India" would be entitled to the property under the "Law of Succession"
- The Central Government does not have absolute power for divesting under section-18 of the Act and the power of the Court is not taken away to pass an appropriate order in a case where the property which vested in the Custodian ceases to be Enemy Property.
- On divestment of the property, the divestee would be entitled to the actual profits by filing a suit, if so advised.
- The Custodian's power is limited to managing, preservation and control of Enemy Property for a limited purpose and for a temporary period only.

The judgment encouraged numerous such 'claimants' who used this judgment to gain control over enemy properties. Following this Supreme Court judgment in Mehmudabad case, there was a spate of court orders that cited this verdict to give ownership to other claimants. As a remedial measure, to thwart various other similar claims, the government of India promulgated an Ordinance, but it lapsed on September 6, 2010 and subsequently Union ministry for home affairs drafted a bill "the Enemy Property" (Amendment and Validation) Second Bill, 2010

A number of court judgments have raised concerns regarding the terms evacuee or enemy. For instance, in Allahuddin and others vs the Union of India, a 2009 case in the Allahabad High Court, the issue in question was that in 1957, the then-custodian of evacuee property declared the property of one Swaleha Begum, the mother of Allahuddin, as "evacuee property." In 1984, the then-custodian of enemy property declared this same property "enemy." In its judgment, the court strongly criticized this order of the custodian of enemy property, which unilaterally declared a property "enemy" 23 years after it was recognized as "evacuee." Moreover, the court argued that the investing of the property with the custodian did not divest the owner of the rights, title and interest in it. This was also reflected in the High Court judgment on Sudhendu Nath Banerjee vs Bhupati Charan Chakravarthy in 1976. In a recent case of India Tourism Development Corporation vs Anil Kumar Khanna in 2015. The petitioners alleged that the property Jiwanroop Mansion, in Connaught Circus in Delhi, was let out to the Pakistan International Airways Corporation and after the 1965 war it was taken over by the custodian because it was deemed to be enemy property despite the owners being residents of India.[24]

---

[24] Pandit, Aishwarya, 'What the new Enemy Act says about Indian Citizenry', The Caravan, Available Online at http://www.caravanmagazine.in/vantage/new-enemy-property-bill-says-indian-citizenry

The problem with the law stemmed from the ambiguity regarding the definition and scope of the enemy property. Moreover, with numerous claims filed by Muslims a few years after the act was passed and was implemented across the country and the stigma of association with Pakistan, the issue assumed political relevance, especially in the context of post-Partition electoral politics where Muslims were an important minority.

Nehru and his party were conscious about this, and this is one of the reasons that the evacuee property and later enemy property laws were passed.

The extant law ignores the tenets of international justice established by the Brussels Declaration, which categorically states that private property cannot be confiscated.[25] In a series of judgments passed by courts in India, such as in the 1975 Hamida Begum vs MK Rangchari, Custodian and others case, the court recognized that right of the custodian as the protector of the property and not as its owner, and ordered the custodian to follow the law while taking control over a property. The court specifically reprimanded the custodian for allowing the sale of the property belonging to Hamida Begum, and clearly stated that, during wartime, the government took over property of an enemy subject to preserve it, and not to take control and sell it as it pleased.

The Enemy Property: A Humanitarian Aspect

Many of the people affected by the Enemy Property law are, in fact, victims of fate, their destiny, partition and now, government action. The spirit of this law is to take over the property of the alleged enemies of the state, but in reality, it is a means to brand certain individuals as "enemies," and to use their claim to property as a proof of their "enemy" status.[26] The enemy property act has gained notoriety for properties still being under the control of the custodian even after the wars have ended. It also raises the questions of justice, as private property cannot be seized indefinitely—this is in conflict with the fundamental rights to property, and does not tackle the question of the fate of individuals who are Indian citizens, but yet were deemed as enemies because their forefathers took the citizenship of Pakistan.[27] This injustice ensures that heirs of alleged enemy subjects continue to bear the burden and stigma of their family's association with Pakistan – something that

---

[25] IBID

[26] Chaturvedi, A and Chiksu Roy, 'Enemy Property: what it is, how the new law changes its status', The Indian Express, 17 March 2017 Available Online: http://indianexpress.com/article/explained/enemy-property-what-it-is-how-the-new-law-changes- its-status-4572372/

[27] Pandit, Aishwarya, 'What the new Enemy Act says about Indian Citizenry', The Caravan, Available Online at http://www.caravanmagazine.in/vantage/new-enemy-property-bill-says-indian-citizenry

thousands of Muslims experience on a daily basis. This is a stereotype that feeds into a certain narrative—that Muslims have no territorial loyalties but their loyalty is with a Muslim brotherhood. This idea discounts the numerous cultural, social and economic differences among Muslims in India.

Lesser Economic Integration and Enemy Property

The maximum 'enemy' properties are situated in Uttar Pradesh, West Bengal, and Delhi. These enemy properties can also contribute as an agent of economic prosperity not only for these states but for the whole nation as there circle rates have increased many folds since the independence and at present there value have become thousands of crores. Many of these properties are not only commercially viable but also have great potential to be conserved as heritage monuments and which can be developed as an important tourism destination which not only help in the economic growth of the nation but also rejuvenate the cultural image of the country worldwide. Political and border tensions between Pakistan and India over the past seven decades, and the ensuing deep-seated mutual mistrust and hatred, have spilled over into the economic arena, hindering any meaningful commercial partnership between them. The bitterness and suspicion between the two sides have also contributed to their committing enormous financial resources toward defence and national security, thus resulting in far lower resources available for other areas such as education and health in a region where millions still live on less than two dollars a day. Furthermore, they have pushed South Asia behind others in terms of economic integration. The region is plagued by high trade barriers, underdeveloped transport infrastructure and regulatory hurdles, among a slew of other problems. And it remains much less integrated into global manufacturing supply chains. For the situation to improve, analysts say, both countries need to find a more peaceful coexistence built on bilateral trade and investment flows. According to an economist, the EU example, whereby Germany's relations with other European nations have been built on peace and stability with steadily improving economic and political ties in the aftermath of two devastating world wars, should serve as a role model for future India-Pakistan relations.[28]

The Way Forward

One of the cases that were prominent while considering amendments in the bill was the enemy property of Raja Sahib of Mahmudabad who was a famous politician

---

[28] HowhaveIndiaandPakistanfaredeconomicallysincepartition?AvailableOnlineathttp://www. dw.com/en/how-have-india-and-pakistan-fared-economically-since-partition/a-40072801

and leader of All India Muslim League during the Pakistan movement. He is said to have properties which cover half of Uttar Pradesh and Uttarakhand which the real heirs of Raja Sahib are claiming from India. Pakistan was also seeking monetary value of the property, but after the amended bill Pakistan can no more claim these properties.

- Strong relations between the nations can help in resolve the problem.
- It is responsibility of the people to respect the decision of Apex Court.
- Both governments will have to work together.
- It is not only the government responsibility to resolve this problem we should also work for it.
- There is a necessity embrace an overarching strategic solidity regime and to shun aggressive security doctrines to reduce the possibility of a nuclear conflict.
- The difficulties of violence and non- state actors need to be addressed jointly through institutionalized mechanisms.
- Self-assurance- build measures should be followed to alleviate the faith but should not be used as a substitute for the resolution of disputes.

CONCLUSION

The issue of Enemy Property is an important manifestation of the enduring legacy of partition on defining citizenship and property rights it entails.[29] Problem of enemy property will also harm our social benefits and relation with our neighbour country Pakistan. For some of the quality things both are dependent on each other. India is the 2nd largest populated country in the world and it is the responsibility of government to fulfil the wants and needs of people. If we want to become the next super power of the world we should have the resolve to solve problems like Enemy Property, Social Conflicts, and Terrorism and so on.

Future of India and Pakistan relations is far from certain. There are both major problems and opportunities that could tilt the relationship either way. The protracted issues of Kashmir and terrorism will remain a thorn in the side of both states and will continue to hamper the normalization of relations into the future. In order to improve their economic and security ties they should capitalize on. Economic ties continue to gain momentum with piecemeal initiatives and reforms, and there is much hope on both sides that trade will continue to grow. Afghanistan appears less certain, but both states would do well to fashion a security agreement

---

[29] Jayal, N.G (2013), Citizenship and its Discontents: An Indian History, Harvard University Press, London

that promotes peace and security in the region while taking into account the various national interests of all the states involved. If that can be achieved, then the problem of militant insurgency, especially in Pakistan's north, which continues to concern India, would become less significant. That, too, would certainly contribute to better relations between Pakistan and India in the future.

*   *   *

REFERENCES

- Chaturvedi, A and Chiksu Roy, 'Enemy Property: what it is, how the new law changes its status', The Indian Express, 17 March 2017 Available Online: http://indianexpress.com/article/explained/enemy-property-what-it-is-how-the-new- law-changes-its-status-4572372/.
- Jayal, N.G (2013), Citizenship and its Discontents: An Indian History, Harvard University Press, London.
- How have India and Pakistan fared economically since partition? Available Online at http://www.dw.com/en/how-have-india-and-pakistan -fared-economically-since- partition/a-40072801.
- Pandey, Onkareshwar and Manmohan Sharma (2015),'The Issue of Enemy Property and India's National Interest', Intervention Paper, India Policy Foundation, pp. 10 Available Online. at http://www.indiapolicyfoundation. org/Encyc/2015/1/14/351_05_03_16_The_Issue_of_Enemy_Property_ and_Indias_National_Interest.pdf.
- Pandit, Aishwarya, 'What the new Enemy Act says about Indian Citizenry', The Caravan, Available Online at http://www.caravanmagazine.in/vantage/ new-enemy- property-bill-says-indian-citizenry
- Parliament passes Enemy Property Bill, The Hindu, 14 March 2017. Available Online at http://www.thehindu.com/news/national/parliament-passes-enemy-property- bill/article17461600.ece
- Why the Enemy Property Ordinance needed Parliaments Reconsideration, The Wire, 26 December 2016. Available online at https://thewire.in/89572/ pranab-mukherjee- enemy-property-ordinance/
- Report of the Select Committee on Enemy Property (Amendment and Validation) Bill 2016, Rajya Sabha, Parliament of India, pp.2 Available Online at http://rajyasabha.nic.in/rsnew/bill/enemy_property_bill_2016. pdf.

Benefits of Big Data Business Analytics for Online Applications in IoT

AUTHOR BIO

Dr. Kamal Gulati
Associate Professor – Amity University Noida

Dr. Gulati is currently working as Associate Professor with Amity University, Noida. He has worked as Visiting Professor & Research Scholar (Under Faculty Exchange Program) CSIT Department at Stratford University, USA for two-quarters from January 2016 to May 2016. Dr. Gulati has also worked at Bahrain University in Kingdom of Bahrain as Sr. I.T. Faculty (Computer Science Department) for two years.

Dr. Gulati has rich experience of over 16 years in the field of teaching and research in Computer Science and Information Technology. He has worked with both private and public institutions and universities as faculty and has also written self-instruction material for Information Technology courses. He has a number of research papers published in national and international journals and conference proceedings. Dr. Gulati is also associate as Visiting Professor with Stratford University (Delhi & USA), FMS - University of Delhi, ICFAI, KKMII, AIMA, Asian Business School, CDAC, Asia Pacific Institute of Management, IMT - Ghaziabad, IIHT, SMU, IIFP, Centre for Policy Research, Career Power, AON Hewitt, Honda-Seil, Ericsson, Vodafone, Reliance, Amity University Gwalior and Jaipur, India.

He has chaired various National and International Conferences of repute and is associated as Editorial Board Member for International and National journals and also as, Academic Adviser and Research Paper Reviewer for them.

Dr. Gulati had visited various countries including USA, Canada, UAE, Bahrain, Oman, Nepal for teaching and research purposes.

Benefits of Big Data Business Analytics for Online Applications in IoT

Dr. Kamal Gulati

ABSTRACT

Huge information platforms primarily are centered on the volumes of information management. The developing pervasiveness of Internet of Things (IoT) applications, alongside their connected capacity should gather information from physical elements. Furthermore, virtual sensors continuously generate enormous information. In this chapter, we would define analytics requirement of IoT applications in Big Data Platforms using the different platforms of Distributed Stream Processing and Complex Event Processing's systems and the need for IoT applications.

"Big data and the internet of things could add £322bn to the London economy by 2020, new research from industry analysts and economists reveals today.

The internet of things – the network of everyday items fitted with electronics to allow them to collect and exchange data – could lead to £72bn of efficiency gains and 67,000 new jobs.

The research from the Centre of Economics and Business Research (CEBR) also said using new techniques to crunch massive data sets could provide a much bigger boost of £220m and 157,000 new jobs.

Adoption rates for big data analytics are estimated to rise from 58 per cent in 2017 to 67 per cent by 2020. Internet of things adoption will increase from 33 per cent in 2017 to 43 per cent by 2020. The biggest beneficiary is expected to be the UK's struggling manufacturing sector. UK factory output declined last year and is still below pre-recession levels. Yet the report says there could be big improvements in supply chain management and customer intelligence.

However, the key is making sure those solutions are extracting maximum insight which is then turned into business actions. IoT is in the initial stages of its life cycle, and will provide more data for analysis in areas that may be new to analytics, reinforcing the potential benefits to the London economy."

Keywords: *Big Data, IoT, Distributed Stream Processing, Complex Event Processing, Analytics*

INTRODUCTION

Internet of Things (IoT) is an emerging architectural model that allows diverse sensors, controllers, devices, and appliances to be connected as part of wider Internet. IoT is driven by the growing prevalence of network-connected devices or "Things" that are present as part of physical infrastructure (e.g., Smart Meters that connect to Power Grids and Smart Appliances at residences), which observe the natural environment (e.g., Air Quality Monitors in Urban Settings), or monitor humans and society at large (e.g., FitBit for individual fitness tracking and Surveillance Cameras at event venues). In addition to monitoring and transmitting observations over the network, these "Things" may also be controlled remotely, say to turn off a smart air conditioning unit or to turn on a smart vehicle, through signals over the network. As such, estimates on the number of such things which are a part of the IoT range is in the billions, and these things may be generic, such as a smartphone, or specialized to a domain, as in the case of a smart cart in a grocery store. Some definitions of IoT include Humans as first-class entities within the Internet of Things (IoT), and Internet of Things and Humans (IoTH) and Internet of Everything (IoE).

IoT enables the generation of enormous volumes of data observed from sensing devices, and this begets a key question of how to meaningfully make use of this information. Promise of IoT lies in being able to optimize the network-connected system or improve the quality of life of humans who use or interact with the system. This helps to analyze, understand, and act on this information. This opens up fundamental questions on big data analytics that are still in the process of being characterized.

Such analytics may be simple correlations between the outside air temperature and the load on the power grid (i.e., hot days lead to increased use of air conditioners, and hence greater load on the power grid), to more complex causal relationships, such as an evening accident on a freeway or leading to a progressive neighborhood which delays the jump in power usage caused by electric vehicles being recharged when commuters reach home.

The ability to observe IoT systems does not mean that we can understand or reason about such complex systems, just as in the "butterfly effect," the ability to observe butterflies does not allow us to link the flapping of their wings to a future tornado at a remote location. However, the unprecedented ability to sense physical and natural systems does offer a unique opportunity to apply, extend, and invent data analytics techniques, algorithms, and platforms to help make decisions to improve and optimize such systems. In particular, it places emphasis on the Velocity dimension of big data and consequently, on the temporal aspect of data generation and its analysis. IoT devices are often active continuously, leading to a perpetual stream of time series data being emitted from them. Such temporal data are transient in value and IoT systems benefit if this data is analyzed and acted upon in real time to close the loop from network to knowledge. In the rest of the chapter, we introduce use cases and scenarios of emerging IoT domains that are grappling with big data and have a tangible societal impact. We use these to motivate specific analytics and techniques that are required by such domains to operate effectively. Subsequently, we discuss big data platforms that are making headway in offering such tools and technologies, and provide case studies of such analytics in action for IoT applications. We finally conclude with open problems we foresee for big data analytics in IoT, as this nascent field matures beyond its hype.

IoT Domains Generating Big Data

Smart Cities

There is intense global interest in enhancing the quality and sustainability of urban life. This is driven by the growing urbanization in developing countries, particularly highly populated ones like China, India, and Brazil, which is stressing the urban infrastructure and affecting the livability of residents, as well as the need to seamlessly integrate the urban ecosystem with a technology-driven lifestyle. The Smart Cities concept attempts to infuse sensing, control, and decision-making into different utilities offered in cities, such as smart transportation, smart power grids, and smart water management. Currently, it also attempts to improve safety and health through urban surveillance and environmental monitoring for air and noise pollution.

Smart power grids monitor the consumers of power using advanced metering infrastructure (AMI), also called Smart Meters, to provide real-time information about the amount of power consumed, typically at 15 minute intervals. This, combined with metering at neighborhood transformers and community sub-stations, allows the power utility to get a realistic view of their distribution network. The goal for the utility is to use this data to manage their supply and demand to avoid a mismatch that could cause brownouts and blackouts, as well as to switch their supply mix from reliable but polluting coal and gas-based power plants to less-reliable solar- and wind-based generation. Data-driven targeting of specific consumers helps in reducing consumption through demand-response optimization, rather than increase production, which is another goal. This requires intelligent shifting, shaving, and shedding of loads from household appliances, electric vehicles, and industrial units based on their load profiles. Smart water management likewise attempts this intelligent resource management for water, with the additional goal of ensuring adequate water quality to mitigate health concerns.

Smart transportation uses sensors that monitor road traffic conditions, using inductive-loop traffic detectors on roads, traffic cameras, and in-vehicle and in-person monitoring devices, with the goal of using such data to efficiently managing traffic flow through smart traffic signaling. This also extends to managing public transport by optimizing the schedule of buses and trains on-demand, based on real-time data, and planning the routing of freight vehicles in transport hubs and port cities to ease the traffic. Such data collection, particularly through surveillance cameras, also helps with vehicular safety (tracking hit-and-run accidents, or auto- mobile theft), public safety (burglaries or attacks), and disaster management (tornadoes, earthquakes, urban flooding). Users already see the benefits of smart transportation through apps like Waze and Google Maps that offer directions based on real-time traffic conditions monitored through their smartphone apps, but getting a more integrated view over diverse sensor and human data for smart transport management is a challenge.

Smart Agriculture

With global warming affecting food supply and the increasing affordability of the world's population to food affecting its demand, there is starting to be a stress on the agricultural output. While mechanized farming by industry-scale farmers is the norm in developed countries, a majority of farming in developing countries is still human-intensive with low to negative profit margins. As such, technology and particularly IoT can play a role in improving practices at both these scales and maturity levels.

One of the key challenges in farming is to decide when to water the crops. Cash crops like vineyards are very sensitive to the soil moisture and humidity. The quality of the produce is affected by over or under irrigation, which also depends on weather conditions such as sunlight and warmth, rainfall, and dew conditions. On the other hand, irrigation in developing countries like India relies on pumping groundwater, and the frequency of this depends on availability of intermittent electricity supply to operate pumps. As such, IoT can make it possible to use soil moisture data from ground sensors, remote sensing data from satellite imagery, and data from weather prediction models as well as supply schedule of power utilities to intelligently plan the irrigation of crops.

Smart Health and Lifestyle

Sports provide natural use cases for IoT, which, while less critical than other social scenarios, do provide early insight into emerging ideas due to rapid technology penetration. Common uses of IoT in sports rely on sensors placed in a player's shoes, helmet, or clothing, which provide high-resolution data (e.g., x, y, z location, speed, acceleration) about the player's actions coupled with vitals like heart rate. For example, the DEBS 2013 Conference's Grand Challenge is based on a data collected from players' shoes and the ball in a soccer game. Also, American football teams have started placing cameras and sensors in players' helmets to detect concussions, and one can even buy basketballs off-the-shelf with sensors embedded within to track plays. The potential benefits of having such fine-grained data on the players and the equipment can ensure player's safety from injuries suffered at game time, better referee decisions, data-driven player selection (e.g., MoneyBall), augmented TV broadcast with the enhanced game analysis, and even embedded virtual reality views for the audience.

Health and lifestyle examples range from activity monitors and smart watches such as FitBit, Withings, and Apple Watch to in-home care for the elderly. There is a growth in electronic devices that track people's behavior and basic health metrics, and enables them to get warnings about potential illness or a health condition, or just for personal analytics that help people reach fitness goals as part of a "quantified self" movement. The increasing prevalence of smart watches and smart health devices is leading to individual health data being collected, and generic or specialized apps that can monitor and analyze them.

At the same time, such inexpensive sensors would make it possible to have sustainable in-home care for the elderly, recuperating patients, and those with long-term medical conditions to live at their home while having their health-monitored remotely. Also, IoT devices can improve the quality of hospital care and closer integration of case handling by monitoring medication to ensure patients are given the dosages consistent with their prescription, and avoid nosocomial ailments by ensuring caregivers wash their hands after procedures. In developing countries that rely largely on tertiary care by community nurses, neo-natal monitoring through bracelets coupled with smartphones can help detect if a baby shows signs of trauma that needs immediate medical attention.

Smart Retail and Logistics

Retail and logistics domains have a vital need to track their supply chain activity. For example, retailers are interested to track their inventory, shipping, and even the behavior of customers in their stores. RFID tags have been a major part of the supply chain for a while, with Walmart using them to handle their logistics. It enables them to automatically track what items move in and out of the store without having to scan them, and to reliably know where each item is, avoiding operator errors. More generally, "Smart things" like RFID tags, GPS trackers, iBeacons, etc., can track items that are being transported and avoid costly errors in domains like airline baggage, postal vehicles, and even livestock and wildlife.

In logistics, speed and accuracy are vital. Within a retail store, smart tracking can reveal a wealth of information about consumer behavior and provide a rich interactive experience. Strategically placed sensors in store shelves and aisles can track what area of the store gets most attention and what regions confuse shoppers. One often-overlooked sensor that is present in most stores is a video camera, typically used for security but which can, through streaming video analysis, also reveal customer behavior. On the other hand, mobile devices and Bluetooth low-energy (BLE) beacons can provide an interactive experience to the consumer, greeting them by name, helping them locate items, and even making suggestions on related products and discount coupons. These can provide mutually beneficial value to consumers and retailers, increase the sales volume for retailers, and help with efficient inventory management.

Despite their huge potential, IoT devices and the communication technology that connect them are just enabling tools—only as effective as how they are used and the decisions that they empower. As a result, deriving actionable insights from data collected through IoT devices and carrying out appropriate actions though IoT devices or by other means is an open challenge for IoT-based systems.

Role of Big Data Analytics in IoT

The above scenarios present an overview of the potential application domains that would benefit from big data being generated through IoT infrastructure. Next, we explore in greater detail the role of analytics and decision systems in these use cases.

IoT systems are an example of autonomic systems that garnered significant attention in the early 2000s. Autonomic system design has resulted in several types of control loops, which often follow the MEAP model of Monitor, Analyze, Plan, and Execute operations. This is similar to the Observe, Orient, Decide and Act (OODA) control loop used in other domains. These are often closed loops, since the Execute or Act step would likely cause the environment to change, which would trigger the loop again, and so on.

These feedback and control models are relevant within IoT applications as well. For example, a smart power grid application that performs home energy management may monitor the power consumption in the household and observe that the residents have just entered their home (e.g., the garage door opens), analyze their preferences, and decide to start the air conditioning unit that is configured to the optimum temperature level and even plan for coffee to be brewed in 15 min, by "talking" to smart appliances. Some of these scenarios are indeed possible, even at the present.

However, there are many challenges in building intelligent systems that can make automated decisions and executing them. Some of the questions to consider are:

- How does it effectively learn from data, and dissociate signal from noise?
- How can it integrate expert knowledge with observed patterns?

- How can it understand the context (Where, When, Who, Where) and act accordingly?
- How can it comprehend the consequences of and interference between different actions?
- How does it plan for causality that are not instantaneous, but take place over time, across control iterations, and can fail?

Of course, these are challenging problems not unique just for IoT but fundamentally to many domains that can benefit from artificial intelligence, machine learning, and expert systems. However, the availability of big data in IoT domains makes them a particularly interesting candidate for exploration.

There is a great deal of diversity in IoT use cases and their underlying decision systems, and these systems frequently contend with the above challenges. We can classify decision systems based on increasing levels of complexity. While this classification is not meant to be comprehensive, it illustrates the different degrees of control capabilities that are possible, and analytics that are required.

1. Visual Analytics: Such techniques help humans analyze the data and present information to them in a meaningful form through a dashboard interface. They are designed to augment the human decision process with more information, presented in a cohesive and easily interpretable manner. An example is FitBit, which collects personal activity data using an in-person device and presents a summary of a user's effort levels, estimated calories burnt, and progress toward monthly goals, through a mobile or web application.

2. Alerts and Warnings: These engines allow decision logic to be provided by end users, and then uses these to interpret and classify data that arrives to raise alerts or warning. These perform a certain degree of automated predefined analysis to help highlight situations of interest, which becomes critical when users must deal with large volumes of data. For example, an environmental monitoring system may track the level of pollution or chemicals in an industrial city and send notifications on health hazards or chemical leaks to the citizens.

3. Reactive Systems: Systems may also go one step further by taking concrete actions (beyond notifications) based on their decisions. Generally, they are designed with a rule-based language that describes actions to be carried out when certain conditions are met. For example, a smart lighting system may turn off the lights when nobody is present in a room. Here, there is a tight coupling between just two physical components—an infrared sensor and light bulbs, and along a single data dimension—the IR level that indicates

human presence, i.e., the system is not aware of the bigger picture but just the local, unidimensional situation.

4. Control and Optimize: Control systems operate in a closed loop where decisions lead to actions that are instantaneous, with the possibility that the actions can fail to meet the optimization goal. Control loop decision systems attempt to optimize the behavior of specific variables and also consider failure cases when deciding action outcomes. As discussed before, such MEAP or OODA systems can generate a plan of action, executing the action, observing the response in a control loop, and recovering from a failure to meet a goal. For example, many electro-mechanical systems such as cruise control in a car or even a simple air conditioner thermostat operate on such a closed loop to either maintain the speed of the car or the ambient temperature.

5. Complex Systems: Such systems understand the context and interaction between several decision loops and can make high-level decisions that span multiple dimensions within a single domain. For example, systems that manage city traffic can discern interaction between multimodal transports such as Bus, Metro, and Trains, in scheduling the road and rail traffic signaling for efficient transit.

6. Knowledge-driven Intelligent Systems: Complex infrastructure has cross-domain impact, with decisions in one domain impacting the other. Knowledge-based intelligent systems attempt to capture the relationship between different domains, such as transportation and power, or environmental conditions and healthcare, and optimize the decisions across these domains. The knowledge base itself is often specified by experts, and these may partially guide automated "deep learning" of correlations and causations within and across domains.

7. Behavioral and Probabilistic Systems: Human being are an intrinsic part of IoT though they are often overlooked. As such, they are both sources of data and means for control, through messaging, suggestions, and incentives. Behavioral systems attempt to include human models as a part of the overall IoT system, with likely nonuniform behavior. As a generalization, probabilistic and fuzzy systems incorporate nondeterminism as an integral part of decision-making, which goes above and beyond failures.

8. Real-time decision-making: These systems vary from simple analytics performed in a batch mode, to real-time detection of patterns over data to issue alerts, to make complex plans and decisions that may have downstream consequences over time. The temporal dimension and the context are two characteristics that make these systems challenging. In the next sections we discuss some of these concepts in detail. However, behavioral systems and beyond are still in their infancy.

Real-Time Big Data Analytics Platforms

Decision systems that go beyond visual analytics have an intrinsic need to analyze data and respond to situations. Depending on the sophistication, such systems may have to act rapidly on incoming information, grapple with heterogeneous knowledge bases, work across multiple domains, and often in a distributed manner. Big data platforms offer programming and software infrastructure to help perform analytics to support the performance and scalability needs of such decision support systems for IoT domains.

There has been significant focus on big data analytics platforms on the volume dimension of big data. In such platforms, such as MapReduce, data is staged and aggregated over time, and analytics are performed in a batch mode on these large data corpus. These platforms weakly scale with the size of the input data, as more distributed compute resources are made available. However, as we have motivated before, IoT applications place an emphasis on online analytics, where data that arrives rapidly needs to be processed and analyzed with low latency to drive autonomic decision-making.

Classification of Platforms by Latency and Throughput

We classify the existing big data platforms along two dimensions: the average throughput of data processed per unit time (along the Y axis) and the latency time to process a unit of data and emit a result (X axis). Volume-driven platforms such as MapReduce scale to terabytes of data, and on an average, are able to process 100 MB/s of data per second (top right of figure). But this is in a batch processing mode, so the minimum time taken to generate a result (even for small data sizes, such as in the bottom right of figure) is on the order of minutes. This is forced by the need to store data on distributed disks, which introduces I/O and network overheads but also ensures persistence of data for repeated analysis. As a result, the time between data arriving and useful decision being made is in the order of minutes or more.

Databases, both relational and NoSQL, also use disk storage but can be used with indexes to support interactive searches. This guarantees persistence while avoiding the brute-force table scans of MapReduce platforms. OLAP technologies (e.g., Pentaho) and projects like Apache drill build a layer on top of databases for interactive processing. For large datasets, indexing needs to be done a priori, introducing some additional latencies. In such platforms, the scalability of data throughput is sacrificed (10 KB–1 MB/s) in return for faster query response times on the order of seconds to minutes.

Stream Processing systems are also called "Real-Time processing" although they are in fact only low-latency (but not real-time) processing, in the strict sense of the word. Such systems can process data as they arrive at high rates by only keeping a small subset of the data in memory or on disk for the duration of processing, and can produce results in milliseconds. Here, the incoming data is transient and once processed is discarded (or separately stored in a NoSQL database for offline processing). Such platforms may operate on a single machine or on distributed systems. These are the focus of further discussion in this chapter.

Categorizing big data platforms based on latency of processing and size of data processed

Finally, In-Memory Computing uses the idea of loading all the data into distributed memory and processing them while avoiding random access to distributed disks during the computation. Platforms like Apache Spark offer a streaming batch model that groups events within a window for batch processing. This, while sacrificing some latency, helps achieve a higher throughput across distributed memory and can be 100's to 1000's of times faster than stream processing.

Among these technologies, streaming analytics plays a key role as a layer that can perform initial, low-latency processing of data available from IoT devices. Their results may directly lead to actions, stored for future processing, or feed into models that take decisions.

We next introduce specific technologies to support real-time analytics, and consider two use case scenarios as running examples. (1) Sports Analytics for Soccer Games, where sensors placed in the football players' boots and the goal- keeper's gloves generate event streams at 60 Hz frequency that contain time, location, and speed information. This is motivated by the DEBS 2013 Challenge. (2) Analytics for Smart Energy Management in buildings that identify real-time opportunities for energy reduction using events from smart power meters and electrical equipment. This is motivated by the Los Angeles Smart Grid Project. In the subsequent section, we discuss how these big data stream processing technologies are integrated into these use cases.

Online Analytics to Detect Exact Temporal Patterns

In many domains, the knowledge from domain experts and from past experiences provide us with interesting patterns that can occur, and such patterns (or signatures) may indicate situations of interest that require a response as part of a decision support system. We can detect the occurrence of such patterns and conditions using Complex Event Processing (CEP). CEP allows the specification of queries over one or more event streams, and consequently helps define such patterns in a formal manner. The queries are described through an Event Query Language (EQL) that is specific to the CEP engine, such as WSO2's CEP Siddhi language or Esper's EQL.

Following are examples of some such patterns of interest:

- Filter ambient temperature measurement events from an Air Conditioner (AC) unit if it crosses a threshold temperature.
- Maintain a moving average of the energy consumption over 1 hour time windows.
- Correlate events from multiple streams by performing a Join operation across them based on an attribute, such as the room location of a power meter generating consumption events and an AC unit generating temperature events.
- Detect a temporal sequence of event patterns specified as a state machine over events, such as the occurrence of several power consumption events of a low value followed by a spike in their value indicating a heavier energy load.
- Preprocess events, such as transforming their units or dropping unused attributes of the events.
- Track the change in state over space and time of an entity, such as the location of a football.
- Detect trends captured by sequences, missing events, thresholds, outliers, and even complex ones like "triple bottom" used in algorithmic financial trading.

Distributed Stream Processing

While CEP allows analytics of interest to be captured and detected in real time from streams of events, the process of ensuring the event streams is made available in an appropriate form falls within the space of stream processing. Stream processing allows composition of real-time applications as a Directed Acyclic Graph (DAG), where vertices are application logic tasks, while edges are streams of events.

Two distinctions between stream and complex event processing are that the events in CEP are strongly typed, and the queries conform to well-defined logic that operate on typed events and are visible to the CEP engine to perform optimizations. In stream processing, on the other hand, the event contents as well as the application logic are opaque to the stream processing engine, and the engine is primarily responsible for moving event payload between application logic and the execution of the logic over the events. The events are just a binary or text payload that the engine does not examine. In that sense, one can consider CEP as specialization of stream processing systems.

Distributed Stream Processing (DSP) has gained interest recently due to the increasing quanta of real-time data that arrives and the hardware limits of single-machine, shared-memory execution. In DSP, the tasks of the DAG can be distributed across different machines in a local area network (LAN) or a Cloud data center, with event streams passing between them. Apache Storm is an example of such a system.

DSP are faster than CEP and offer a lower latency for processing since they avoid the overheads of introspecting the contents of the message. Consequently, they are used as preprocessors for cleaning and ingesting data from sensors and their outputs can be passed onto online analytics platforms such as CEP, or stored for offline analytics. Such preprocessing often takes the form of an Extract–Transform–Load (ETL) pipeline used in data warehousing or Extract–Transform–Analyze; except that it is done in near real time. These pipelines can help convert the format and representation of the data, detect and clean outliers, perform sanity checks and quality control, etc. on the incoming data. DSP also allow analytic logic to be embedded within them as a task, so that a CEP engine or a machine learning logic can be a task within a DSP application.

For example, data streaming from hunDreds of building sensors in a binary format is parsed to extract relevant information, and then transformed into a standard format necessary for analysis, a copy stored in a NoSQL archive for future processing, while a duplicate copy is forked for real-time analytics by a CEP engine.

Despite the events and task logic of the DAG themselves being opaque, DSP engines support several different semantics when composing streaming applications. These include whether to perform a duplicate or interleave/split of outgoing events from a task, and using transparent keys with opaque values to perform a map operation from one task to a set of downstream tasks. Tasks may also perform either a merge or a join of multiple incoming messages, where the former interleaves incoming messages while the latter aligns messages based on arrival order. Tasks may be stateful or stateless, which determines whether the state from processing a message is available to upstream events that arrive. Often, DSPs do not guarantee ordering of events as distributed coordination is more difficult and favors faster execution instead.

The selectivity of a task determines the number of events it generates when consuming a single event and its latency is an estimate of time taken to process one event. DSPs have a natural ability to pipeline execution of events. The length and the width of the DAG, respectively, determine the total latency of the critical path of execution, and the number of parallel tasks at the widest width of the DAG which can be exploited for task parallelism, if preceded by a duplicate task semantic. Stateless tasks can also leverage data parallelism by adding more processors to execute a single task, either on multiple threads in a machine, or across different machines in a cluster or virtual machines in the Cloud. This is more challenging for stateful tasks.

More recently, there is interest in distributing such stream processing engines to go beyond a single data center into distributed execution across edge devices and the Cloud. This Edge + Cloud model of execution is motivated by the growing prevalence of generating data from distributed IoT sensor devices that themselves have computing capabilities, albeit limited. Devices like smartphones, Raspberry Pi, and Arduino running mobile processors and hosting sensors can perform part of the data filtering on-board rather than push all data to the Cloud or to a centralized data center for processing. This has several benefits. It limits the need to transfer large quantities of data that can incur communication costs. It also reduces the network round-trip latency that is paid when sending the data to the Cloud for analysis and receiving a response to take action. Finally, it enhances the privacy of the data sources as it allows for local analysis on-site rather than pushing it to a public Cloud. At the same time, there may be some analytics such as aggregation and comparisons across sensors/devices that require limited event streams to be centrally accumulated for analysis. This distribution of the computation across edge and the Cloud to meet the different metrics of costs, time, and privacy is of growing research interest as IoT applications start to actively utilize DSPs.

Real-Time Analytics Case Studies

We next expand on the earlier example IoT domains of Smart Energy Management and Sports Analytics, and discuss how CEP and DSP systems are used for real-time analytics within these applications.

Analytics for Smart Energy Management

Smart power grids use information gathered from sensors that monitor the electricity transmission and distribution infrastructure to ensure reliable, efficient, and sustainable generation and supply of power. In addition to individual residences in a city-scale electric grid, there are also islands of micro-grids that are operated by large institutional campuses such as universities, office parks, and heavy industry. Such micro-grids control the power distribution within their campus, with local cogeneration as well as electricity supply from the city grid, and offer the ability to deploy IoT solutions to instrument, monitor, and control the micro-grid behavior in an intelligent manner.

The University of Southern California's (USC) Campus Micro-grid, part of the Los Angeles Smart Grid project, is an example of such a model where stream and CEP platforms are used with similar efforts taking place at other institutional campuses worldwide. Diverse sensors to monitor the micro-grid range from smart power meters that measure KWh, power load, and quality, to building area net- works that can monitor and control HVAC (heating, ventilation, air conditioning) units, lighting, and elevators. In addition, organization, spatial and schedule information on the departments, people, buildings, and class schedules are also available.

These provide a mix of slow (buildings, departments) and fast (sensor readings, schedules) changing data that must be analyzed in real time for smart power management. Specifically, the analytics aims to perform demand-response optimization, wherein the power consumption of the micro-grid has to be curtailed on- demand when a mismatch between the available power supply and expected power demand is identified. Stream and complex event processing platforms play vital a role in this decision-making process.

1.   Information integration pipeline: Data coming from thousands of diverse sensors have to be preprocessed before analysis can be performed on them. Preprocessing includes extracting relevant fields from the sensor event stream, applying quality correction, performing unit transformations, and annotating them with static information available about that sensor. These steps are performed by an information processing pipeline that is composed using a distributed stream processing platform. The outcome of the preprocessing is further forked into three paths: One, for semantic annotation and archival in a RDF data store for offline querying, analysis, and visualization; Two, for performing demand forecasting over KWh events that arrive from smart power meters; and Three, for detecting power demand and curtailment situations using a CEP engine to aid decision-making.

2.   Demand forecasting using time series: One of the paths taken from the information processing pipeline is to predict future energy demand by each building in the micro-grid based on past behavior. For this, we use the ARIMA time series forecasting model that uses the recent history of KWh events from a building for its prediction. The ARIMA model is included as a logic block within the distributed stream processing pipeline and the forecasts are generated as a series of events. These are further analyzed in real time as part of the DSP to see if the sum of impending demand from different buildings is greater than the available generation capacity during that future period. This helps in deciding if a power curtailment action is required within the micro-grid.

3.   Detecting power demand and curtailment opportunities: Another event stream that forks from the preprocessing pipeline is to a CEP engine, which appears as a logic block within the DSP. This CEP engine has two types of analytics queries registered with it, one to detect energy spikes that may occur due to special circumstances that cannot be captured by

the time series model, and another to detect potential energy leaks that can be plugged to reduce energy consumption when required. We offer a few examples of these two classes of CEP queries.

Sports Analytics

The Distributed Event-Based Systems (DEBS) Conference 2013's Event Processing Grand Challenge offers a novel IoT use case for soccer analytics that is addressed using CEP platforms. Data for this use case came from a Soccer game that was played with sensors placed in the ball, the players' boots, and the goal keeper's gloves. Each sensor generates events which describes the current location (x, y, z), the timestamp, velocity (vx, vy, vz), and acceleration (ax, ay, az), at the rate of 60 Hz.

This data can provide complete information of the game play. However, understanding and deriving higher levels events such as kicks, passes, ball possession, and offside requires detecting complicated temporal queries from these raw events. As part of the challenge, we implemented those queries using the Siddhi Complex Event Processing engine, and achieved throughput in excess of 140,000 events/sec. We look at some example queries to understand how the aforementioned CEP operators are combined to detect such complex sport strategies.

Discussion and Open Problems

The use cases we have presented exemplify the rich and novel information space that IoT applications offer for analytics and decision-making. These have a tangible impact on both technology and human lifestyle. Real-time big data platforms such as distributed stream processing and complex event processing that we have discussed are two of many platforms that can help coordinate, process, and analyze such information to offer actionable intelligence that offer the "smarts" to these IoT applications. However, as we have observed, these platforms need to work in tandem with other advances in computing, in areas like machine learning, data mining, knowledge harvesting, deep learning, behavioral modeling, etc. to provide holistic solutions that are robust and sustainable.

There are several open challenges on fast data processing platforms themselves. Incorporating semantics into processing events is important to bring in contextual information about diverse domains into the queries and combine offline knowledge bases with online data that stream in. Such contextual information includes schedule and environmental information, habits, and interests that are learned, and proximity with other entities in the virtual and physical space that help integrate with an active world of humans, their agents, and things.

While the scalability of high-velocity big data platforms on captive commodity clusters is well studied, making use of elastic cloud computing resources to on-demand adapt the execution to runtime changes in the application logic or incoming data rates is still being investigated. The nominal utility cost of stream and event processing and the real cost paid for cloud computing resources will also come into play.

Smart devices that we carry on our person or are deployed on physical infrastructure have capable computing power despite their low power footprint. Enabling DSP and CEP engines to effectively leverage their compute capability, in conjunction with more capable computing resources at centralized data centers and Clouds, is important. This is sometimes referred to as fog computing or mobile Clouds. This has the advantage of reducing the round-trip latency for processing events that are often generated by the sensors, and actions taken based on the events have to be communicated back to actuators that are collocated with the sensors. This can also be robust to remote failures by localizing the closed-loop decision-making. Further, issues of data privacy can also be handled in a personalized manner by offering the ability to select the computing resource to perform the analytics and decision-making on.

Decisions that are driven by these analytics can have an immediate effect or may impact future actions. Defining performance requirements for such fast data processing platforms that take into account the lead time for decision-making and the resulting actions themselves can help prioritize processing of information streams. Having policy languages that can capture such dependencies, and real-time processing engines that can interpret and adapt to such needs, will help.

There are several open challenges specific to CEP engines too. First is scaling CEP execution beyond single machine. Several systems use data partitions, either derived automatically or given explicitly by the users, to break the execution into multiple nodes. For IoT use cases, handling out of order events is a major challenge. With thousands of sensors without a globally synchronized clock, events can arrive from sensors out of sync, and many CEP operators that are sensitive to the event ordering will find it challenging to enforce order and ensure runtime scalability. Google's MillWheel is an effort to address this problem. Finally, it is unavoidable that some of the sensors or readings may be faulty in an IoT deployment. Taking decisions despite those uncertainties is another challenge.

*   *   *

REFERENCES

E. Vera, L. Mancera, S.D. Babacan, R. Molina, A.K. Katsaggelos, Bayesian compressive sensing of wavelet coefficients using multiscale Laplacian priors, in:

Statistical Signal G. IEEE Transactions on Intelligent Transportation Systems, 6 (2005), pp. 43-53

M. Botterman, Internet of things: an early reality of the future internet, in: Workshop Report prepared for European Commission, Information Society and Media Directorate General, Networked Enterprise & RFID Unit (D4), Prague, May 2009.

P. Kumar, S. Ranganath, W. Huang, K. Sengupta Framework for real-time behavior interpretation from traffic video

Point-to-Multipoint RF Modules <http://www.digi.com/products/wireless-wired-embedded-solutions/zigbee-rf-modules/point-multipoint-rfmodules/>.

Processing, 2009, SSP'09, IEEE/SP 15th Workshop on., 2009, pp. 229–232.

Real World Internet Position Paper <http://rwi.future-internet.eu/images/c/c3/Real_World_Internet_Position_Paper_vFINAL.pdf>.

S. Kuznetsov, E. Paulos, Participatory sensing in public spaces: activating urban surfaces with sensor probes, in: ACM Request Permissions, 2010.

S. Lohr. The age of big data. New York Times (http://www.nytimes.com/2012/02/12/sunday-review/bigdatas-impact-in-the-world.html), Feb 2012.

Santucci, Internet of the future and internet of things: what is at stake and how are we getting prepared for them?, eMatch conference, Oslo, September 2009.

Y. Bengio Learning Deep Architectures for AI (first ed.), Now Publishers Inc. (2009)

http://www.nedapavi.com/products/sensit/sensit.html.

http://www.tst-sistemas.es/en/solutions/parking/.

http://www.streetline.com/parksight/.

Assessment of Ease of Doing Business in India: Survey of India based UK Companies

AUTHOR BIO

Havish Madhvapaty
Co – Founder | Head of Research and Analytics
Decode Research and Analytics

Havish has diverse experience across sales and marketing, academia and market research. He is a Ph.D. scholar researching experiential marketing. His qualifications include Microsoft certified Microsoft Office Specialist (MOS) Master [2013 + 2016], Google Analytics & Google AdWords Certified, and VSkills Certified Digital Marketing Master. He has also been an MBA Gold Medallist and Scholarship Awardee.

At Decode, he leads a team of analysts, spearheading research work. Traverse Strategy Consultants, a group company, where he worked as Head of Research and Analytics, was listed as Top 10 Most Promising Market Research Firms in India. He has had the opportunity to work on projects for Government of India (Ministry of Tourism, Ministry of Finance, Ministry of Commerce etc.)

He is a corporate and academic trainer in quantitative analysis, focusing on Advanced Microsoft Excel and SPSS. He has trained organizations such as S&P, PWC, EY, UBER, ITC, TATA MOTORS, S. CHAND, WIPRO, EXL etc. In addition to Microsoft Excel, he is also proficient in MS PowerPoint, MS Word and MS Project. He is active on the Microsoft community as an expert contributor and also contributes to Stack Overflow.

Havish has over 25 academic publications in national and international journals, and has acted as a reviewer for IGI Global. He has authored three books. His research assignments have been featured regularly in BW|Businessworld, BW|Applause, BW|Education, IMPACT, Pitch; and on websites of Amagi, Businessworld, CMO. com, Colgate Palmolive, Goa Tourism, Indiantelevision, Marico, SEBI, Yahoo News and so on.

AUTHOR BIO
Prof. (Dr.) Anupama Rajesh
Professor
Amity Business School, Amity University Uttar Pradesh, India

Prof. (Dr.) Anupama Rajesh is Professor at Amity Business School, Amity University, India. Her qualifications include Ph.D. in the area of Technology in Education, M.Phil. (IT), M.Phil. (Mgmt.), M.Ed., M.Sc. (IT), PGDCA, PGDBA. She has also been trained for Case Writing at INSEAD Paris. She has a teaching experience of about 20 years including international assignments which include a teaching stint in London and Singapore and training of Italian and French delegates and students. She has written more than 40 research papers and case studies for prestigious international journals and has eight books and several book chapters to her credit. She is reviewer of renowned Sage and Emerald journals. Her research interests are Business Intelligence, Educational Technology, Marketing Analytics etc. while her teaching interests are Business Intelligence, E-Commerce, IT enabled processes and so on.

She is an avid trainer and has trained Union Bank of India, NHPC, ILFS, TATA Motors, Bhutan Power Company employees as well as Commonwealth Games Volunteers and army personnel. She is a Master Trainer from Microsoft, Infosys Partner for Business Intelligence and Academic Partner for SAP ERM Sim.

She has recently won the ADMA Research Award and has also been awarded several Outstanding Paper Awards at prestigious conferences at institutes such as IIM Ahmedabad. She also has a MOOC to her credit.

Assessment of Ease of Doing Business in India: Survey of India based UK Companies

Havish Madhvapaty
Co – Founder | Head of Research and Analytics
Prof. (Dr.) Anupama Rajesh
Professor, Amity Business School, Amity University

INTRODUCTION

India and United Kingdom share a historical association. UK was India's largest trading partner in the European Union (pre-Brexit). Indian companies in the UK reached an annual growth rate of 31% in 2016 (CII, 2017). Some noteworthy points are:

- There are over 800 Indian companies in the United Kingdom.
- Their combined revenue is of USD 63.07 billion.
- 55 of the most rapidly growing Indian companies had an average growth rate of 31%.

UK has continued to remain a highly attractive destination for Indian investors.

Fastest-growing Indian companies in UK

Domestic ultimate owner	Global ultimate owner	Latest Growth %
Datamatics Infotech Limited	Datamatics Global Services Ltd	103%
Ksk power Ventur Plc	Sayi Energy Ventur Limited	90%
Bharti Airtel (UK) Limited	Bharti Airtel Limited	84%
The Bio Agency Ltd	Tech Mahindra Limited	77%
Oakus Limited	Enzen Global Solutions Limited	76%
Secure Meters (UK) Limited	Secure Meters Limited	69%
Aegis Outsourcing UK Limited	Essar Global Fund Limited	55%

Kotak Mahindra (UK) Limited	Kotak Mahindra Bank Limited	55%
Y International (UK) Limited	Yousuf-Ali Masaliam -Veetil Abdulqader	54%
Apollo Tyres (UK) Pvt Limited	Apollo Tyres Limited	52%

UK India Business Council

UK India Business Council was set up with the aim of supporting UK businesses with insights and services. Network building and policy advocacy are other key areas.

They support businesses which are well-established, as well as those, in early stages of engagement. They work closely with The UK Government and other influential partners. They undertake the task of conveying to India's union and state legislators business interest of companies in the UK. The end goal is to make it easier for UK businesses to engage and operate in India.

Key services provided by their team include sector-specific research, market entry and expansion strategies.

UK Companies in India

FTSE (Financial Times Stock Exchange) 100 companies are looking to invest increasingly in emerging markets, and India is a prime destination. Ten UK-based companies pledged to invest USD 40 million to train about 2 million people in India. These companies have committed to support initatives such as "Make in India" and "Skill India". These companies include HSBC, Vodafone, Reckitt Benckiser, Rolls Royce, OCS, Mott Macdonald, G4S, Aviva, Marks & Spencer and GSK.

Ease of Doing Business Survey

The *Doing Business* project is an objective measure of business regulations and enforcement across 190 economies and selected cities. It is done at the subnational and regional level. It is administered by The World Bank. In the last ranking in 2016, India's ranking had improved from 131 to 130 among the 190 countries evaluated. In light of new policy regulations, Goods and Services Tax and impact of

Brexit; a survey was conducted with Chartered Accountants and Lawyers handling accounting and legal work for these UK companies based in India.

There were 6 questionnaires administered to a total of 120 Chartered Accountants and 120 Lawyers in Mumbai and New Delhi whose clients include these UK companies based in India.

The results were a part of the Ease of Doing Business Ranking.

Questionnaire 1: Enforcing Contracts

1.1 Score on a scale of 1 to 5 (Strongly Disagree to Strongly Agree)

- Can the initial complaint be filed electronically through a dedicated platform.
- When the initial complaint is filed electronically, do you have to submit a hard copy as well?
- Can the initial complaint filed be served on the defendant electronically?
- Can court fees be paid electronically?
- In your city is there a small claims court/division or a fast-track procedure for small claims?

1.2 Is an electronic case management system in place within the District Court/ High Court/ Civil Court in where the judges can perform the following functions:

Score on a scale of 1 to 5 (Strongly Disagree to Strongly Agree)

- Judges can access laws, regulations and case-law.
- System can do automatic generation of a hearing schedule for all cases on the judge's docket.
- System can send notifications (e.g. emails) to lawyers.
- Judges can track status of a case on the judge's docket.
- Judges can view and manage case documents (briefs, motions, etc.).
- Judges can get assistance in judgment writing.
- System can do Semi-automatic generation of court orders.
- Judges can view court orders and judgments in a particular case.

1.3 Which of the following actions can lawyers perform through the electronic system?

Score on a scale of 1 to 5 (Strongly Disagree to Strongly Agree)

- Lawyers can access laws, regulations and case law.
- Lawyers can access forms to be submitted to the court.
- Lawyers can receive notifications (for example, e-mails).
- Lawyers can track the status of a case.
- Lawyers can view and manage case documents (briefs, motions).
- Lawyers can file briefs and documents with the court.
- Lawyers can view court orders and decisions in a particular case.

1.4 What are your thoughts on policy persuasion?

Score on a scale of 1 to 5 (Strongly Disagree to Strongly Agree)

- Commercial benches in High Courts should be dedicated for commercial cases.
- No commercial court shall be constituted for the territory over which the High Court has ordinary original civil jurisdiction.

1.5 What, in your opinion, are the barriers present in enforcing contracts?

_____

_____

1.6 What are your suggestions on the following?

Reforms Required	Comments / Suggestions
• Nature of reforms required	
• Policy/ regulation change required	
• Reforms required to make Service easy to access	
• Reforms required to make service transparent	
• Reforms required to make service timely	

1.7 How difficult/easy it is to enforce a contract for your business in your location?

Score on a scale of 1 to 5 (Very Easy to Most Difficult)

Questionnaire 2: Protecting Minority Investors

2.1 Score on a scale of 1 to 5 (Strongly Disagree to Strongly Agree)

- A shareholder having controlling stakes in both buyer and seller businesses must not vote for the large value transactions, equivalent to 10% of buyers assets (Section 188 of the Companies Act, 2013).
- Making provision for immediate disclosure of transaction to the public, the regulator or the shareholders is required both on terms and conflict of interest.
- Making provision for holding the controlling shareholder liable for the damage the buyer-seller transaction causes to the company, when the transaction is unfair or prejudicial to the other shareholders.
- Making provision for controlling shareholder to be fined and imprisoned or if he is disqualified i.e. disallowed from representing or holding a managerial position in any company for a year or more.
- Making provision that plaintiff can obtain categories of relevant documents from the defendant without identifying each document specifically.
- Making provision for plaintiffs to be able to recover their legal expenses from the company regardless of the outcome of their legal action (Section 242 of the Companies Act, 2013).
- Making it forbidden to appoint the same individual as CEO and chair of the board of directors (Section 149 and 203 the Companies Act, 2013).
- Making provision for a potential acquirer to compulsorily make a tender offer to all shareholders upon acquiring 50% of Buyer (assuming that Buyer is a limited company).
- Allowing shareholders representing 5% of buyer's share capital to put items on the agenda for the general meeting (Section 100 the Companies Act, 2013).
- Make provision allowing members representing 5% to put items on the meeting agenda (assuming that Buyer is a limited company).

2.2 What, in your opinion, are the barriers present in protecting minority investors?

_____

_____

2.3 What are your suggestions on the following?

Reforms Required	Comments / Suggestions
• Nature of reforms required	
• Policy/ regulation change required	
• Reforms required to make Service easy to access	
• Reforms required to make service transparent	
• Reforms required to make service timely	

2.4 How difficult/easy it is to protect minority investors for business in your location?

Score on a scale of 1 to 5 (Very Easy to Most Difficult)

_____

_____

Questionnaire 3: Registering a Property

3.1 Score on a scale of 1 to 5 (Strongly Disagree to Strongly Agree)

- Has there been any administrative or legal change since October 2016 affecting the process for transferring a property or the land administration system?
- Has this change simplified your daily work related to property transfers?
- Can this procedure be completed online?
- Can this procedure take place simultaneously with another procedure?

- Are majority of title/deed records in your city held in a paper format or in a computerized format?
- If title deeds are held in computerized format, are they scanned documents or fully digital documents?
- Is there an Electronic database for checking for encumbrance's liens, mortgages, restrictions, etc.?
- Are property plans in your state held in a paper format or in a computerized format?
- If property plans are held in computerized format, are they scanned documents or fully digital documents?
- Is there any Electronic database for recording boundaries, checking plans and providing cadastral information (Geographic Information System)?
- Are the information recorded by the immovable property registration agency and the mapping agency kept in a single database?
- Do the Immovable property registration agency and cadastral/mapping agency use the same identification number for properties?

3.2 Score on a scale of 1 to 5 (Strongly Disagree to Strongly Agree)

- Mechanism for filing complaints for any grievance related to immovable property registration and cadastral or cadastral maps.
- Official statistics tracking the transactions at Sub Registrar Office being available publicly.
- Maps of land plots being publicly available.
- Setting service delivery standards for providing updated map within a specific time frame and making it available online.
- All privately held land plots to be formally registered and mapped in your city.
- All privately held land plots to be formally registered and mapped in India.
- Integrating registry offices with Permanent Account Number (PAN) and Aadhar data to create a national property database.
- Ensuring cases/disputes are adjudicated in the first instance (without appeal) Court within one year.
- Having statistics of land disputes maintained in each Registrar Office and Land Revenue Department and available on the website.
- Fixed Timelines which are accessible online for delivering a legally binding document that proves property ownership.
- Having a Fee schedule which is publicly online for accessing maps.

3.3 What, in your opinion, are the barriers present in registering a property?

_____

_____

3.4 What are your suggestions on the following?

Reforms Required	Comments / Suggestions
• Nature of reforms required	
• Policy/ regulation change required	
• Reforms required to make Service easy to access	
• Reforms required to make service transparent	
• Reforms required to make service timely	

3.5 How difficult/easy it is register a property for your business in your location?

Score on a scale of 1 to 5 (Very Easy to Most Difficult)

_____

_____

Questionnaire 4: Paying Taxes

4.1 Score on a scale of 1 to 5 (Strongly Disagree to Strongly Agree)

- Were there any major changes to the tax laws, regulations implemented in the country in the last 6 months?
- Were any new taxes introduced between October 2016 to February 2017?
- Were any taxes eliminated or merged with other taxes between October 2016 to February 2017?
- Did tax rates or tax bases change between October 2016 to February 2017?

  i. *Corporate Income Tax*
  ii. *Labor Taxes and mandatory contributions*

iii. *Sales Tax, Value Added Tax, Goods and Service Tax or other Consumption Tax*

iv. *Any other taxes*

- Did tax payment or filing schedules change between October 2016 to February 2017?

  i. *Corporate Income Tax*

  ii. *Labor taxes and mandatory contributions*

  iii. *Sales Tax, Value Added Tax, Goods and Service Tax or other Consumption Tax*

  iv. *Any other taxes*

- Were there any legal or regulatory changes that increased/ reduced the time for preparing, filing or paying these taxes between October 2016 to February 2017?

  i. *Corporate Income tax*

  ii. *Labor taxes and mandatory contributions*

  iii. *Sales Tax, Value Added Tax, Goods and Service Tax or other Consumption Tax*

  iv. *Any other taxes*

- Were there any changes to the method (e.g., online) of preparing, filing or paying any of the following taxes that increased or reduced the time required between October 2016 to February 2017?

  i. *Corporate Income Tax*

  ii. *Labor taxes and mandatory contributions*

  iii. *Sales Tax, Value Added Tax, Goods and Service Tax or other Consumption Tax*

  iv. *Any other taxes*

- Have any changes to tax rates, associated rules or tax administration become effective or are expected to become effective between October 2016 to February 2017?

  i. *Corporate Income Tax*

  ii. *Labor taxes and mandatory contributions*

    iii. Sales Tax, Value Added Tax, Goods and Service Tax or other Consumption Tax

    iv. Any other taxes

4.2 Have the forms for filing Income Tax return, VAT returns, CST returns and GST return, EPFO and ESIC return simplified?

• Yes	
• No	
• Other (Specify)	

4.3 What has been the impact of online return filing made mandatory?

_____

_____

4.4 Has single return, single challan and online payment of fees for EPFO (Employees' Provident Fund Organisation) and ESIC (Employees' State Insurance) been implemented?

• Yes	
• No	
• Other (Specify)	

4.5 Has unified e-filing, returns and payment of contributions for EPFO and ESIC by eliminating offline filing of returns and payment been implemented?

• Yes	
• No	
• Other (Specify)	

4.6 What, in your opinion, are the barriers present in registering a property?

_____

_____

4.7 What are your suggestions on the following?

Reforms Required	Comments / Suggestions
• Nature of reforms required	
• Policy/ regulation change required	
• Reforms required to make Service easy to access	
• Reforms required to make service transparent	
• Reforms required to make service timely	

4.8 How difficult/easy it is pay taxes for your business in your location?

Score on a scale of 1 to 5 (Very Easy to Most Difficult)

_____

_____

Questionnaire 5: Resolving Insolvency

5.1 Score on a scale of 1 to 5 (Strongly Disagree to Strongly Agree)

- Debtors to initiate both liquidation and reorganization proceedings.
- Creditors to initiate both liquidation and reorganization proceedings.
- Debtor or an insolvency representative on its behalf to continue performing contracts essential to the debtor's survival.
- Allowing the debtor or an insolvency representative on its behalf, after commencement of insolvency proceedings, to obtain financing necessary to function during the proceedings.
- Post-commencement finance to receive priority over ordinary unsecured creditors during distribution of assets.
- Reorganization plan to be voted on only by the creditors whose rights are modified or affected by the plan.
- Creditors entitled to vote on the plan are divided into classes, each class votes separately and the creditors within each class are treated equally.
- Dissenting creditors to receive as much under the reorganization plan as they would have received in liquidation.

- Creditors to participate in the selection of an insolvency representative.
- Creditors to approve the sale of substantial assets of the debtor in the course of insolvency proceedings.
- Individual creditor to object to a decision of the court or of the insolvency representative to approve or reject claims against the debtor brought by the creditor itself and by other creditors.

5.2 What, in your opinion, are the barriers present in resolving insolvency?

_____

_____

5.3 What are your suggestions on the following?

Reforms Required	Comments / Suggestions
• Nature of reforms required	
• Policy/ regulation change required	
• Reforms required to make Service easy to access	
• Reforms required to make service transparent	
• Reforms required to make service timely	

5.4 How difficult/easy is it to resolve insolvency for your business in your location?

Score on a scale of 1 to 5 (Very Easy to Most Difficult)

_____

_____

Questionnaire 6: Starting a Business

6.1 Score on a scale of 1 to 5 (Strongly Disagree to Strongly Agree)

- Have you witnessed any reforms in last 6 months, related to the process of Starting a Business?
- Are you aware of any reform that was expected to be adopted in last 3 months?
- Can married women legally register any type of business in the same way as a married man?
- Is a company legally required to hire a lawyer/ notary/ any other professional to complete any part of business registration?
- If not legally required, do majority of companies still hire services of lawyer/ notary/ any other professional to complete any part of the business registration?
- Does any government agency require a bank account for a new company at or within 3 months of incorporation?
- Is company seal required by law or in practice in a company's interaction with any government agency?
- Is a company required to register with competent tax authority?

6.2 Mention the Time and Cost required for the following:

- Obtain Digital signature online.
- Obtain Director Identification Number online.
- Reserve the Company Name online.
- Pay stamp duty online, file all incorporation forms and documents online and obtain the Certificate of Incorporation.
- Make a Company Seal and Stamp.
- Obtain a Permanent Account Number.
- Open a Bank Account.
- Register with Employees' Provident Fund organization.
- Register for medical insurance with Employees' State Insurance Corporation.
- Register for Value Added tax.
- Obtain a Tax Account Number.
- Register online with State Shops and Establishment Act.
- Additional Procedure, if any.

6.3 Are you aware of the initiative of e-spice as the only option for registering of company?

• Yes	
• No	

6.4 What, in your opinion, are the barriers present in starting a business?

6.5 What are your suggestions on the following?

Reforms Required	Comments / Suggestions
• Nature of reforms required	
• Policy/ regulation change required	
• Reforms required to make Service easy to access	
• Reforms required to make service transparent	
• Reforms required to make service timely	

6.6 How difficult/easy is it to register start a business in your location?

Score on a scale of 1 to 5 (Very Easy to Most Difficult)

CONCLUSION

Globally, as per World Bank ranking for 2017, UK has the following ranks: Enforcing Contracts (31), Protecting minority Investors (10), Registering a Property (47), Paying Taxes (23), Resolving Insolvency (14) and Starting a Business (14). UK overall ranking is 7.

For India, the ranks are: Enforcing Contracts (164), Protecting minority Investors (4), Registering a Property (154), Paying Taxes (119), Resolving Insolvency (103) and Starting a Business (156). India overall ranking is 100.

The distance to frontier (DTF) measure shows the distance of each economy to the "frontier," which represents the best performance observed on each of the indicators across all economies in the Doing Business sample since 2005. An economy's distance to frontier is reflected on a scale from 0 to 100, where 0 represents the lowest performance and 100 represents the frontier. The ease of doing business ranking ranges from 1 to 190.

UK's score is 82.22 and India's score is 60.76.

While India is trailing behind UK by a significant margin, it has made significant improvement since the last ranking (where it was rated 130). Another change being brought is a Subnational Ranking, which will includes states other than political and financial capital. The last such survey with 17 Indian cities happened in 2009, with one expected in 2018. It is expected that it will be a more accurate representation of India's ranking.

*   *   *

REFERENCES

http://www.hindustantimes.com/business-news/indian-companies-in-uk-growth-up-31/story-wFI2GUZAcPZmiUijqVLYlI.html
https://www.ukibc.com/

mHealth in India and United Kingdom

Havish Madhvapaty
Co-Founder – Decode Research & Analytics

Prof. (Dr.) Anupama Rajesh
Professor, Amity Business School, Amity University

Executive Summary

The healthcare industry is moving towards a delivery model that is more patient-centered, value-based and accessible in even remote environments. Mobile and communications allow both the power and the reach to enable mHealth to become a revolutionary approach to healthcare. Multi-layer partnerships for mHealth smartphone applications are poised to become an essential foundation in the bridge to augment the continuum of care to the neediest patients, whilst also providing management information and real time surveillance data.

Enterprise healthcare is not bound by the same requirements or revenue models that direct-to-consumer Applications (apps for short) are. Enterprise healthcare solutions looking to engage patients aren't looking to generate revenue with mobile apps – and hence – any app development they do is an enterprise cost which is usually associated with large IT budgets. This isn't remotely comparable to an early stage software venture eager to impress venture capitalists with simple download and usage metrics.

Barriers exist – and in different forms. They differ from the developed world to the developing world and from region to region. The collaborative effort of different players is required to deal with them.

Key Takeaways

- mHealth will grow unabated. Major stakeholders are: Mobile Operators, Government, Funders, Service providers, Private Healthcare, and end users.
- The focus should be two – fold: to enable health providers to integrate and complement traditional health systems with mHealth systems.
- Growth in health and fitness apps is unabated. Magnitude of the wearables market is huge.
- Setting of standards and interoperability between systems is very crucial.

- Relationship between mobile and health stakeholders has to be simplified.
- Pharmaceutical and health providers need to figure out their role in the app ecosystem.

Key Topics Explored

- What is the scope, and key applications of mHealth?
- What is the global outlook and investment interest in mHealth from technological players?
- What opportunities does mHealth offer to different players in the value chain?
- What are the barriers to the mHealth market?
- What sort of alliances can we foresee in the future?

Scope of mHealth

mHealth is a component of eHealth. There is no standardized definition of mHealth. It can be expressed as the use of information and communication technology to provide better access to health services for practitioners and patients. mHealth has applications for both industrialized and developing nations. The added element of services make mHealth vary greatly in their level of sophistication. It includes everything ranging from static information about a disease to providing comprehensive healthcare management. mHealth services can be differentiated across different levels of the value chain as:

- Information services
- Enabling Services
- Transformative Services

PwC in a report for the GSMA (Global System for Mobile Communication Association) has said that mobile technology will play a significant role in the provision of healthcare services globally. It has predicted that the growth of the mHealth market led to a revenue opportunity worth INR 3 trillion (USD 0.6 billion) for India and USD 23 billion for the world in 2017.

Sectors where mHealth can have an impact are manifold. These include, but are not restricted to:

- Personal Health Records (PHRs)
- Aging / Elderly

- New born / Maternal Care
- Mental health

Market Drivers and Key Benefits

There are some key trends in the market today. Digital health was the buzzword that caught up in the mid 2000's with several start-up companies. Blogs and social networks for patient empowerment were also started. These were the pioneers with no funding. Today the ecosystem has expanded. There are thousands of funded companies in the digital health space.

With smart phones becoming smarter and the go-to device, one of the biggest trends to have emerged is that self – tracking has gone mainstream. Consumers have become more engaged and the sensors in a smartphone now enable continual accumulation of data. The Internet of Things (IoT) – aimed at connecting all sorts of devices to the internet – will accelerate the data integration.

Benefits to Patients and Health Providers

- Formalizing linkages between patients and primary health centers
- Managing patient registration information and records
- Strengthening health system response and remote diagnostics
- Managing health conditions – including informational and encouraging messages
- Communication of guidelines and protocols to patients
- Digitizing monitoring systems

Benefits to Health Providers (From Administrative Viewpoint)

- Staff communication
- Training and management
- Research
- Supply chain and Inventory management

Current mHealth Ecosystem

Adoption and Alliances

Use of mobile technology has tremendous potential to improve access, affordability and quality of healthcare delivery in the developing world. Growing amounts of attention over the years have resulted in an increasing amount of experimentation and commitments from funding agencies and other stake holders of global health.

mHealth Alliance

mHealth Alliance was launched in 2008. Since then, the mHealth Alliance has provided a critical voice and served as a catalytic force for the mHealth field, resulting in significant progress in scaling up mHealth solutions and increasing knowledge and capacity within the global health and mHealth communities.

The evaluation findings showed that the Alliance's contributions to the field of mHealth are widely acknowledged as being significant. The Innovation Working Group mHealth Catalytic Grant program has provided 26 grants in 14 countries to support efforts aiming to reach over 31 million people. The Alliance produced over 20 publications and played a constructive role in incubating global initiatives and platforms that have since spun off in the form of the Mobile Alliance for Maternal Action (MAMA) and the mHealth and eHealth Expert Learning Program (mHELP). The Alliance facilitated the mainstreaming of mHealth into global health issues ranging from maternal, new-born, and child health to aging. More recently, the Alliance has pioneered work in Nigeria on the ICT for Saving One Million Lives initiative (ICT4SOML) in a way that is poised to make a significant contribution to the sector.

UNICEF mHealth

For under-served communities, where households need to be able to access essential services and information for pregnant mothers and children, UNICEF and partners have integrated mobile technologies into health systems. They focus on capturing transactions real-time which allows for aggregation of data at district and national levels.

Their areas of work include:

- Safe pregnancy and delivery
- Patient tracing and results delivery
- Nutrition monitoring

- Health information and reminders
- Health systems management
- Coordination, monitoring and accountability tools
- Citizen reporting

Open mHealth

Open mHealth is a nonprofit start-up. It works on an open-source philosophy. The code produced is open-sourced through the Apache 2.0 license, and the code base can be adapted and evolved by community members. As non-profit, Open mHealth is sustained in three ways: grants, sponsorship, and services.

Indian Government Policy

India has a sixth of the world population but less than 1% of the world's total health expenditure. India has one of the biggest healthcare burdens in the world. One of the reasons for this is the high rural population and the consequent difficulty in accessing specialists. Addressing this demand required major endeavours and a huge expectation from the exchequer. An investment in mHealth can contribute towards lessening this burden.

For mHealth to scale up in India, the government needs to create an mHealth policy and create a strong public push for its adoption. Healthcare is too regulated a sector for mobile solutions to achieve scale just through successful private sector pilots and initiatives. The National Telecom Policy (NTP) 2011 refers to mHealth and the government has undertaken some projects already, but so far it has not shown any real seriousness about mHealth, and no service has scaled up in India.

The Nation Health Portal[30] website has a section on mHealth which provides useful external links to apps and other websites.

Health care represents a major challenge as rising health care costs, aging populations, access disparities and chronic illnesses threaten traditional health care systems. Four key benefits of mHealth are:

- Mobile devices will improve affordability of health care by lowering disparities based on geography and income.
- Health providers who offer services like consultations, diagnosis and treatment through remote monitoring devices can be provided reimbursement by the government.
- Patient experience can be enhanced by providing reminders and diagnostic information to patients and physicians.

---

[30] http://www.nhp.gov.in/miscellaneous/m-health

- Policymakers can be aided by the health data collection and analysis that mHealth offers.

Technological and Legal Issues

When technology is used for medical purposes, it gives rise to medico legal and techno legal issues. In United States, the Health Insurance Portability and Accountability Act of 1996 (HIPAA), Health Information Technology for Economic and Clinical Health Act (HITECH Act), etc. are some of the laws that take care of medico legal and techno legal issues of e-health and telemedicine.

mHealth in India is still in infancy and therefore technological and legal issues are still evolving. Telemedicine laws and online pharmacies laws in India and their legal implications also need to be understood well. The privacy rights in India in the information age have also posed many legal challenges before m-health companies and entrepreneurs in India. Although we have no dedicated privacy laws in India and data protection laws in India yet there are certain legislations in India that govern both privacy and data protection aspects of m-health industry in India.

Indian Examples in mHealth

Both government and private examples are available:

- Non-emergency help lines (Government): Large states in India are looking to set up these helpline for consumers and people who live in rural areas and do not have access to basic health.
- Emergency help lines (Private Set UP): 1066 - A National 24 hour emergency and trauma care helpline by Apollo Hospitals Group.
- Apollo - Aircel Mobile Health Care: Aircel customers can call 55104 from their mobile and talk to Health Experts from Apollo for any health related queries.
- Apollo M.I.N.D Line: Apollo M.I.N.D. Line is a psychological tele-counselling helpline to support individuals who are dealing with complications faced in everyday life.
- B positive: BPositive, a health and lifestyle magazine, initiated by Apollo Hospitals Group, was launched in 2008. B Positive conforms to the mission of empowering the people to conquer the world with a positive attitude, by creating awareness about health.
- Apollo Telemedicine: Telemedicine brings healthcare within reach of population residing in medically inaccessible areas. They will also be able to share their medical re- ports and images to ensure an all-round investigation

and an accurate diagnosis. Doctors can get in touch with their peers to discuss complicated cases or to get specialized help remotely.

- Apollo Prism: Apollo Prism is a patient-controlled Personal Health Record with which the users can import and manage health records created during various doctor visits and can also access their online health record and medical reports anytime and anywhere.
- Airtel - Doctor: A consultancy based doctor helpline and toll free helpline service on 54321 in which call @ INR 3/minute for Airtel users.
- Apollo Munich, ICICI Lombard Health Insurance Companies: SMS and Health Line Services for their customers.
- MedIndia web site: Services to ask health questions on their mobile site.
- Mobile Clinics: Similarly, mobile clinics, telemedicine centers and health information on mobile phones is catching up as priorities amongst Indian Government.
- Heart Helplines: Asian Heart Institute (AHI) Mumbai has started an emergency service based on mobile communication which also has air-lift capability to AHI by helicopter from distant parts of India.
- Dr. SMS: An initiative by Kerala Government.

Examples of mHealth in United Kingdom

- The mobile health services market in the UK is projected to be worth £27 billion by 2020.
- From the NHS (National Health Service) annual budget of £113bn, 70% is allocated to care for long term illnesses.
- As the number of mobile health apps increase in the UK, patients are becoming more engaged. The rise in the use of mobile health applications is not just restricted to patients; physicians are seeing the vast benefits these applications provide.
- Some numbers presented from a Deloitte Report:
  - The global market for digital health was worth £23bn in 2014 and is expected to almost double to £43bn by 2018
  - The UK market size for digital health is £2bn and is expected to grow to £2.9bn by 2018, predominately driven by mHealth apps
  - The UK represented a 9% share of the global health market in 2014, which the report predicts will fall to 7% by 2018, due to strong growth in other markets
  - Digital health systems represent the largest market both globally and in the UK, where they contribute 66% of digital health sales

- The most promising market for growth is mHealth apps, which although is currently the smallest digital health market sub-sector, is predicted to grow at 35% in the UK and 49% globally from by 2018.

- NHS has decided to provide patients with free mobile apps and devices to aid in the management of their chronic diseases and promoting their overall initiative to increase self-care interventions as part of their drive towards personalized, precise, predictive and preventative medicine.
- NHS England have piloted a COPD (Chronic Obstructive Pulmonary Disease) app in Portsmouth called MyCOPD to help patients with chronic obstructive airways diseases to help manage and support their conditions. This has had some good results.

Synergy of mHealth and Mobile Financial Services (MFS)

One of the most promising opportunities for positive socio-economic change lies in the scaling of mobile health and Mobile Financial Services (MFS). More people have access to a mobile phone today than to clean water or the electrical grid. While reduced costs and advances in network coverage are accelerating, the underlying business models to sustain this growth are unclear.

Mobile Health efforts are also highly fragmented. Because of the lack of platform standardization, many providers are building discreet and independent systems from ground up. As a result, systems are costly, inefficient, unable to achieve scale and often not interoperable. MFS is an umbrella term, often referred to as mobile money. MFS uses a "mobile wallet" or a separate electronic money account used for payments other than prepaid or postpaid mobile airtime. Within MFS, there are three main categories: mobile payments, mobile credit/savings/insurance and mobile banking. Payments in mHealth fall into three main categories:

- those for health services and supplies,
- those associated with systems administration, and
- those associated with use of the electronic healthcare record and aggregated data.

Due to the fact that payments are a vital component throughout the healthcare delivery continuum, a means to securely, reliably and cost-effectively transact is valued by both industry sectors. Along with the need to accelerate transactions, both industries have common users, digital infrastructure elements, business processes and policy concerns. Recognizing these synergies and working cross-sector, stakeholders in both industries are positioned to achieve greater impact, ultimately establishing a more robust ecosystem for servicing the needs of the poor.

Mobile Financial Service for Providers

The various ways in which this can be used are:

- Salary disbursement - Healthcare employers can pay a healthcare worker automatically into the healthcare worker's mobile financial service account rather than paying in cash or cheque, which is both cumbersome and costly to manage.
- Performance-based funding - Providers of performance-based funding can pay healthcare workers electronically into their mobile financial services account based on services that were performed on patients.
- Vouchers or Conditional Aid - Mobile financial services can be the settlement mechanism between payers and providers of healthcare services or products given to patients who use vouchers.
- Supply Chain Settlement and Credit - Supply chain participants can settle payment electronically between their mobile financial service accounts.

Mobile Financial Service for Patients

The various ways in which this can be used are:

- Mobile Pre-paid Savings - The majority of the world's population has no access to healthcare insurance. Access to mobile-based savings may assist with this issue. Patients can accrue assets in a prepaid mobile savings account to prepare for upcoming healthcare costs.
- Mobile Micro-Insurance - In addition to savings accounts, patients can pay for micro- insurance premiums through a mobile phone and receive claims into the mobile financial services account. By taking the friction out of saving and making regular payments, opportunities are created for individuals to manage small amounts of money more effectively.

Key Stakeholders

mHealth and MFS have a number of ecosystem constituents, which include policy-makers, large corporations, donor communities and agent networks.

- Policy-Makers: Core concerns to policy-makers for mHealth and MFS involve the degree of regulatory policy to enact to ensure adequate safeguards for health and finance without stifling innovation and free market competition.

- Constituent parties involved include ministries associated with:
  - Communications: Focused on broadband data, data encryption, security (networks, devices, adoption and utilization), privacy and reliability of networks
  - Central Bank: Focused on money supplies, banking regulations, consumer privacy, money laundering and terrorism financing concerns, and electronic money transfer regulations
  - Health: Focused on enabling ubiquitous, affordable access to healthcare based on population needs assessment and consumer healthcare information privacy

- Private Sector Large Corporations:
  - Mobile Network Operators (MNOs)
  - Companies in health services
  - Mobile money providers
  - Donor Communities
  - Health Service agents
  - Mobile financial service agents

Role of Mobile Phone and Network Providers

We suggest a strategic framework which will act as a guideline to implement mobile and wireless technologies. This should include:

- ROI (Return on Investment) model and payment methods
- Standards and Interoperability
- Privacy and Security
- Technology advancements

mHealth Apps

mHealth app market has made significant strides in the last few years. Apps are targeted either to chronically ill patients, to health and fitness oriented people, or to physicians. Pharma and hospitals have the longest way ahead of themselves to find a role in the mHealth ecosystem.

The most relevant revenue stream is linked to services that are offered via the apps. Even though fitness apps are the biggest group presently, it is expected that in the mHealth category remote monitoring and consultation shall become big in a few years.

Traditional healthcare players will need to understand the working and impact of health API and data aggregators.

A cursory glance tells us that there are a plethora of apps – mostly catering to fitness. The health apps are made by small publishers and seldom by actual medical practitioners.

Wearables and Technology

Fitness devices and smartwatches is at a turning point. As a category, Fitness and Sport tech has gone mainstream. The market offers huge potential – and the amount of investment is stupendous. It remains to be seen whether market growth keeps pace or not. The winners who come out at the end will be the ones who can marry technology innovation with intimacy and personalization. While we have seen some indie manufacturers like Pebble tasting success – with the big players like Google, LG, Samsung, Apple now entering full force – the market is likely to be dominated by the big players since the small manufacturers like Pebble cannot command significant discounts or custom parts from the supply chain without incurring significant costs on relatively small production runs. Hence Pebble is now closed.

As far as their relation to health is concerned, we feel that we are still figuring out the potential that it offers for mHealth. A consumer product will go a long way in promoting mHealth – and the myriad ways in which different players in the market use the potential offered by mHealth is immense.

Our key findings are:

- Technology innovation is critical – but social acceptance and driving adoption of wearables is step one.
- Various sensors used in watches will drop in pricing once economy of scale is reached.
- Apple watch is the first attempt at cross – fertilization between fashion and technology.
- All data collected by smartwatches will also develop market for fitness tracking.

CONCLUSION

New opportunities in mHealth will keep on emerging. Partners have to aim to simplify the relationships between mobile and health stakeholders, while maximizing the ubiquitous nature of mobile technology and its capabilities for health providers and, ultimately, for patients. Health content, patient registration, data collection and critical diagnostics will increase the access to health care while providing the delivery mechanism for mHealth services that are commercially sustainable and scalable.

Challenges and opportunities

From the experience gained from implementation across the world – it is prudent to sit and take stock of mHealth. Some observations:

- In African countries – one can now see that there are too many pilot tests – and the government has finally put all new initiatives on hold. The delivery system is there – but there is a lack of clarity as to what exactly to deliver.
- The technology behind mHealth is evident. But one should not lose sight of the fact that it is the people element behind it that matters.
- Setting of health informatics standards and interoperability between devices is crucial. Various players are working on mHealth and there seems to be proprietary standards everywhere.
- The pricing system needs to be kept such that consumers do not mind paying for the benefit they get. The payment system should be seamless.
- Privacy issues might also be a touchy point.
- There might be a disinterest from healthcare professionals.

Our Opinion

We feel that there needs to be synergy in research in terms of:

- Mobile Network Operators/Connectivity Providers
- Mobile & mHealth Device OEMs
- Content & Application Providers
- Healthcare Service Providers
- Pharmaceutical Industry

In terms of specifically identifying and documenting, we can research:

- The current status and maturity of various geographies
- The specific types of mHealth initiatives in practice
- Barriers to implementation

We also feel that mobile payments are also a huge topic of discussion today with massive technological investment in the sector. Even though mHealth has been there for some time now – right now seems to be a fantastic opportunity for all players in mHealth to really up the ante and gain the first mover advantage. Especially owing to the fact that customers regarding their health would not tend to be fickle, and would show some loyalty – a first mover advantage would go a long way. Broadly speaking – a multitude of options for the customers is excellent. There is ample room in the market for all players to play. Also – competition would encourage more focus on development and improving customer experience and using mHealth in ways hitherto unexplored.

It is also interesting to see that even though universally there is a concern for high health care costs, the concern does not seem to be translating into more cost-conscious behavior on part of the consumers. Consumers definitely are embracing a more active role in medical decision making. The traditional model of doctors possessing most of the decision-making authority is now slowly decreasing.

*   *   *

MarTech Trends in India – A Perspective of UK Companies Based in India

Havish Madhvapaty
Co-Founder – Decode Research & Analytics

Prof. (Dr.) Anupama Rajesh
Professor, Amity Business School, Amity University

Executive Summary

Growth in Marketing Technology has led to an expanding number of marketing tech offerings, but has also resulted in a new set of challenges for the marketer. Marketers seem to be displaying greater efforts towards tactics, rather than strategy. Compounding the problem is the fact that a low barrier to entry has led to immense fragmentation in an ever expanding universe of marketing technology.

In early 2012 technology research and advisory firm Gartner predicted that CMOs will spend more on information technology than CIOs. We are now seeing an accelerated trend towards the adoption of technology in marketing. MarTech – a whole new stream of technology has emerged that brings together data, analytics, technology, digital marketing, CRM and social media to help marketers manage their digital and customer side marketing at scale.

Companies like IBM, Adobe, Oracle, Salesforce and SAP have invested in buying, building and customizing MarTech solutions that can give CMOs the tools to help leverage the opportunities that data, digital, social content and CRM are offering them.

This report was designed to understand how technology is changing the Indian marketing landscape, and how UK companies based in India are leveraging the MarTech movement.

The survey results have led us to identify key Indian MarTech (Marketing Technology) trends across industries, as well as learn about their strategic approach to marketing technology adoption and discover how its implementation is transforming businesses.

Methodology

The survey was conducted to understand how companies are employing MarTech. The responses were gathered by direct interactions with decision makers for MarTech in the organization.

The survey covered:

1. Strategic Approach to MarTech
2. Data Collection, Management and Use
3. Analytics and Insight
4. Technology Driven Campaign Management
5. Mobile Marketing
6. Social Media Marketing
7. Content Marketing

Questionnaire with Responses

Dear Marketer

Your company has been chosen from among hundreds of companies we studied to identify the leaders in the use of marketing technology. By spending a few minutes on this survey, we will be able to further understand how you and your team are adopting, implementing and profiting from the use of MarTech.

In early 2012 technology research and advisory Gartner predicted that CMOs will spend more on information technology than CIOs. We are now seeing an accelerated trend towards the adoption of technology in marketing. MarTech - a whole new stream of technology has emerged that brings together data, analytics, technology, digital marketing, CRM and social media to help marketers manage their digital and customer-side marketing at scale. Companies like IBM, Adobe, Oracle, Salesforce and SAP have invested in buying, building and customizing MarTech solutions that can give CMOs the tools to help leverage the opportunities that data, digital, social content and CRM are offering them.

Decode Research and Analytics have created the India MarTech Rankings Study. The study is designed to understand how technology is changing the Indian marketing landscape. It will identify companies who are at the forefront of the MarTech movement, learn about their strategic approach to marketing technology adoption and discover how its implementation is transforming their businesses.

1. **Your role in the company:**
    - • I head the marketing function in the company.
- I am a member of the marketing team and report in to my department head.
- I am part of the digital marketing team and report in to my department head.
- I am part of the CRM and loyalty marketing team and report in to my department head.
- I do not work directly in the marketing department. Please specify your department.

MarTech within your organisation

2. Does your organisation have a strategy for the following? (Choose all that apply):

- Collection, management and use of prospect and customer data. [97%]
- An approach to use analytics and prospect and customer data-driven insights. [100%]
- A structured approach to run 1 to 1 digital marketing campaigns to prospects and customers. [87%]
- A CRM program or a customer lifecycle management program. [87%]
- A structured approach to social media marketing. [93%]
- Investing in and using marketing technology tool(s). [87%]

3. Please rate the six statements below by order of strategic importance to your organisation:

- Use of analytics and prospect and customer data-driven insights. [57%]
- Collection, management and use of prospect and customer data. [70%]
- Investing in and using marketing technology tool(s). [37%]
- Structured 1 to 1 digital marketing campaigns to prospects and customers. [50%]
- Structured approach to social media marketing. [37%]
- CRM program or a customer lifecycle management program. [50%]

4. Imagine three years from now. Please rate once again the same six statements by order of strategic importance to your organisation.

- Structured 1 to 1 digital marketing campaigns to prospects and customers. [43%]

- CRM program or a customer lifecycle management program. [43%]
- Investing in and using marketing technology tool(s). [67%]
- Collection, management and use of prospect and customer data. [63%]
- Structured approach to social media marketing. [27%]
- Use of analytics and prospect and customer data-driven insights. [57%]

Strategic approach to MarTech

5. Thinking of the level of alignment for adopting and using of MarTech in your organisation (Choose the most appropriate answer):

- We are aligned at the board level for adopting and implementing MarTech in our organisation. [30%]
- Our CEO is committed to bringing MarTech tools into the company to drive his future vision. [50%]
- We have multiple departments (Marketing, Customer Service, IT etc) working together to implement MarTech solutions within our company. [17%]
- We are evaluating MarTech and its tools for use by the marketing department. [4%]

6. Use of MarTech as a strategic business tool within your organisation. (Choose the most appropriate answer):

- We actively use MarTech to drive positive business outcomes across our organization. [17%]
- MarTech is used to drive specific outcomes in some departments. [50%]
- The use of MarTech is limited to the marketing department at the moment. [24%]
- We are still evaluating the use of MarTech and how it will be used strategically. [10%]

7. Teams and departments involved in evaluating, adopting and implementing MarTech within your organisation. (Choose the most appropriate answer):

- All our alignments are driven from the CEO's office. [4%]
- Marketing leads an interdepartmental approach to investing in MarTech into our company. [80%]
- Some other department (e.g.: IT/customer service) takes the lead in evaluating and deploying. [17%]

8. Expected business outcomes when adopting and using MarTech within your organisation (Choose the most appropriate answer):

- We have set clear and measurable goals that we report into business. [20%]
- We measure and evaluate goals that help improve marketing outcomes. [70%]
- We use MarTech to support our digital marketing efforts. [7%]
- We are currently evaluating MarTech. [4%]

9. Budget allocation for MarTech in your organisation (Choose the most appropriate answer):

- We have MarTech budget approvals from our board. [10%]
- Our CEO and CFO have agreed to clear allocations for MarTech. [44%]
- Multiple departments have come together and pooled in resources for us to deploy in MarTech. [7%]
- Our MarTech investments come in from the budgets we have set aside for digital marketing. [30%]
- We don't directly invest in MarTech. We hire an agency which brings in the appropriate technologies. [4%]
- At the moment we have not invested in MarTech. [7%]

Data collection, management and use

10. Do you have a well defined data use policy in our organisation?

- Yes. [63%]
- We use data for marketing. Not sure if we have a structured data policy though. [30%]
- Not that I am aware of. [3%]
- No. [3%]

11. Collecting and managing prospect and customer information:

Excellent [80%]
Non-Existent [20%]

12. Where/how does your organisation collect prospect data (Choose all that apply):

- We run online lead generation campaigns. [74%]
- We have a call centre where leads come into. [50%]
- We collect leads at point of sale (POS). [84%]
- We run onground activation programs to capture leads. [87%]
- We work with third party agencies and vendors to help generate leads. [44%]

13. When you collect prospect and customer information, does your organisation do any of the following? (Choose all that apply):

- Integrated lead and customer data management. [57%]
- Lead and customer data cleaning and enrichment. [54%]
- Lead and customer data analysis and segmentation. [64%]
- Lead and customer data driven campaigns. [67%]
- Data driven personalization of campaigns to leads and customers. [70%]
- Data integrated social media campaigns. [67%]

14. What is the primary reason for your organisation collecting customer information (Choose up to three):

- We have a loyalty program. [47%]
- We do not have a loyalty program but use customer information to run structured lifecycle management campaigns. [24%]
- We run email and SMS campaigns at our customers. [47%]
- We use customer data to segment and understand customer behavior. [70%]
- We use customer data to build analytical models. [67%]

15. Has your organisation built a customer data mart?

- Yes. [57%]
- We are in the process of setting up one. [40%]
- No. [3%]

16. Has your organisation integrated customer data from multiple sources into a customer data mart? (Choose all that apply):

- We capture and integrate leads that come in from across all digital media. [37%]

- We capture and integrate customer information coming in from the point of sale. [54%]
- We capture and integrate data that come from visitors who come onto our website(s). [47%]
- We capture and integrate data from social media. [47%]
- We capture and integrate prospect data from our call centre. [50%]
- We capture and integrate customers who call in for service or write in to our help desk. [30%]
- We capture and integrate customer data from partners. [37%]
- We capture and integrate prospect and customer data from third party sources. [7%]

17. Does you organisation have a strategy for big data?

- Yes. [97%]
- No. [3%]

18. We are in the process of putting together a big data strategy:

- No. [50%]
- Don't know/Can't say. [50%]

19. Is data helping your organisation improve marketing outcomes?

- Yes. [74%]
- We currently do not measure this metric. [20%]
- No. [3%]
- Don't know/Can't say. [3%]

Analytics and insights

20. Does your organisation have a structured approach to analytics and generating customer driven insights?

- Yes. [94%]
- Not a very structured approach, but we use analytics from time to time. [3%]
- Don't know/Can't say. [3%]

21. Does your organisation use analytics to take strategic business decisions?

- Yes. [93%]
- Not sure. [2%]
- No. [2%]
- Don't know. [3%]

22. Which of the following analytics approaches do you use? (Choose all that apply):

- Descriptive. [84%]
- Prescriptive. [87%]
- Predictive. [84%]
- Cognitive. [30%]

23. Do you use analytics across the organisation?

- Yes. [53%]
- Some departments use analytics but not marketing. [7%]
- Marketing uses analytics but other departments don't/may not. [40%]

24. Has your organisation invested in building an analytics team (Choose one):

- Yes, we have a full in-house team which handles all the analytics work across the organization. [27%]
- Yes, we have a full in-house analytics team but we outsource some projects from time to time. [30%]
- Yes, we have a full in-house analytics team but we have also outsourced some of the analytics work to full-time agency/vendors(s). [3%]
- We work with external agency/vendor(s) to handle our full-time analytics needs. [20%]
- We only do ad-hoc analytics work and this is done by our internal team(s). [10%]
- We only do ad-hoc analytics work and these are outsourced to external agency/vendor(s). [7%]
- We don't do any structured analytics work at the moment. [3%]

25. Does your organisation do web analytics? (Choose One):

- Yes, we have invested in an in-house web analytics team who use a paid tool. [43%]

- We have a paid analytics tool that is managed by an external agency/vendor. [33%]
- We use a free tool that is managed internally. [10%]
- We use a free tool that is managed by an external agency/vendor. [4%]
- We don't use web analytics at the moment. [10%]

Technology driven campaign management

26. Do you run structured digital marketing campaigns in your organisation? (Choose one):

- Yes. [53%]
- We run digital marketing campaigns, but they may not be very structured. [30%]
- We have not run any digital marketing campaigns of note. [17%]

27. Who is responsible for digital marketing in your organisation? (Choose one):

- We have specialized digital marketing team(s) as part of marketing that handle this. [73%]
- We have a specialised digital marketing team that works in another department to handle the same. [23%]
- Brands/departments manage digital marketing independently. [4%]

28. What kinds of digital marketing campaigns do you run? (Choose all that apply):

- Online display campaigns to acquire new customers. [90%]
- Online display campaigns to amplify offline campaigns. [90%]
- Online search marketing campaigns. [90%]
- E-mail marketing campaigns to existing customers. [97%]
- E-mail marketing campaigns to acquire new customers. [87%]
- SMS Campaigns. [100%]
- Social media campaigns. [100%]

29. For managing digital marketing does your organisation use the following tools and services (Choose all that apply):

- E-mail service provider. [47%]
- SMS short code and gateway. [70%]

- Own campaign management tool. [20%]
- Not own, but a campaign management tool that is used by our vendor. [30%]
- Your own data management platform (DMP). [25%]
- A data management platform provided by a media agency/vendor(s). [50%]
- Digital media buying platforms. [80%]
- Any other tool that you may be using to support your digital marketing efforts. Please specify. [4%]

30. When running digital marketing campaigns in your organisation do you (Choose all that apply):

- Segment your databases and run intelligent 1 to 1 campaigns. [57%]
- Do you use personalization. [37%]
- Do you capture and track responses to your campaigns. [77%]
- Do you A/B test campaigns or do multivariate tests. [70%]
- Do adhoc/tactical campaigns only. [50%]
- At the moment, we do not run any digital campaigns of note. [2%]

Mobile marketing

31. Does your company have a branded mobile app? (Choose one).

- Yes. [30%]
- Yes, we have multiple mobile apps. [17%]
- We don't have a mobile app but a mobile optimized website. [50%]
- No, we neither have a mobile app nor is our site mobile optimized. [3%]

32. Does the branded mobile app you run have push notifications?

- Yes. [57%]
- No. [43%]

33. Does your branded mobile app run in-app advertising?

- Yes. [7%]
- No. [93%]

34. Does your company do mobile advertising?

- Yes, we do structured mobile marketing campaigns. [53%]
- We do adhoc/tactical mobile campaigns from time to time. [30%]
- No. [17%]

Social media marketing

35. Creating and managing social media communities (Choose one):

- We have a structured social media strategy that has been rolled out across many social networks. [40%]
- We have built social media communities which we manage. [16%]
- We have a few communities on social media but we don't know what they are doing for us. [17%]
- We have built independent social media communities to support marketing campaigns from time to time. [17%]
- We do not have our business on social media. [10%]

36. Which social media platforms does your organisation use? (Choose all that apply):

- Facebook. [100%]
- Twitter. [100%]
- YouTube. [47%]
- Linkedin. [80%]
- Blog(s). [17%]
- Instagram. [94%]
- Quora. [7%]
- Pinterest. [4%]
- Snapchat. [14%]

37. Who manages social media in your organisation? (Choose one):

- We have a specialized social media team as part of marketing which handles social media. [54%]
- We have a specialized social media team that works in another department that handles social media. [23%]

- One/some of the members of the marketing team handle social media as part of their role. [20%]
- Brands/departments manage social media independently. [3%]

38. Does you organisation encourage employees to use social media? (Choose one):

- Yes. [53%]
- We don't actively encourage our employees to use social media, but we have no norms against them using it personally. [20%]
- We restrict our employees' use of social media. [23%]
- We currently don't have a social media policy for our employees. [4%]

39. Does your organisation listen and respond to online conversations (ORM)? (Choose one):

- Yes, we are actively listening to online conversations and responding to them. [67%]
- We listen to online conversations that are relevant to our company and brands and respond to them on a case by case basis. [17%]
- We are monitoring online conversations, but we do not respond to them. [13%]
- At this moment we do not listen to online conversations. [3%]

40. Does your organisation use tools to manage social media marketing? (Choose all that apply):

- We use an online listening tool. [60%]
- We have invested in tools that help us automate social media management. [47%]
- We don't directly invest in these tools but our agencies or vendors have invested in them. [40%]
- We are currently evaluating investments in social media management tools. [10%]
- At the moment, we do not have any plans to invest in tools for social media management. [2%]

Content marketing

41. Does your organisation invest in creating original content? (Choose one):

- Yes, we have a content strategy and make investments in producing original content. [60%]
- We do not have a clear content strategy but invest in creating content from time to time. [17%]
- Our social media/digital agency generates content for us as part of their deliverables. [17%]
- When necessary we use borrowed content. [6%]
- At the moment, we do not create original content for digital marketing. [3%]

42. What kinds of original content do you create (Choose all that apply):

- Video. [70%]
- Audio. [44%]
- Static visual content. [80%]
- Written content. [90%]

43. Does your organisation use a content management tool?

- Yes, we have invested in a content management tool. [30%]
- Yes, we use a content management tool through our agency/vendor(s). [60%]
- No, we don't use a content management tool. [23%]

44. Has your organisation done influencer* marketing program(s)?

*Influencer marketing program is a term used to describe a digital marketing technique that use members of public who by their presence in social media have garnered a large fan following

- Yes, we work with social media influencers. [50%]
- No, we have not worked with bloggers or other social media influencers. [50%]

Customer side digital transformation

45. Is your organisation planning to integrate multiple digital technologies that are used to engage with prospects and customers? (Choose one):

- Yes, we have integrated a few areas where we use digital technologies and are working towards an organization wide customer side digital transformation project. [23%]
- Yes, we are in the process of formalizing a customer side digital transformation strategy. [40%]
- Yes, we are in the planning stages of unifying our customer side digital touchpoints. [20%]
- No, we don't have any immediate plans to integrate the digital technologies we use. [14%]
- Does not apply. [3%]

About you

Name: _____

Designation: _____

Department: _____

Organisation: _____

Years of work experience: _____

Current city of work: _____

Thank you for taking time to fill out the Decode MarTech research questionnaire. We appreciate your time and believe that your contribution will help us and other marketers get a perspective of how the best companies are using technology to transform their marketing

Thank you once again for your time and participation.

Pain Points in the MarTech Ecosystem Implementation

Marketing is becoming a technology-oriented discipline, and good organizations understand that it is not merely about embedding IT services within marketing. Organisations need to understand the context of technology as well.

Basis the survey results, UK companies based in India can be put into 3 broad categories on the basis of the current stage of marketing technology implementation.

Figure: Distribution of Marketing Technology Sophistication Among Organizations

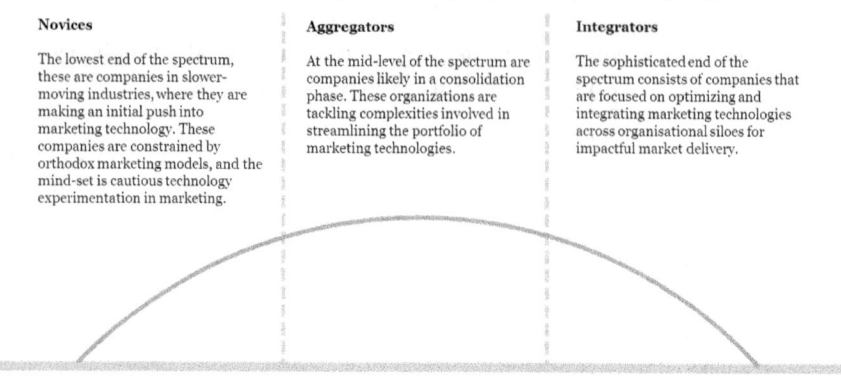

Figure: Major Pain Points in Marketing Technology Implementation

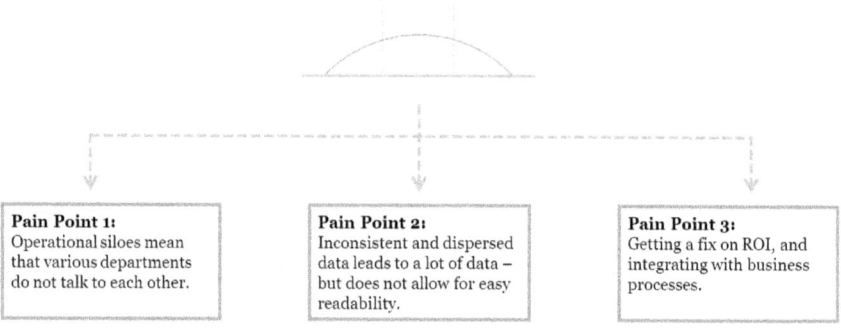

The average UK SME owner will be putting around 16% of their 2018/19 on marketing, according to a study by performance marketing network affilinet. They polled over 1,000 SME business owners in UK. UK companies in India will be rolling their digital marketing spend, with several companies relooking their ad spend allocated on Google and Facebook. While overall the marketing technology market is expected to grow, areas like Artifical Intelligence, Machine Learning, Augmented Reality / Virtual Reality and so on might seem more interesting to markteres than generic social media.

Clean-up of the River Ganga – What East Can Learn From the West

AUTHOR BIO

Prateek Mangal
Director, SSR Management Consultants Pvt. Ltd.

Prateek works as the Director – Client Services, for SSR Management Consultants Pvt. Ltd. and is also a founding partner in an entrepreneurial venture – Shilp Metals Pvt. Ltd. An MBA from Indian Institute of Foreign Trade - Kolkata, and International University in Geneva, Switzerland; he is also a Diploma holder in Cyber Law from Asian School of Cyber Laws, Pune and has taken several courses on Big Data and Blockchain. He started his corporate journey with Triton Management Services and served the FMCG giant in Africa and India. He has eight years of experience in FMCG and Manufacturing Industry and is widely travelled across Asia, Africa and Europe and is an expert of International Trade.

Prateek has co-authored and edited a casebook titled "Compendium: Management Cases from Emerging Markets". He has edited and authored several Book Chapters, Case Studies, and has presented and published research papers on key FMCG and manufacturing issues. He is also a prominent Social Worker and runs an NGO 'Neelabh Foundation' to finance studies of underprivileged children in eastern Uttar Pradesh.

Clean-up of the Ganga – What East Can Learn from the West

Prateek Mangal
Director, SSR Management Consultants Pvt. Ltd.

INTRODUCTION

Sir Thomas Roe intertwined the fates of two great nations in the early 1610's when he approached the Mughal Dynasty ruler Jahangir, under the instruction of King James I. The purpose of the visit was to arrange for a commercial treaty and secure land for commercial agencies called 'factories'. He was successful in his endeavour and The East India Company established factories in Ahmedabad, Broach and Agra. This was the advent of a historical timeline bejewelled with prosperous trade, technology sharing (during the Industrial Revolution) and cordial relations, but also marred with hate, war and bloodshed; which India and United Kingdom had to share.

The Rivers Ganga and Thames share the same grandeur being the providers of their respective lands - River Ganga being the sustenance of millions of people of Northern India, and Thames supporting the magnificent city of London. However, sadly they were meted a similar fate by mankind, being fed with garbage, untreated sewage and other human and animal waste. Today, stretches of over 600 kilometres of the river Ganga are ecologically dead zones; Thames faced this situation some 50 years back, being highly polluted and reduced to a fermenting sewer.

Nonetheless, due to the endeavours of the UK Government and unrelenting support of the people Thames bounced back to being the cleanest river flowing through a major city. This article attempts to draw a parallel between the two rivers and highlight the steps taken for the decontamination of the Thames, so that they can be replicated in India for the cleaning of the river Ganga. With the advances in technology, and methods that have been tried and tested; all being well the Ganga will also follow suit as Thames, and be as pure as it is holy within our lifetime.

Ganga: Mythology

In Hinduism, river Ganga is sacred and personified, and worshipped as 'The Goddess Ganga'. Hindu people believe that bathing in the river Ganga will cleanse them of their sins and set them on the path to '*Moksha*' i.e. freedom from the cycle of 'Birth and Death'. Pilgrims also immerse the ashes of their dead as they believe doing so will bring the spirits closer to moksha. Water of river Ganga is considered not only pure but holy and is used in all Hindu rituals and ceremonies.

Story of descent of the cosmic river Ganga on Earth begins with a sage, Kapila. Sage Kapila was in deep meditation but was disturbed by the sixty thousand sons of King Sagara. Enraged at being disturbed, the sage burned them with his angry gaze, reducing them to ashes, and sent them to the netherworld. Only the 'Holy Waters' of the river Ganges, then in heaven could bring the dead sons of King Sagara to their salvation or moksha. King Bhagirath, a descendant of these sons, took on the mammoth task of bringing the water of river Ganga on Earth to restore his ancestors. Bhagirath pledges to undertake penance, and after years of rigorous penance Goddess Ganga is pleased and grants him the boon of salvation of his ancestors. However, the Goddess put up a condition; since her turbulent force upon descent from heaven would shatter the earth, King Bhagiratha had to persuade Lord Shiva to receive Ganga in the coils of his tangled hair and break her fall. Bhagirath travelled to the abode of Shiva – *Mount Kailash* in the Himalayas and prayed to Lord Shiva. Shiva accepts the prayer and gladly accepts to receive the mighty river. Ganga descends and is tamed in Lord Shiva's matted locks and flows in the Himalayas. Ganga is then led by the waiting Bhagirath to the ashes of his ancestors, who achieve salvation by the waters of Ganga. In honor of King Bhagirath's pivotal role in the descent; the source stream of Ganga in the Himalayas is named Bhagirathi.

Ganga: Origin

In March 2017, The High Court of Uttarakhand (India) accorded the status of 'living human entity' to the river Ganga, making any crime against Ganga to be tried as crime against a human being. Ganga is the lifeline and a source of livelihood to Northern India, and millions of people who live along its course depend on it.

The river Ganges, popularly known as river Ganga flows in India and Bangladesh. The river covers a length in excess of 2500 kilometres; starting in the Eastern Himalayas in the Indian state of Uttarakhand, covering the plains in Uttar Pradesh, Bihar, Jharkhand, West Bengal and finally emptying into the Bay of Bengal to meet the Indian Ocean.

The confluence of *Bhagirathi* and *Alaknanda* creates the main stream of the river Ganga, this happens at *Devprayag* in Uttarakhand. However, Bhagirathi is considered to be the source of Ganga in Hindu culture and mythology, despite the fact that Alaknanda is the longer stream and hydrologically the source stream. Melting snow from the peaks like *Nanda Devi, Trishul,* and *Kamet* form the headwaters of Alaknanda. Bhagirathi stream is born at the foot of *Gangotri* Glacier at *Gomukh*; and is mythologically known to reside in the matted locks of Hindu God Shiva.

Pollution of the Ganga

Pollution in any form is harmful, not just to humans but to flora and fauna alike. Pollution in the River Ganga - the largest river and major source of drinking water in northern India - has posed a huge challenge since the late 1970's. Statistics show that Ganga provides water to approximately 40% of the Indian population spread across 11 states; more than any other river in the world. Ganga is now severely polluted with industrial waste, human and animal waste; by the time people realized that pollution in the river needs some control measures, stretches of over 600kms of the river were essentially ecologically dead zones. Oxygen level was so low that the river was unable to sustain any life in those stretches.

Various factors contributing to the pollution in the river are: increase in population density, various human activities like bathing, washing clothes, bathing of animals, releasing of waste water from industries and institutions. In case of Ganga, waste generated from religious activities is also a significant factor. Human waste water is contaminated with soaps and detergents, and sewage laden with faecal matter which is a carrier of numerous strains of disease causing bacteria. Industrial waste comes from different manufacturing units, tanneries, chemical factories, textile manufacturing units, distilleries and coal based power generation plants; as well as biological waste matter from hospitals and nursing homes along the banks of Ganga in the cities like Kanpur, Allahabad, Varanasi, Patna and Kolkata. This untreated industrial waste which can be toxic and non-biodegradable, is overloaded with chemicals and heavy metals like mercury, lead and copper, which are harmful to marine life as well as human and animal life.

Thames: Origin

Thames supports and provides about 8.8 million (2016 estimate) people in London, and is the primary source of water for drinking as well as daily chores. The source of Thames is about 1.5 kilometre north of the village of Kemble, near Cirencester. The river trickles out of the earth in a Gloucestershire field near Cirencester. It travels six counties and a distance of 346 kilometres and finally pours into the North Sea.

It is often considered that the River might be taking its name from the Sanskrit word '*Tamas*' meaning "dark" as its waters were often dark and cloudy; however there is also an alternative school of thought saying it is named after the Roman word '*Tam*' meaning "Wide" and '*Isis*' meaning "Water". The countryside along the length of Thames is mainly rolling hills; farming and grazing cattle are the main use of the land till it reaches London. In London the river becomes urbanized, it is a point of recreation, a place for inspiration. It provides water to the city as well as a passage for transportation. The lengths of Thames have frozen over many times, the earliest record of the Thames being frozen dates back to 1150 AD. Post the cleaning efforts, more than 100 fish species, several birds and aquatic mammals like seals have been spotted in the Thames river over the past 30 years, many of these in the river within London.

London Bridge on Thames

For about a thousand years now, the London Bridge is joining the banks of Thames and providing passage for trade and culture to flourish. The London Bridge as we see today was opened in the year 1973; however the site of the current bridge is the same place where the romans built the first bridge when they invaded Britain in AD 43. At the time of the invasion the current London was a swampy marsh. The first bridge was probably made of wood but it was vital for the Romans to expand their reach further in Britain; as it was needed for troops and supplies to reach the other side of Thames. The bridge has been rebuilt several times after it was first constructed. It is probably the first wooden bridge constructed by the Romans that the Nursery Rhyme – 'London Bridge is falling down' refers to.

Thames: It's Myths and Legends

Thames has its fair share of myths and legends through its history; there have been innumerable myths, legends and ghost stories. It is said to be a place of magic, mystery, urban legends and natural power. It has witnessed and supported pre-historic civilizations to the modern era; seeing the dark ages, renaissance and industrial revolution. Thames has also been a witness to pagan rituals to popular festivities and celebrations on its banks since ancient times, ghosts, ghouls, dreams and strange stories - from the suicidal ghost of Waterloo Bridge to the phantom willies of Westminster Bridge, and the traitor's heads of London Bridge; all gather on the bridges on Thames and lurk within its tunnels, tributaries and sewers.

Pollution of the River Thames

Thames River is supposed to be the cleanest river flowing through a major city. It is a major achievement considering the fact that just some 50 years ago it was considered badly polluted and biologically dead, i.e. the oxygen levels in the river were too low to support any form of life. During the reign of William IV (1830-1837) and the early years of the reign of Queen Victoria (1837 -1901) till about 1860's several thousands of people had died of cholera resultant of the pollution in

Thames. Untreated sewage was being discharged directly in the river. Despite the dirty water and foul smell, people continued using the water of Thames for washing and bathing and even drinking.

The British 'House of Parliament' building situated at the bank of Thames saw a time when the curtains of the building had to be soaked in lime, to prevent the stench from halting the proceedings of the house. In the late 1870's there was an incident which became a black mark on the history of Thames. A pleasure steamship named 'Princess Alice' sunk in the Thames after a collision; about 600 passengers lost their life in the incident. Most of the people who died had not drowned but died because of the extensive pollution in the river.

Charles Dickens, the renowned novelist described the Thames as 'a dank, stinking sludge, the scene of murders and crime' in several of his works. In the middle of the 20th Century, when the world was reeling under the impact of the Second World War (1939-45), United Kingdom had seen a lot of destruction too. Many treatment plants were destroyed by German bombs and a lot dirty water polluted by gun powder and other explosives was released in the river killing a lot of aquatic animal and plant life.

Revival of the Thames

Steps were taken as early as the Victorian era for the revival of Thames; two of the most successful steps were setting up of the embankments and later the treatment plants.

The Embankments

In the year 1861, the Thames embankments were built under the supervision of Sir Joseph Bazalgette. The embankments were made over what were earlier the tidal foreshores of the Thames; they helped by narrowing the river and increasing the rate of flow. Increased rate of flow helped to get rid of all the pollutants and waste materials faster. Since the embankments were essentially raised platforms limiting the sideways flow of the river, they allowed for building of raised riverside roads and walkways and also helped by concealing the huge sewage pipes and water mains.

Treatment Plants

Even after the embankments were made, water borne diseases were still a cause for concern, it led to the decision to construct water 'Treatment Plants' to clean the water of Thames before it was supplied to the households. The waste water after usage along with the sewage was also treated at the treatment plants before being released back into the Thames. This practice significantly improved the health of the people and also cleaning the water in Thames. After the destruction caused during the

Second World War New treatments plants were set up in the 1950's. Post that, the 1960s decade saw new laws being made to stop industries letting their waste water go into the Thames. In the 1970's and 1980's with the increasing general awareness about environment, people were getting concerned and efforts were made to make tabs on the amount of pesticides and fertilizers getting washed into the river.

Everyday newer methods are being developed to control the pollution levels in air and water, one of the contemporary methods prevalent in the United Kingdom is turning the sewage sludge to fertilizer pellets and using it for agricultural purposes. However, concerns are rising over a new pollutant that has caught the world off guard and the Thames is also not immune to its ill effects – Plastic. It's so convenient to use that it has made inroads in most of the aspects of human life but when discarded, it takes hundreds of years to breakdown and many varieties of plastics are poisonous for the environment.

CONCLUSION

Though the visionaries in India were proactive regarding Hindu sentiments and their faith in the Ganga; Pt. Madan Mohan Malviya formed the Ganga Mahasabha as early as 1905 and it took the Mahasabha about a decade of struggle to get British India to accept the uninterrupted flow of Ganga is the elementary right of Hindus.

Other steps such as the *"Ganga Action Plan"* started in 1986 by then Prime Minister Rajeev Gandhi; *"Namami Gange Programme"* launched in 2014 with an allocation of over INR 20 billion. However these steps proved to be inadequate due to lack of execution and rampant corruption.

Thames though much smaller in length than the Ganga, faced the same problems and emerged triumphant, steps taken for the cleaning of the Thames can be reproduced in India on a larger level to control the pollution situation in the Ganga. Construction of embankments on the river in the cities and setting up of water treatment and sewage treatment plants of appropriate capacity in every city by the river banks should be considered as pollution control methods. There is an inherent need to put tabs on illegal sand mining from the river as it also disturbs the aquatic ecosystem. Control measures should be ensured in place where illegal dumping of untreated waste is done.

With collective efforts of government and people, coupled with the use of contemporary technology and strategy; Thames will stay clean as it is and Ganga will be clean and holy within the years to come.

*   *   *

REFERENCES

https://en.wikipedia.org/wiki/Ganges
https://en.wikipedia.org/wiki/Ganges_in_Hinduism
https://en.wikipedia.org/wiki/London_Bridge
https://en.wikipedia.org/wiki/Pollution_of_the_Ganges#Ganga_Action_Plan
https://en.wikipedia.org/wiki/River_Thames
http://www.gatewayforindia.com/history/british_history1.htm
http://primaryhomeworkhelp.co.uk/riverthames/intro.htm
http://primaryhomeworkhelp.co.uk/riverthames/pollution.htm
http://primaryhomeworkhelp.co.uk/riverthames/londonbr.htm
https://vibhanshu.wordpress.com/2010/03/20/bhagiratha-who-brought-river-ganga-to-earth/
http://www.bbc.com/earth/story/20151111-how-the-river-thames-was-brought-back-from-the-dead

I, Koh - i - Noor

AUTHOR BIO

Prateek Mangal
Director, SSR Management Consultants Pvt. Ltd.

Prateek works as the Director – Client Services, for SSR Management Consultants Pvt. Ltd. and is also a founding partner in an entrepreneurial venture – Shilp Metals Pvt. Ltd. An MBA from Indian Institute of Foreign Trade - Kolkata, and International University in Geneva, Switzerland; he is also a Diploma holder in Cyber Law from Asian School of Cyber Laws, Pune and has taken several courses on Big Data and Blockchain. He started his corporate journey with Triton Management Services and served the FMCG giant in Africa and India. He has eight years of experience in FMCG and Manufacturing Industry and is widely travelled across Asia, Africa and Europe and is an expert of International Trade.

Prateek has co-authored and edited a casebook titled "Compendium: Management Cases from Emerging Markets". He has authored several Book Chapters, Case Studies, and has presented and published research papers on key FMCG and manufacturing issues. He is also a prominent Social Worker and runs an NGO 'Neelabh Foundation' to finance studies of underprivileged children in eastern Uttar Pradesh.

Richa Gond
Principal, Neelabh Public School

Richa is currently working as the Principal of Neelabh Public School, Ratasia Kothi, Deoria. An erudite herself, she has made a mark for herself as an educationist at the young age of twenty six. She's also a part of Board of Directors at SSR Management Consultants Pvt. Ltd. She did her graduation form Magadh Mahila College, Patna Univesity and post-graduation from Nalanda Open Univesity. She has also done B.Ed. from Women's Training College, Patna University. She has been a part of the education field for the last six year.

Richa is also a proud mother of a baby girl, and her conviction to contribute to the society powers her to balance her personal and work life effortlessly.

I, Koh - *i* - Noor

Prateek Mangal
Director, SSR Management Consultants Pvt. Ltd.

Richa Gond
Principal, Neelabh Public School

I, Koh - *i* - Noor

As I sit today, glittering atop the British crown amongst the crown jewels; I bask in the splendour of the appellation, notoriety and worth I have earned through my existence so far. I have been a witness to unparalleled glory for Maharajas, Nawaabs, Nizams, Monarchs, and some have even told me, of Gods. I have also been a spectator to several dead, disfigured or maddened rulers, sacrificed queens, slaughtered masses, ruined lives and plundered and devastated cities and provinces. History has revered me as the symbol of supremacy; I am a living testament of man's lust for riches, power and absolute domination. Even today nations like India, Pakistan, and Iran fight to prove their stake over me. I am Koh-i-Noor.

Syamantaka

I have always had a fascination for the mighty lands of India; it is also my birth place. The ancient scriptures of Hindus, namely *Vishnu Purana* and *Bhagvata Purana* name me as '*Syamantaka*'. I was owned by the Sun god '*Surya*' and he wore me around his neck. I was believed to be the source of dazzling appearance of the Sun God. Ancient scriptures mentioned whichever land would possess me, will be free from all calamities and natural disasters as earthquake, flood, drought or famine and will always be prosperous with plentiful resources.

The Sun God offered me to *Satrajit*, a *Yadava* nobleman, as a boon for his devotion and ardent prayers. When Satrajit returned to his home in Dwarka, with me hanging in his neck, people mistook him for Sun God. When Lord *Krishna*, incarnation of Lord *Vishnu*; asked Satrajit to present me to *Ugrasen* - the supreme leader of the Yadava clan, he did not comply. Instead he presented me to his brother *Prasen*, who was also the ruler of a Yadava province. Prasen also valued me and often wore me on his neck.

One day when Prasen went hunting, he met a Lion, a fierce battle ensued but the beast emerged victorious; and took me with him. However the lion could not take me very far, its stride was cut short by *Jambavant*, the king of bears. Jambavant was a brute himself and easily defeated the lion and took me home. He gave me to his kids who used to play different games with me; I stayed there for many days until one day Lord Krishna himself came looking for me.

When Krishna challenged Jambavant, there was a furious combat which went on for 28 days. Jambavant who was a devotee of Lord *Rama* and the strongest being at that time realized; he was fighting Lord Rama himself (Rama and Krishna are both incarnation of Lord Vishnu). Jambavant was ferocious but pious by nature; he returned me to Krishna and also married his daughter Jambavati to Krishna. Krishna took me and Jambavati to Dwarka. Later, Lord Krishna told me, when Prasen mysteriously disappeared with me, people accused him of killing Prasen and stealing me and he was out looking for me to prove his innocence.

I stayed in Dwarka for ages after that, however I don't remember much. Scriptures also don't mention me for the next few thousand years.

Kollur Mines

My next memories are that of a shallow river of mud or a gravel-clay pit to be specific. I was lying there for millions of years before someone came looking for me. I believe I was swept there by the river current after I was ejected from my host rock by some primeval volcano. I was transported along the river and came to rest when finally the river dried up.

The place where I was found was called Kollur Mines, in Golconda region, present day Andhra Pradesh and Telangana on the banks of river Krishna. I was supposedly mined during the rule of the Kakatiya Dynasty. Thousands of men, women and children of all ages worked in the mines, looking for diamonds of all shapes and sizes. Me and my sister diamonds *Daria-i-Noor* (Sea of Light) and The Great Mughal Diamond (a.k.a Orlov) were found there.

Daria-i-Noor was 242 old carats when she was found. In her current weight 182 Carats in a square cut, she is one of the world's largest diamonds and her pale pink colour makes her one of the rarest. Separated at birth we were united for some time at the house of *Maharaja Ranjit Singh* but later she was also taken away by the East India Company like me, and she somehow ended as the part of Iranian crown jewels, in Iran.

My other sibling, the Great Mughal Diamond, at 787 carats was even bigger than the two of us put together. She was in the shape of a half egg. She was gifted by *Emir Jemla* to the Mughal ruler *Shah Jahan* as a token of friendship between the two families. Shah Jahan entrusted Venetian lapidary *Ortensio Borgio* with the cutting of my sister. Borgio, supposedly in an attempt to preserve the size of the diamond, decided to grind it rather than cut into smaller stones. This did more bad than good; Shah Jahan was enraged, though he spared the life of Borgio, he fined him all his money for his ineptness. We spent a lot of time together in the Mughal treasury together until *Nader Shah Afsar* took us all with him to Iran. Many of Nader Shah's diamonds and other precious stones ended up being the part of Persian crown jewels and several were sold to the Ottomans. My sister I think is now part of the Kremlin Diamond Fund in Russia with the name Orlov.

My Story and My Curse

When I was found, my weight was just over 186 old carats (191 metric carats), in the shape of a hen's egg. Contrary to popular belief, I was not a perfect diamond. In my original uncut form, I was 'flawed at heart' in the words of gemmologists. Yellow flecks ran through a plane inside me, one of which was actually big and reduced my ability to refract light. Nevertheless my original cut was like that of the 'Mughal Era' diamonds many of which are now a part of the Iranian crown jewels.

Some people say, I was first mentioned in writings in the year 1306 when I was taken from a King of Malwa; whose family had hosted me for centuries. I was described then as weighing 186 carats with an oval cut – the shape and size of a small hen's egg.

My curse dates back to a Hindu text from the time of my first authenticated appearance, in 1306. My Curse read:

> "He who owns this diamond will own the world,
> but will also know all its misfortunes.
> Only God, or a woman, can wear it with impunity."

Baburnama

According to historians the first dependable written records of my existence were the writings of the Mughal ruler *Babur*. In his autobiography '*Baburnama*', he mentions a 'famous' diamond weighing just over 187 carats, he called it 'Diamond of Babur'. According to his writings, he received me as tribute in the year 1526 as an accolade for his conquest of Delhi and Agra provinces at the Battle of Panipat. The writings also state that I was originally acquired by *Alauddin Khilji* of the *Khilji* dynasty of the Delhi Sultanate (Province) after his invasion of the Kingdoms of Southern India in the early 14th century. I was later passed on to the succeeding dynasties of the Sultanate till I reached the hands of Babur and made the Mughal dynasty my guardians for the years to come. This was the initiation of my becoming an icon of domination.

The Peacock Throne

Shah Jahan was the fifth ruler of the Mughal dynasty; he was an art connoisseur and architecture aficionado. His rule was during the golden age of the Mughal Era, when the Mughals were ruling almost the entire Indian subcontinent. Such a ruler was deemed worthy of the '*Takth-e-Sulaiman*' or the 'Throne of Solomon' to accentuate his position as a just king. In the early 17th Century, Shah Jahan commissioned the 'Peacock throne' or the '*Takth-e-Taus*'; perhaps the most stunning and valuable throne ever built by the hands of a man. This magnificent gemstone encrusted 'work of art' took seven years to build and costed 4 times as much as the Taj Mahal; it was entirely covered in gold and inlaid with diamonds, emeralds and rubies. I was lodged at the top of this exquisite throne, in the head of a glimmering gemstone peacock overlooking the entire Mughal Empire from the '*Diwan-e-Khas*' in the Red Fort at Delhi, for a little over 100 years. My first verifiable appearance was here on the top of the Peacock Throne.

The Sands of Persia

Nader Shah Afsar, one of the most powerful Iranian rulers (also known as Persia), attacked the Mughal Empire ruled by *Muhammad Shah Rangila* in the year 1739. The invasion wreaked havoc over the Mughal king; subsequent carnage resulted in loss of tens of thousands of lives, and the treasury was plundered. The looted wealth was so much that it took 700 elephants, 4,000 camels and 12,000 horses to pull it. Nader Shah also took the Peacock Throne as part of his treasure, but he removed the Timur Ruby and me to wear on an armband. It was him that gave me the name: Koh-i-Noor, meaning 'Mountain of Light'.

Nader shah was killed in 1747 and his empire was vanquished; I was taken by his grandson *Shah Rukh*, who gave me to *Ahmad Shah Durrani* of the Afghan Dynasty in lieu of his support. Shah Rukh was later killed by pouring molten lead over his head. I remained a part of Afghan Dynasty for about 70 years. It was during this stay an Afghan Queen, *Wufa Begum* tried her best to describe my worth. She said "If a strong man were to throw four stones, one north, one south, one east, one west, and a fifth stone up into the air, and if the space between them were to be filled with gold, all would not equal the value of the Koh-i-Noor." *Shah Zaman Durrani* a descendant of Ahmad Shah was blinded by needles to gain control over me. I was now beginning to gain the notoriety of truly being cursed as most of my new owners were gaining possession over me by vanquishing my previous owner.

Shuja Shah Durrani, one of the descendants of Ahmad Shah wore me in a bracelet on Mountstuart Elphinstone's visit to Peshawar in 1808. About a year later there was a looming threat of invasion of Afganistan, by the Russians. Shuja Shah formed an alliance with the United Kingdom to thwart the attack, but the Russians were victorious in the battle and Shuja Shah escaped to Lahore with me in his possession.

Lahore was under the rule of the *Sikh Maharaja Ranjit Singh*, who was also the founder of the Sikh Empire. Shuja took refuge from Maharaja Ranjit Singh, and the Maharaja insisted that I, the Koh-i-Noor diamond, an invaluable gem; be bestowed to him in return of his hospitality. He gained possession over me in the year 1813.

The East India Company

The new owner Maharaja Ranjit Singh had wanted to offer me to Lord Jagannath at the Jagannath Temple in Puri, modern day state of Odisha. The British were outraged at the idea of the most invaluable diamond, a symbol of absolute domination to be committed to priests. The British media urged the East India Company to do everything in their power to keep a track of me. After the death of Ranjit Singh in 1839, his will was not executed and I was passed on to his four successors in four years along with the throne. Finally, after the violent period ended, the only successor remaining in line to the throne was his son – five year old *Duleep Singh* and his mother *Rani Jindan*. In 1849, at the conclusion of the second Anglo-Sikh War, Rani Jindan was imprisoned and Duleep Singh was forced to sign a treaty with the British to annex the kingdom to the East India Company and hand me over to them. Duleep Singh was a mere 10 years old at the time.

My Journey to the United Kingdom

The treaty was signed by Duleep Singh and The Earl of Dalhousie - James Andrew Broun-Ramsay. Though most of the officials of the East India Company were of the opinion that I, the diamond, should be presented to the Queen as a gift from the East India Company but Dalhousie treated me as spoils of war and ensured that I be surrendered to Her Majesty The Queen by Duleep Singh Himself. He placed Ranjit Singh under the guardianship of Dr. John Login, a Surgeon in the British Army.

Early in the year 1850, I was sealed inside a small iron safe and placed in a red dispatch box, it was taped and sealed with a wax and kept at Bombay Treasury awaiting a steamer ship from China. I was placed under the care of Captain J. Ramsay and Brevet Lt. Col F. Mackeson and shipped to England on the ship HMS Medea, captained by Captain Lockyer under taut security arrangements. Upon reaching England, I was to be passed on to the chairman and deputy chairman of the East India Company in the City of London, to be presented to Queen Victoria.

On 3rd July 1850, the 250th anniversary of formation of the East India Company; I was formally presented to Queen Victoria. I immediately became one of the most prized possessions of the Queen; she even wore me on her dress in a broach.

The Great Exhibition

In the year 1851, The Great Exhibition was held at Hyde Park, London. General public was for the first time given a chance to see me, one of the most valuable gems of the times. The British media trumpeted about me as the symbol of Victorian Britain's imperial domination of the world. Some three million people, about ten percent of the population of United Kingdom turned up to see me up close. At first I was displayed in gilded bird cage, the public was not happy with my presentation; so I was then shifted to a case with black velvet and gas lamps so that I would refract the light better.

The Re-cutting

In my original Mughal Era cut with my flaws I was 169 facets and was 4.1 centimeters long, 3.26 centimeters wide, and 1.62 centimeters deep. I was high-domed, with a flat base and both triangular and rectangular facets. Prince Albert, husband of Queen Victoria was upset by the disappointment of the public over my appearance. He with the consent of the government ordered that I be re-cut. One of the most famous Dutch diamond merchants of the time *Mozes Coster* was chosen for the task. He sent his most experienced artisan *Levie Benjamin Voorzanger* and his team for the job.

On 17 July 1852, I was taken to the factory of Garrard & Co. in Haymarket; I was cut further using a steam-powered mill built specially for the job by Maudslay, Sons and Field. It was all done under the supervision of Prince Albert and the Duke of Wellington. The cutting reduced my weight from 186 old carats (191 modern carats) to my current weight of 105.6 carats. My new dimensions were 3.6 centimetres long, 3.2 centimetres wide and 1.3 cm deep. Normally brilliant-cut diamonds have fifty-eight facets, but I was given eight additional "star" facets around the culet (flat face on the bottom), making a total of sixty-six facets.

Prince Albert was highly dissatisfied with the huge reduction in my weight and size, Voorzanger however elucidated that he found several flaws in me that he needed to file away. Various other experts were in agreement with Voorzanger and believed he did a great job with me. When Queen Victoria showed the new me to my last non-British owner Maharaja Duleep Singh, he was left speechless for several minutes!

Queen Victoria

The new lighter but much more dazzling me was mounted in a honeysuckle brooch and a circlet worn by the Queen herself. At this time I was property of the Queen and yet not a part of the crown jewels. Although the Queen wore me often, she became extremely upset about the way I had been acquired. In the 1870's she wrote a letter to her eldest daughter, Victoria, Princess Royal, she mentioned "No one feels more strongly than I do about India or how much I opposed our taking those countries and I think no more will be taken, for it is very wrong and no advantage to us. You know also how I dislike wearing the Koh-i-Noor."

Queen Victoria wears me, the Koh-i-Noor as a brooch in 1887.
(Image Source: Wikimedia Commons/Alexander Bassano)

Crown Jewel

After the death of Queen Victoria, I was set in the Crown of Queen Alexandra, wife of King Edward VII; the crown was presented to her at their coronation in 1902. I was again transferred to Queen Mary's Crown in 1911, and finally to The Queen Mother's Crown in the year 1937, which is my current abode. When The Queen Mother passed away in 2002, the crown was placed on top of her coffin for the lying-in-state and funeral.

All the previous crowns that I was a part of are on display in the Jewel House at the Tower of London with crystal replicas of me and other diamonds set in the older crowns. The original bracelet in which I was studded and presented to Queen Victoria is also kept there. A glass replica of me shows visitors how I looked when I was brought to the United Kingdom.

Flawed Account of my History

When the British Governor General, Lord Dalhousie first seized me from Duleep Singh after the conquest of Punjab by the East India Company in 1849; he was fascinated with my story and commissioned a report on my history. An Englishman Theophilus John Metcalfe, was delegated with the responsibility and was instructed "to collect and to record as much accurate and interesting information regarding the Koh-i-Noor" from the goldsmiths, jewellers and courtiers of Delhi. Sadly, the probe was done more than 100 years after I was taken away from Delhi by Nader Shah. Even Metcalfe accepted that report was more or less heresy. His report is still safe in the vaults of National Archives of India.

At the moment

Today, I sit glittering in my case at the Tower of London, beside the Cullinan Diamond and some other gems. They say I'm invaluable; I don't carry an estimated value because I'm not insured. However, the crown that I'm set in is valued at $10-$12 billion dollars. Though, I am only the 90th biggest stone in the world, I am still at the centre of contention for at least three governments; India, Pakistan and Iran constantly attempt to take me from the English, not like the older time but by diplomacy.

*   *   *

REFERENCES

https://en.wikipedia.org/wiki/Crown_of_Queen_Elizabeth_The_Queen_Mother

https://en.wikipedia.org/wiki/Daria-i-Noor

https://en.wikipedia.org/wiki/Golconda_Diamonds

https://en.wikipedia.org/wiki/Great_Mogul_Diamond

https://en.wikipedia.org/wiki/James_Broun-Ramsay,_1st_Marquess_of_Dalhousie

https://en.wikipedia.org/wiki/Koh-i-Noor

https://en.wikipedia.org/wiki/Kollur_Mine

https://en.wikipedia.org/wiki/Peacock_Throne

http://www.bbc.com/news/world-asia-india-38218308

http://www.firstpost.com/living/the-kohinoors-true-and-bloody-history-is-traced-by-william-dalrymple-anita-anand-in-new-book-3150398.html

https://www.ft.com/content/0f17f436-5089-11e7-bfb8-997009366969

http://kohinoordiamond.org/history-of-kohinoor-diamond/

http://themystery2012.blogspot.in/2012/07/kohinoor-diamond.html

https://www.smithsonianmag.com/history/true-story-koh-i-noor-diamondand-why-british-wont-give-it-back-180964660/

https://www.theguardian.com/commentisfree/2016/feb/16/koh-i-noor-diamond-britain-illegally-india-pakistan-afghanistan-history-tower

https://www.internetstones.com/darya-i-nur-diamond-famous-jewelry.html

https://www.livehistoryindia.com/forgotten-treasures/2017/06/01/darya-i-noor-the-sea-of-light

A Study of London Payment Systems Growth and lessons learnt by Indian Digital Banking Payment System

AUTHOR BIO

Dr. Narinder Kumar Bhasin
Faculty - ASIBAS

Dr. Bhasin is a distinguished senior banking professional and research scholar with 31 years in the banking industry and academic experience as visiting / adjunct faculty. He is pursuing his second Ph.D. from Amity University. He is a qualified CAIIB, MBA and Certified Bank Trainer with expertise in establishing and restructuring banking systems and processes, objectives and goals.

He has worked in foreign banks like ANZ Grindlays and Standard Chartered as well as private sector banks like ING Vysya Bank and HDFC Bank Ltd. His last assignment was as Vice President, Axis Bank. He is presently working as a Professor in Amity School of Insurance, Banking and Actuarial Science (ASIBAS) at Amity University, Noida, Uttar Pradesh.

He was a part of Reserve Bank of India as member of Reconciliation Group and Working Group for settlement of clearing disputes and writing procedural guidelines of Cheque Truncation System respectively. He has been an eminent speaker, panelist and presenter at reputed national and international conferences, seminars and forums. He has authored multiple publications related to the BFSI industry and is a fellow member of Indian Institute of Banking and Finance.

A Study of London Payment Systems Growth and lessons learnt by Indian Digital Banking Payment System

Dr. Narinder Kumar Bhasin
Faculty - ASIBAS

INTRODUCTION

A clearing house is a traditional organization and financial institution formed by banks where representatives of banks can exchange cheques deposited by the customers for payment and settlement for credit to customer account. It should not be confused with Central Counterparty Clearing (CCP) which also provides clearing services, but very differently by taking on the settlement risks of the counterparties (member banks and broker-dealers). Clearing houses were instituted for the convenience of the customers. For example let us take the case of a city / town with 10 banks. Customers of every bank who receive cheques from their customers for any commercial transactions will deposit cheques with the bank where they maintain accounts every day, drawn on any of the ten banks. Those drawn on the same bank as the depositor are easily processed but cheques drawn on the other banks need to be presented to each bank in order to receive payments. This was a lengthy procedure and very cumbersome. Representatives of all ten banks who are participating in clearing house will have representatives who will carry all the cheques from the banks to hand over to representatives of drawee banks. Clearing houses solve the issues involved in long cycle of clearing settlement. The clearing system reduced the reconciliation problem of cheques.

With the development of cheques in England in the 1600s it was customary to return the cheque to the issuing bank for payment. However, with the passage of time the awareness of banking started growing and the volume of cheque usage start increasing. Many customers used to fill the cheque deposit and would deposit a cheque with their bank where they maintain the account. The collecting bank would depute their representatives who present the cheques and arrange for collection by returning to the drawee bank for payment.

176

Evolution of Payment Systems in London

History of London Payment System can be traced to 1770 when an unorganized and informal exchange of financial instruments like cheques, pay orders, drafts used to get exchanged between London banks. Executives and clerks of banks used to visit the banks daily in nearby areas and deposit the cheques deposited by their customers drawn on other banks. No formal records of cheque number, amount, payee names were kept on the records. No reconciliation was done - they settled the cheque drawn on each other. There were no time limits or defined turnaround times when the clearing settlement is to be done.

There was no formal and daily process of cheque clearings in 1770. Bank clerks from different banks fixed a particular time every day and started meeting at the Five Bells, a tavern in Lombard Street in the City of London. Their main objective was that instead of giving and collecting cheques individually to all the banks, they could meet at one place and settle the balances in cash. This was a major challenge to meet the customer's demand for faster settlement of funds to their account, to start a formal and organized clearing system. It was in early 19th century, when London Bankers and Bank of England took the decision to start an organization for clearing cheques. This organization was named as Bankers Clearing House (BACH). Founder of BACH was Lubbock's Bank on Lombard Street which initially started in one room. The uniform rules and procedures for clearing house was formulated and the clerks for London banks were required to meet twice daily in a fixed place for exchange of cheques, cheque returns and account settlement. In 1832, Charles Babbage published a book on operations, process and guidelines on functioning of clearing house titled "The Economy of Machinery and Manufactures".

The Process of Banker's Clearing House

In Lombard Street of London one large room was hired where around 30 clerks engaged in processing of cheques from the different banks that are the members of London Bankers Clearing House and used to visit daily. Each bank has been allotted a particular workstation with one desk placed in the rooms like a roundtable. The names of the banks are arranged in alphabetical order and one pigeon box is kept on the table. Name of the firm is written in the bold characters on the wall and desk to which the clerks belong.

As the clerks from different banks start visiting the BACH room, they start putting the cheques in the drop-box of different banks which were drawn on them. When the cut-off time for clearing house is over and all the member banks have dropped the cheques against each other, they will open the drop-box and count the cheques. After counting the cheques, they will sum up the amount due by that firm to the house from which the distributor is sent.

At 5 pm, after total amount of cheques drawn against each other by the banks, the net amount due by the clerk for each debtor bank would be announced by the clearing house incharge and they have to go to a rostrum to pay the net amount due by them in cash. The Inspector of the Clearing House is responsible for managing and settlement of the amount their bank owed to other banks on that particular day of net settlement.

Once all of the bankers who are debtor against clearing settlement had paid the clearing house inspector, the creditor bank who owed money was asked to go to rostrum to collect the money owed to their bank. Then total cash reconciliation was done by tallying the total amount paid by debtor banks which had to be equal to the total cash collected by the creditor banks.

Sometimes, there was a difference in the total amount paid by debtors' bank in the total collections and receipts as compared to total amount to be paid to creditor banks. In such cases all the member banks clerks re-tallied their total amount of cheques and tried to locate the difference. Clearing house incharge or the Inspector would also examine the paper trail of cheques so that any totalling or numerical errors could be located and corrected. All the members of clearing house had to wait till the total amount is tallied and house is reconciled.

This was an evolution of traditional bankers clearing house that started as a concept in London and lessons were learnt by many countries in the world. Jumping forward several centuries, the Cheque and Credit Clearing Company is the United Kingdom's clearing house.

BACS, EFTPOS, CHAPS and Faster Payments

The participant banks of London Clearing House have moved on from the manual clearing systems to electronic payment systems. London Clearing Banks (LCBs) have very smartly and successfully adopted payment systems to provide efficient customer services and business development to attract low cost CASA retail deposits and retail lending by establishing customer franchises. The major challenges which they faced were cost and pricing of the service rationally. Market growth has dramatically increased the volume of payments, exacerbating the cost problem. To counter this, the LCBs have introduced additional payment mechanisms such as credit cards and Bankers Automated Clearing Service (BACS); are introducing Electronic Fund Transfer at Point of Sale (EFTPOS); and are further automating the existing cash and cheque-based system. Development of the clearing house, BACS and EFTPOS demonstrates how payment systems impose co-operative policies to facilitate the transfer of funds and reduce costs, but such enforced co-operation and to lead to perfect competition, with uniform pricing policies. Competitors are in a strong position to operate more efficient and less expensive payments media for their customers. The dilemma facing the LCBs is therefore how to match this challenge and maintain their market position through further investment in payments technology, while maintaining their existing less efficient and more expensive payments media.

Clearing House Accepted Payment Systems (CHAPS) is a United Kingdom sterling high value and same-day payment and settlement system for corporate clients to settle wholesale payments. CHAPS also ensured to settle time-sensitive lower-value payments like buying or paying a deposit on a property. In November 2017, responsibility for the CHAPS system transferred to the Bank of England.

CHAPS is one of the most efficient, risk free, largest, irrevocable, real time and gross high value payment systems in the world. There are over 5000 banks and financial institutions with 25 direct participants that process CHAPS transactions and payments without any intervention of third parties or outsource payment companies through one of the direct participants. Direct participants in CHAPS include the traditional high-street banks and a number of international and custody banks. Agency or correspondent banks are those financial institutions that adopt the CHAPS Payment system indirectly and make their payments via direct participants.

CHAPS payments have various uses:

- Settlement of foreign exchange, money market, clearing funds by many big corporates, businesses houses through CHAPS
- Corporates needs to settle their business and commercial transaction and vendor payment which are very time sensitive and high value. These transactions also include Tax payments, Forex, Domestic, International and Suppliers payment.
- CHAPS is commonly used by solicitors and conveyancers to complete housing and other properly transactions.
- Retail individuals also use CHAPS to settle their daily life purchases of buy high-price and value items such as a home purchase, car and consumer finance items.

CHAPS Direct Participants

Bank of America N.A. (London branch)
Bank of China Limited (London branch)
Bank of England
Bank of New York Mellon (London branch)
Bank of Scotland plc (part of the Lloyds Banking Group)
Barclays Bank plc
BNP Paribas SA (London branch)

Citibank N.A. (London branch)
ClearBank Limited
CLS Bank International (an Edge Act Bank based in New York)
Clydesdale Bank plc
Danske Bank (a trading name of Northern Bank Limited, part of the Danske Bank Group)
Deutsche Bank AG (London branch)
HSBC Bank plc
J.P. Morgan Chase Bank N.A. (London branch)
Lloyds Bank plc (part of the Lloyds Banking Group)
National Westminster Bank plc (part of the Royal Bank of Scotland Group)
Northern Trust Company (London branch)
Royal Bank of Scotland plc (part of the Royal Bank of Scotland Group)
Santander UK plc (part of the Banco Santander Group)
Societe Generale (Paris Head Office)
Standard Chartered Bank plc
State Street Bank and Trust Company (London branch)
Svenska Handelsbanken AB (London branch)

Real Time Gross Settlement (RTGS) settled a payment obligation individually on gross basis between direct participants on the same day that they are submitted. The transfer of funds is irrevocable between the direct participants. The CHAPS system opens at 6am each working day. Participants must be open to receive by 8am and must send by 10am. CHAPS closes at 6pm for bank-to-bank payments. Customer payments must be submitted by 5:40pm.

Faster Payments – Bank of England Settlement

The Faster Payments Scheme (FPS) is a Deferred Net Settlement (DNS) in which banks continue to exchange payments to the customer in real time during 24 hours with final transfer occurring at the end of the processing time. During the entire process record is kept of net debits and credits. In DNS, net settlement takes place three times a day with Bank of England, being the regulator and central bank of England.

In order to ensure the settlement is being done in time, all direct participants need to maintain balances and reserves with Bank of England in their current accounts. Based on the MIS of daily funds payment volume, banks need to maintain their own Net Sender Cap (NSC) for settling transactions against them. The banks have to set the mechanism to limit the credit exposure and control mechanism. The NSC should be set at a level that more than covers the anticipated maximum intra-cycle debit position for that Participant, recognizing that the flow of funds in and out of each participant may vary during each settlement cycle.

This pre-funded settlement model ensures that settlement risk will be taken care of during the process of faster payment system. If any bank is not in a position to meet the financial obligations during the settlement then FPS will instruct the Central Bank viz. Bank of England to debit the Reserve Collaterisation Account (RCA) of the participant. Every participant bank has to meet the cash sum equal to the value of NSC so in case of emergency situation Bank of England can debit the same so no participant is impacted. Participants bank will be allowed to add more funds in RCA as FPS would have deduct the NSC to complete the transaction to eliminate the financial settlement risk exists between the different FPS participants. This means that each participant must have a robust system in place to ensure to meet their settlement obligations in time whilst protecting all other participants as well as ensuring the underlying associated settlement and faster payment transactions.

Steps in Faster Payment Systems

- PSP A – PSP A is a Net Receiver and therefore has no requirement to fund its Bank of England Settlement Account or RCA as it will be the recipient of credit funds.
- PSP B – With the pending £20m settlement to occur, this could leave PSP B close to its current NSC. If for example this was over a busy period and a weekend (Easter Bank Holiday), PSP B may want to increase its NSC to handle the higher than normal level of transactions and avoid hitting their cap (as payments would reject if the cap was reached). This example would only work if PSP B has sufficient excess funds in its RCA and potentially would have funded this in anticipation of the busy period.
- PSP C – with this example, PSP C has sufficient funds on its settlement account and can therefore settle its Faster Payment obligations accordingly.
- FPSL Operations then has the ability to increase the NSC to the desired level (as long as this mirrors funds held on the RCA) and notify the Bank of England accordingly so that at the beginning of the next Banking Day the Bank of England can action their records.

Lessons Learnt by Indian Banking Payment System

The progress and journey of Payment System in India has been termed as a silent revolution which has been evolving and growing for last three and half decades. This silent revolution has undergone many changes in the banking needs of the customer and accordingly to satisfy the customer's needs, banks have adopted different level of technology and introduced different types of products. Payment system is a very important aspect of the financial system because it focuses on faster and accurate transfer and movement of funds and thus push the economic activities in an economy at large scale. Reserve Bank of India has taken many initiatives to convert the manual clearing house system of settlement to Machine based processed of cheques through Magnetic Ink Character Recognition (MICR) Technology in 1985.

With the increasing volumes of cheques and long time taken for processing the same in giving the final credit to the beneficiary, MICR Technology was replaced with Image based Settlement called Cheque Truncation System in 2009. While the RBI vision was always to promote cash less and cheque less business transactions in Indian Economy and Banking System, E-Banking and Digital Banking was the recent important agenda in the hand of Government of India and Reserve Bank of India. Indian payment System has learnt many lessons from London Payment System and Indian RTGS system is similar to CHAPS and Faster Payment Systems. Bankers Automated Clearing House of London is similar to National payment Corporation of India who is responsible for clearing bulk electronic transfers. The following modern payment systems exist in India:

Cheque Truncation System

In 2008, an image based cheque clearing settlement system was introduced in New Delhi in which the physical movements of the cheques from the bank branches to clearing houses were stopped. CTS was introduced after 20 years of MICR Clearing as the cheque volumes increased and clearing differences reconciliation problems started arising. Benefit of CTS was a faster clearing settlement cycle, cost reduction, restricted loss of instruments in transit and no reconciliation problem. In CTS electronic image of the cheque is captured and data is saved and the credit is given to the customer within 24 hours i.e. T + 1 Basis. CTS was introduced in Chennai in 2011 and in Mumbai in 2013.

Cheque Truncation System was different as compared to Manual clearing, Microprocessor and MICR Settlement because here the movement of the cheques were stopped. The images of cheques are digitally secured and ensure safety of funds in the CTS Process and transfer from branches to clearing house electronically.

Digital banking / Payment System

With the growth of usage of cheque payment system and development in banking, role of technology changed from a support function to an enabler function.

New types of payment instruments were developed all over the globe and customers started using the same for faster and accurate settlement of commercial and economic activity. Indian story of strong payment systems also evolved after 1990's with introduction of various electronic payment systems by Reserve bank of India. RBI formulated a payment system vision to achieve these milestones since 2008 and the latest one is Vision 2015-2018 to create awareness among the customer and modernization of payment system with advanced technology. Rangarajan Committee on computerization in early 1980's suggested a phased plan for mechanization and computerization. This was followed by various initiatives taken by RBI through Saraf Committee, Patil Committee, Burwan Working Group.

At present Indian Banking System is having different payment systems to meet the funds transfer and remittance requirements of customers based on their requirements depending upon the cost and time.

National Electronic Funds Transfer (NEFT)

In 2005 Reserve Bank of India started a funds transfer facility one to one basis without any paper instruments like cheques. Every retail branch need to be NEFT enabled and individuals, companies and firms can transfer funds. There is no maximum or minimum limit on the funds transfer through NEFT. NEFT is settled in twelve batches stating from 8am to 7pm from Monday to Friday whereas on Saturdays, there are only 6 settlements from 8am to 1pm.

Real Time Gross Settlement (RTGS)

In March 2004 Reserve Bank of India introduced a new system of online order by order basis funds transfer system on real-time basis. These payment transactions are final and irrevocable and done individually. RTGS is an individual transactions settlement payment system whereas NEFT is deferred net settlement system in batches with particular time. RTGS system is for high value transactions for 2 lacs and above with no maximum amount. RTGS is available for customers between 9:00 am, hours to 4:30 pm from Monday to Friday and from 9:00 am to 2:30pm on Saturdays. The customers need to obtain IFSC code from their bank branch where the account is maintained and there are more than one hundred thousand RTGS enabled bank branches in India.

Immediate Payment Service (IMPS)

IMPS is an interbank instant real time funds transfer system electronically and it offers services through mobile phones. This payment system facility is available 24 by 7 including bank holidays throughout the year. IMPS is designed on the framework of national Financial Switch Network and controlled and supervised by National Payments Corporation. Customer has to save the IFSC Code of Beneficiary and his account number. There is a daily cap limit of two hundred thousand in IMPS and SMS based mobile banking can be used for transactions up to INR 5000.

Aadhaar Enabled Payment System (AEPS)

It is an initiative by Ministry of Electronics and Information to ensure cashless, paperless and faceless payment system. This is bank led model where customer Aadhar number is linked with bank account and allows online interoperable commercial transaction at merchant place / point of sales. Bank Mitra and Business Correspondent plays an important role in AEPS for service activation and operations. Maximum and minimum funds transfer limit is fixed by the banks to individual customers where RBI does not have any capped or limit. Various services offered are funds transfer, cash deposit, withdrawal, funds enquiry and payment transactions. Services are available at more than 118 banks and are interoperable.

Unified Payments Interface

It refers to any participating single mobile application that powers and connects multiple bank accounts. UPI has various banking transactions, merchant payments and fund routing platforms. Customer must have smart mobile phone linked with bank account and have an internet facility. Customers need to have a Debit card for generating m-Pin or resetting whenever required. Funds transfer limit is INR one hundred thousand and virtual address, IFSC and MMID is required by the customer for sending and receiving money.

Electronic Clearing Service (ECS)

This electronic funds transfer mode of payment is used by the customer for payments periodical in nature / repetitive in nature such as monthly salary, payment of utility bills, rent receipts etc. There are two types of ECS – Debit and Credit and includes various transaction processed at NACH – National Automated Clearing

House. ECS is further classified into three categories based on the geographical location – Local, Regional and National ECS. Institution need to obtain one time ECS Registration through their bank and then prepare input file consisting of account number, name, amount, MICR code of bank and branch. There is no limit on the value of ECS Transactions and amount is credited with in 24 hours.

Aadhaar Payment Bridge System (APBS)

This payment system is a way to transfer funds without any cheque and debit card. This system is linked with Aadhar Enabled payment System and not linked to any bank or branch. This initiative has also been taken by NPCI. The major benefits of AEPS are that financial and non-financial transactions can be done through banking correspondent of any branch. It is very secure, fast and a safe payment system as every individual has its own fingerprints and no one can copy the same.

BHIM

Bhart Interface for Money (BHIM) is a unique and recent initiative to promote cash less, fast, reliable and secure financial funds transfer through mobile. This payment system is interoperable with other applications like UPI and bank applications. Bhim is an Indian initiative payment system by NPCI. It works with simple operations by registering with bank and setting the password with UPI Pin. Mobile number of the customer acts as his virtual payment address and one can immediate start the funds transfer.

CONCLUSION

With United Kingdom having set the precedent, a number of initiatives are under way around the globe to implement faster or immediate payments systems. There has been rapid progress in the past decade as smartphones have become ubiquitous and broadband communications have been rolled out across the world. Businesses and consumers have come to expect rapid access to information and want to conduct transactions in real, or near real-time. These developments have not been matched, however, in the payments space. Majority of financial institutions are burdened with ageing core banking systems and myriad regulatory demands are monopolising resources that might otherwise be diverted to upgrade programmes. The relatively slow clearing cycles in the payments world are coming under scrutiny as consumers and businesses demand more agile systems.

Little surprise, then, that the UK's Faster Payment Service (FPS) which launched in May 2008 has been watched with international interest – certainly of late. Generally speaking, faster payment schemes enable customers to make electronic payments almost instantaneously, seven days a week, 24 hours a day. The payments are typically made via a phone or internet-enabled device and involve the transfer of money between accounts, to other people, to pay bills or to make regular standing order payments.

There is a healthy positive growth in electronic payments in India compared to paper-based payments which is indeed a good sign. The continuing efforts of RBI and the banks to migrate from paper to electronic payments had a favourable influence. Among the electronic payment options, RTGS has been widely accepted as the payments mechanism by corporates and banks, and yet on the retail payment side, a lot needs to be done to increase the use of electronic payments. RTGS clearly emerges as the principal payment system in India for wholesale payments. In the short time that it has been in existence, it has bypassed the cheque-based clearing volume in terms of amount and now accounts for over 80 percent of the payment volume (in terms of amount) in India.

*　　*　　*

Impact of Brexit on the Financial Services Industry

AUTHOR BIO

Samrat Kishor

Samrat is a Technology Consultant with a decade of rich experience working with firms like GT, KPMG, Deloitte and presently Accenture Strategy. He advises businesses on Innovative Business Models driven by technology and Design Thinking. He is a strong believer in Open-Innovation and is presently contributing to Blockchain technology as a member of NASSCOM's Blockchain SIG. He is adept at spotting technology trends and has successfully predicted many technology applications to new business models.

Samrat is also a mentor on the Startup India Program and Atal Innovation Mission, both initiatives of Niti Ayog - Government of India. He has a knack for influencing young minds and shaping their thoughts in a way that they are able to think, reason, and debate on a variety of topics outside of their regular curricula. He enjoys presenting real-world concepts in simple ways and has impacted over 2000 students from various backgrounds. He has been quoted in the media multiple times and has made numerous public appearances speaking on topics intersecting business and technology.

Impact of Brexit on the Financial Services Industry

Samrat Kishor

Genesis of Brexit

In a nationwide referendum held in June 2016, a majority of British citizens voted for United Kingdom to leave the European Union. Though the Brexit vote signaled a new low in the relationship between the UK and the EU, the conflict stretches back nearly a century when Britain and the remaining members of European Economic Community (EEC) were at loggerheads regarding matters of trade. It should be noted that a similar referendum was conducted in the UK in 1975 with the question "Do you think the United Kingdom should stay in the European Community (Common Market)?" Wherein, 67 percent of the respondents voted "Yes".

Turnout for the last referendum was 71.8 percent, with more than 30 million people voting. The referendum passed by a slim 51.9 percent to 48.1 percent margin, but there were stark differences across the United Kingdom. Northern Ireland voted to remain in European Union, as did Scotland (where only 38 percent of voters chose "leave"); leading to renewed calls for another referendum on Scottish independence. England and Wales, however, voted in favor of Brexit. Following the verdict, Prime Minister David Cameron, who led the campaign to stay in the EU, resigned.

What's in store for Britons

In October 2016, Prime Minister Theresa May, who had assumed office following David Cameron's resignation, announced her intention to invoke Article 50 of the Treaty on European Union, formally giving notice of Britain's intent to leave the EU. On March 29, 2017, the order, signed by May a day earlier, was delivered to the Council of the European Union, officially starting the two-year countdown to Britain's EU departure, now tentatively set for March 30, 2019.

Theresa May, self-appointed leader in this historic negotiation, has so far revealed little about her strategy. It remains to be known whether beyond this secrecy lies a feasible plan or fluff. Her comments suggest that she has chosen to prioritize the control of immigration, even if it means giving up membership of the single market (she said only that Britain should go on "trading in and operating within" it). This sort of "hard Brexit" is favored by the keenest Brexiteers. However, it is unclear if the public agree. One recent poll found that most would rather have single-market membership than controls on immigration. The matter of not disclosing a concrete plan is seldom backed by the notion that the Government doesn't want to show its hand in the negotiations: if Britain is to outwit its foes in Brussels, it must keep its strategy under wraps. Parliamentary debate would supposedly give the game away. A rapid solution to continued passporting arrangements between UK and EU, and the single market will be a high priority in 'Brexit' negotiations. A favorable outcome is highly relevant to the ability of UK based institutions to export financial services into the EU and may impact future decisions by global institutions on where best to locate.

Impacts of Brexit on the Financial Services Sector

Looking at the macro picture, UK is economically more dependent on the EU; 44% of its exports go there and 48% of its foreign investment comes from them. This also includes the business that is enabled by means of passporting rights to the services sector, which makes up for around 79% of UK GDP. The repealing of these rights may further aggravate the losses to UK. Since financial services continue to be one of the most important net exports from Britain, let's assess the potential impact on the capital markets and money markets. We have attempted to assess the impact of Brexit from the perspectives of regulatory landscape, economic landscape and implications on cross border trade.

The regulatory requirements are a tad complex in the UK. Many financial services and banking related requirements are set by global regulators while in some cases the UK regulatory standards dictate higher or tighter requirements. On the other hand, this also means that the Brexit could reduce overall ease of operating for banks and financial institutions considering unforeseeable responses from the UK and EU regulators.

Irrespective of the changes to the regulatory requirements, there will be an on-going need to comply with new EU regulation in order to continue to conduct business across the European Union. Indeed, even if UK were to exit, it is probable that firms wishing to conduct business across EU and vice versa, via passporting arrangements, would face increasing regulatory demands and will be required to comply with MIFID II rules when they were introduced in January 2018.

Let's now take a look at the economic landscape. Upon the finalization of the Brexit vote, banks took a nosedive on the stock market and other related industries followed; leading to a massive erosion of wealth from the average Briton's pockets.

Members of the public at large generally had their savings in GBPs which saw turmoil with an almost 8 percent decline in response to the country's vote to leave the European Union. The S&P 500 dropped 3.6 percent on the same day, and the pan-European STOXX 600 Index closed down around 7 percent lower. Quite rhetorically, those who had invested in the controversy laden cryptocurrency 'Bitcoin' made an almost 9 percent jump intraday. For the days to come, it was considered to be the 'digital gold' for Britons and the world followed cues by further investing in Bitcoin and taking its price to a new high.

Uncertain markets and weak cues on important sectors was poised to have a domino effect on Britain's ultimate store of wealth and property which could turn into a trap. With a fall in investment and demand from foreigners and interest rates were already at rock bottom, and London's market had already cooled off. Interestingly, what actually happened in the days following the verdict is history; London saw a stark increase in the prices of commercial Real Estate owing to the weak Sterling. Foreign investors wanted a piece of the pie and were buying real estate at inflated valuations. This asset class continued to give stellar returns as compared to money markets during the same investment period.

Considering the impact on cross-border trade it's quite evident that the "passporting" rights of companies are on the line. 'Passporting' is the right of a firm registered in the European Economic Area [EEA] to do business in any other EEA state without needing further authorization in each country. It was a natural outcome of the 'leave' vote that the corporates operating in Britain would lose their passporting rights in the EEA and vice versa. However, it could be argued that this shall boil down to the fact that a lot of work from the British offices will be shipped to the subsidiaries based in EEA countries and vice versa. It is certain that this is bound to create tons of overheads for the corporates and may have indirect implications for the end customers; hence the uncertainty in the markets. One of the biggest attractions to insurers of operating via Lloyd's (insurance market located in London) is that it has passporting rights into the EU. Insurers hold large portfolios of corporate bonds to cover their liabilities. Any fall in the value of the bonds could dent the insurers' solvency ratios in the short term, although as they tend to hold these bonds to maturity there may be no economic damage unless corporate defaults rise. Life assurers' asset management operations are also expected to suffer because of the market turmoil.

A majority of the skilled workforce strengthening the UK's financial services markets come from UK universities which receive an additional 15 per cent in funding from the EU and some believe the UK could lose this if Brexit happens. It could also mean academics will struggle to cooperate on research projects. A change in visa arrangements for other European countries may also deter high-caliber academics from joining British universities.

There's undoubtedly a period of significant change ahead for the further education sector post Brexit but while these are unsettling times, there are certainly good reasons to stay positive. University leaders from 24 countries across Europe have signed a joint statement following the UK's vote to leave, citing the importance of continued

European collaboration and recognizing the need to work together through these uncertain times. Perhaps if these core values can remain at the heart of negotiations, then there is a clear way forward for the UK education market after Brexit.

A research suggests that British universities could increase tuition fee income by 187 million pounds in the first year if the Government decides to charge European students at the international rate.

Considering the impact of Brexit on the job market one may envisage the following two scenarios; first, professionals stay put, nervous of change. When risk increases in one part of our lives, our natural reaction is to seek to reduce it elsewhere. Second, professionals move quickly to beat the rush. Top talent knows it has options and may look to make an international career move soon, preempting any permanent changes that might make it harder to relocate later.

For UK professionals with international ambitions, EU has always been a natural destination given the ease with which they can relocate. Post-Brexit, the barrier to moving could increase significantly, making it just as tricky to move to France as it is to the US. As banks work out their recovery plans and may roll back risky propositions from the market, they should be considerate of the fact that SME's form the backbone of the UK economy, making up 99% of businesses and 60% of private sector jobs. In times of uncertainty if banks reduce or pull back from lending, small businesses can be most easily hit and without large coffers to turn to their expansion and hiring will get restricted. There is every reason for optimism but any change in the availability of small business finance could be an early sign of what lies ahead.

Brexit uncertainty could also scare off some investment and push jobs away. In fact, some firms had already relocating elsewhere in the days following the verdict. With the tightening of borders, the main driving force behind the decision of Brexit, companies within the U.K. may be forced to outsource to the rest of Europe.

* * *

REFERENCES

http://www.bbcactive.com/BBCActiveIdeasandResources/Impactof BrexitonFurtherEducation.aspx

https://www.cnbc.com/2016/06/27/bitcoin-gains-validity-as-digital-gold-after-brexit-vote.html

https://www.forbes.com/sites/cherryreynard/2017/08/31/uk-commercial-property-a-glaring-opportunity-or-a-brexit-disaster/#1ebd750a6a2e

https://www.ft.com/content/518b8902-39e9-11e6-9a05-82a9b15a8ee7

https://www.grantthornton.co.uk/globalassets/1.-member-firms/united-kingdom/
    pdf/brexit-impact-financial-services.pdf
http://www.telegraph.co.uk/education/0/will-brexit-impact-british-universities/
https://www.weforum.org/agenda/2016/07/how-will-brexit-impact-job-market
https://www.weforum.org/agenda/2017/04/brexit-european-union
    -negotiations/

London and International Film Industry

AUTHOR BIO

Arpan Mukherjee

Arpan has completed his B. Com. from University of Mumbai in 2013 in first class. Currently, he is pursuing Master of Business Administration from Amity University Uttar Pradesh, India and currently is in second year of the course. His first paper for a magazine was in the year 2006 titled "What's the point of education if we can't make a difference to other people's lives". It was published when he was in Class IX Hiranandani Foundation School, Thane from where he completed his ICSE exams. His second article was in Class XII when his essay titled, "Traffic! Traffic!" in Hindi was selected for the Hindi Magazine at RA Podar College of Commerce and Economics in Matunga from where he graduated in first class both in Higher Secondary and Bachelors of Commerce.

Since then, he has been working as content writer for a start-up and has also written a case study comparison of Dubai Mall and South China Mall titled "The bigger they are, the harder they fall" for Amity Business School's Retailer Magazine. He is also an avid quizzer and extempore speaker and has won the 2017 Annual Amity Business Quiz for Amity Business School held during Amity Youth Fest along with his friend Siddhant Gautam.

London and International Film Industry

Arpan Mukherjee

"England might be a small country but its contribution to the world is much greater than its size," said the Prime Minister of Great Britain (played by Hugh Grant) in the 2003 movie 'Love Actually'. The point was put quite well. Britain had been ruling more than half of the World (including India) till the early 1950s during which it had created a world relatively more peaceful than what it was since time immemorial. Many would consider the British to have been cruel and unfair to them but few would realise the level of change the British have brought in the world. Before criticising them, one must give a thought that whether he/she is ready to live in a world constantly in fear of being invaded by cruel rulers or whether he/she is ready to live in a war-torn country.

British contribution to India has been in several areas - Railways, Investments, Scientific Research, Arts as well as the Indian Film Industry which the world has lovingly given the name 'Bollywood'. Today, film industry of various countries provides employment to a large number of people either directly or indirectly. There are also several firms which make money through showing movies on television. Let's trace its journey:

Britain has been the centre of learning for the modern world. This has been evident with the way the movie camera has evolved tremendously over the years. The first ever patented design was created by Wordsworth Donisthorpe in 1876. With his patented movie camera, he filmed London's Trafalgar Square. Due to low quality of facilities back then, the film was quite poor in quality. It took a Londoner to open the minds of people to new technology and make them realise the possibilities. The next patent came from Frenchman Louis Le Prince in 1988, followed by one from Lumiere Brothers which opened the technology and made it accessible in many countries including India. Little did anyone realize that one small invention would give birth to two of the world's most influential film industries catering to massive employment: Hollywood and Bollywood.

Dhundiraj Govind Phalke, famously known as Dadasaheb Phalke, may have been known as the 'Father of Indian Cinema' by having created the first ever full length Indian Film titled 'Raja Harishchandra', but it required him to get inspired by various other movies shown in tents back in the day in various parts of the country. It might be hard for people to believe nowadays that working in films was considered a taboo back in the early 20th century. Strange isn't it? One version of Phalke's life story states that when his workers left home to work at his film, they said to their family members that they are working at the factory of someone named Mr. Harishchandra.

During the freedom struggle and post-independence period of India, television became a popular medium along with theatre which showcased speeches by freedom fighters and leaders. It was during this stage that films like 'Alam Ara (1931)' came out which received huge support. Shunning taboo, a change came in and people started accepting work in Movies as a way of earning livelihood and making careers. As a government initiative, Film and Television Institute of India came into origin in 1960 as one of the first of its kind institutes in India, flaunting prestigious alumni like Jaya Bhaduri among its ranks.

Economic liberalization in 1991 through the famous 'LPG' policy (Liberalization, Privatization, Globalization) initiated by the Indian Government under Finance Minister Dr. Manmohan Singh opened doors of the world for Indian Cinema. No longer was there a problem in exporting films to US or UK, as investor assistance was at hand to support film producers. Film production, starting at 100 films in 1930 went up to 1000+ movies from the year 2000 as more and more film production houses came into the market and shooting sets started getting built. It was evident that Indian film industry had crossed the nascent stage and had now become a full-fledged industry with 1% contribution to our nations' GDP and providing employment and business opportunities.

Today, people worldwide are aware of Bollywood and its influence has stretched from Russia to Nigeria, not to forget US and UK. A research article by the consulting firm Deloitte has put the demand for skilled technicians required by Bollywood industry at 5,000 in the next few years. This includes technicians for VFX work, make-up artistes etc.; thereby giving youngsters robust career opportunities.

In a recent agreement signed by dignitaries of India and UK, India has been given new offers from UK and its movie production houses have been made eligible for the UK Creative Tax Relief Initiative provided they follow the additional conditions stipulated in the dossier.

UK Creative Tax Relief Initiative

Star Wars, Thor, James Bond, Harry Potter - the list continues to grow. Over the last few years, there has been a growth spurt in the number of films being produced in UK, both from Hollywood and Bollywood. Pinewood Studios, UK regularly features in the credits of upcoming films.

While Hollywood ranks 2nd in the list of successful movies at the UK Box office, the gap between them and Bollywood films is not that much. While Hollywood films rake in £15 million, Bollywood stands at £13 million.

In 2012, UK Parliament approved a new Tax Relief Benefit initiative for the purpose of encouraging International Media Industry to build and create projects in UK subject to tax benefits of up to 25%. Following is an excerpt taken from the website of British Film Industry (www.bfi.org). It details the rules which prospective film production houses willing to make movies in UK need to follow:

Incentive: For films with a total core expenditure of £20 million or less, the film production company can claim payable cash rebate of up to 25% of UK qualifying film production expenditure. For films with a core expenditure of more than £20 million, the film production company can claim a payable cash rebate of up to 25% of the first £20 million of qualifying UK expenditure, with the remaining qualifying UK expenditure receiving a 20% tax credit.

Qualifying Production:

- Tax relief is available for British qualifying films.
- Films must either pass the Cultural Test or qualify as an official co-production.
- Intended for theatrical release.
- The Film Production Company responsible for the film needs to be within the UK corporation tax net.

Minimum Spend Requirement:

10% minimum UK spend requirement - where a good or service is "used or consumed" in the UK.

Project Cap:

No Cap.

Eligibility:

Must meet the requirements of one of the following:

- The Cultural Test.
- One of the UK's official bilateral co-production treaties.
- The European Convention on Cinematographic Co-production.

Benefits of Initiative:

Tax Benefits in United Kingdom are much more than that in the United States but Foreign Exchange would mean more administrative hassles but the initiative launched by UK has reaped major benefits for their industry. 80% of investments in 2017 were in Film Industry which reaped benefits of £1.5 billion through additional investment from overseas the credit of which goes to the tax benefit provided by the authorities. One statistic states that for every £1 given as tax relief to investors, £12.49 is injected into the economy, which is the highest amongst the three industries which this initiative covers (the others being high-end TV shows and video games).

A 2014 report by BFI stated that investment in UK film industry had grown by 14% to reach £1.075 billion. During shooting for Game of Thrones, on an average 573 personnel were hired per series.

Famous Locations

There are several famous locations in UK which have been visited by Bollywood icons for their films as well as used as shooting locations for many UK films and TV series.

Borough Market

People of London are highly passionate about their Art, Culture, History and Heritage. This is evident when one visits Borough Market, considered the oldest Market existing in London City. Currently located in the midst of Southwark Street and Borough High Street just South of Southwark Cathedral on the southern edge of London Bridge, the market has been operational in the current location since 1756. Though in the history books, it has been said to exist since 1014 AD, often changing its location as London grew; finally settling down at Southwark after an Act passed in 1754 forced the local parishioners to shift to Southern end of London Bridge to restart the market where they are now located.

The market's current location near the riverside wharves of the Pool of London gave it a strategic advantage during the 19th century as one of the most important food markets of London in the South with Covent Garden serving North London. London grew tremendously, so did the Business of traders running their shops in these two markets. The City of London functioned well with Covent Garden serving it and the rest of what was later renamed as 'Greater London' was served by Borough Market. Current Buildings were designed in 1851 with additions made in 1860s. The entrance to the market in Southwark Street was added in 1932. It is currently run by a charitable trust whose volunteers live in the vicinity of the market which today mainly sells speciality foods to the general public. In the 20th century, it was a wholesale market selling produce to greengrocers.

Borough Market is quite famous for having been shown in movies like *Bridget Jones' Diary (2001)* and *Lock, Stock and Two Smoking Barrels (1998)*. More recently, it was considered for shooting of the film *'Jab Tak Hai Jaan'* in 2012 starring Shahrukh

Khan, Katrina Kaif and Anushka Sharma; where the lead character Samar Anand (played by Khan) used to work here while he was in London apart from being a street musician of course. The UK Detective Series 'Sherlock' starring Benedict Cumberbatch and Martin Freeman was also shot here and has been frequented by the actors a lot in the recent past.

The location has undergone massive development, including two buildings being demolished to make way for the viaduct connecting London to Southwark and extension under the Thameslink Programme though such developments haven't stopped the market from functioning with full intensity and vigour. It is this positive energy that has kept the market surviving for 1000 years and continues to motivate and inspire people in a way that, "Passion is important if one has to succeed in life." It is the passion of the traders of Borough Market in their work that has kept the spirit of the market alive all these years.

Waddesdon Manor

It is one of the oldest and rarest French Chateau located in Aylesbury Vale in Buckinghamshire, England. It was built during 1874-1889 using neo-renaissance style of architecture. Even though, the late 19th century was a time when France and England were rivals, yet amongst them there were many who had powerful friends on both sides. One such person was entrepreneur Baron Ferdinand De Rotschild who was the founder of this immensely beautiful piece of architecture.

The journey began in 1874 when Baron Rotschild bought the estate from the Duke of Marlborough after he inherited money from his father. The estate was a barren land, quite beautiful as Baron Rotschild would later go on to say. The foundation stone was laid in 1877 and the manor was completed in 1880.

The credit goes to Alice De Rotschild for the beautiful gardens which envelop the surroundings of the Manor. Miss Rotschild, sister to the Baron had inherited the Manor post his death and was known for her personal initiatives to maintain the gardens as well as interiors of the Manor. Majority of the Manor's collection of antiques was contributed by her. The Manor had also served as asylum for children below the age of five who had been evacuated from Croydon during World War II as well as Jewish Children from Frankfurt. The trees of the park had been planted by many distinguished guests like Queen Victoria and King Edward VII who have visited the Manor and have been part of its legacy.

Common Travellers would know this place as The Home of the Raichand Family in Karan Johar's movie "Kabhi Khushi Kabhi Gham" which was released in 2002. Whatever way, reason or purpose it might be famous for, Mr. Rothschild will be smiling in the heavens with a sigh of relief that even after his death, Waddesdon Manor lives on, and tells the tales of old, of times when royalty and aristocracy was at its prime to the people living in the modern world.

CONCLUSION

UK film industry continues to grow at a steady pace giving another example of the kind of impact it continues to have in the world. As long as it grows, it will continue to provide employment opportunities to millions of people directly or indirectly. Its existence will prove to be beneficial for other relevant industries like tourism and the Indian cuisine industry, as UK films make the country popular amongst modern citizens of the world and encourage people to travel to UK which further boosts employment opportunities for its burgeoning population.

Success and failure of any industry depends on the policies initiated by state government which help its survival. In this case, tax benefit initiatives launched by UK government helped revive the entertainment industry.

Tourism and Media Industry are interdependent. Through popular routes, many historical sites can be made visible, noticeable and worth visiting. Also, success of one industry provides employment and business opportunity to other supporting industries. In this case, it opened business opportunities for several UK Production houses and ancillary industries.

* * *

Self-Employment in the United Kingdom

AUTHOR BIO

Anupoju Prudhvi Kumar

Anupoju Prudhvi Kumar is currently pursuing his Masters in Business Administration with specialization in Marketing and Information Technology from Amity Business School. He has completed his B. Tech. from Mechanical stream from Maharaja VIjayaramaraju College of Engineering. He hails from Vishakhapatnam, Andhra Pradesh. He has done an internship in Vishakhapatnam Steel Plant. He has also done an internship in Future Consumer Group on improving sales and visibility in Modern Trade during post-graduation in the marketing sector. He has completed a certified course in AUTOCAD which is a specialisation in machine drawing and a certified course in CREO software for design engineers. He is also certified in JAVA. He is an avid learner with a keen interest in emerging markets. He is enthusiastic for organising events since he has played a significant role in organising Amity Youth Fest, Amity Sports Meet - Sangathan, etc.

Self-Employment in the United Kingdom

Anupoju Prudhvi Kumar

INTRODUCTION

After the election of the Liberal Government in United Kingdom in 2010, there has been an immense increase of interest in the self-employment policies which mainly concentrate on the youth in the country. After doing a thorough research on self-employment in the country, this paper outlines the most remarkable contemporary private, public and other sector policies that have been envisaged to improve entrepreneur activation among the youth. Few of these designs are planned partially, others completely. The aim is to shield the youth from recession and convert them to self-employed people.

For the betterment of the future of the country, UK government also has formulated several programme and policies. This paper also discusses those policies which are designed to encourage self-employment or build start-ups among the people of youth as well as some minority groups. Due to these policies, the work which is done easily is converted into success factors and also teachings for other people who are willing to leverage from these policies and achieve success.

This paper focuses on the problems. There are several possibilities these policies can create within or between the given schemes. Therefore, some initiatives are planned initially to improve the number of start-ups. Other policies focus on improving the capacity of the people which would enable them to elevate themselves in their career and lower the stress on the labour market.

The main concern for introducing these policies is for the benefit of the youth of UK by increasing their chance of getting self-employed within the economy. It would be pointless though, if the people do not produce quality work and consequently reduce the value of the economy.

AIM OF THE PAPER

The main aim of the paper is to conduct an analysis of self-employment perceived by the residents of UK. The other aim is to discover the ways in which the government is helping the youth to create self-employment. The final objective is to have a look on the quality of work delivered by these self-employed people.

Start-Ups

To build a start-up in UK, no specific qualifications or financial threshold is required. According to the law a person is considered as a self-employed only for tax purposes. To build a start-up, choose the type of business which you want to start and accordingly apply for the different types of licence or permits or insurances. According to the literature, there are two types of start-ups.

Dependency Vs Autonomy

While working, if people are under certain rules and regulations which might affect their quality of work consistently, it is referred to as a condition of dependency. Many factors exist in self-employed work; people will be at their free will not to work according to their comfortable conditions and standards.

Choice Vs Necessity

In this type, people who choose self-employment consider a lot of options, such as whether they have professional opportunities in the field they are good at. People who choose self-employment as a choice put themselves in the self-driven employment mode to improve their entrepreneurial activities.

Statistics of Start-ups

Based on the national statistics given in 2017, 5.2 million people living in UK are self-employed. Percentage of start-ups is given as 15 percent which is the highest rate in last four years. UK has shown an immense growth in the sector of self-employment and start-ups in the recent years. Growth in start-ups and self-employment has played a major role in the increase of the overall employment rate in the UK in recent times. Current growth of self-employment is due to many factors. Mainly there has been an immense rise in female self-employment rate. Rate of self-employment in females has increased by 70.8 percent in the years from 2015 to 2017. Rate of self-employment in males still dominates by having a growth of 79.7 percent in the same years. Newly self-employed people are interested mainly in part-time jobs and are getting low incomes.

Self-employment rate in UK also differs with age. In the year 2012, in the category of young people between the ages 16 to 24, there were only 5 percent of people who were self-employed. According to the survey, people in the middle age group are highly interested in the entrepreneurial opportunities in UK. By 2017, there has been an increased rate of self-employment in every age group 17 percent in 18-24 age group, 5.9 percent in the 55-64 age group and 27 percent in 35-44 year age group.

Financial Support

Main aim of the UK government is to introduce these policies to encourage start-ups in the country. Government created these policies such that they can provide financial support to the people who are not able to afford building start-ups. Young people are majorly affected and find it difficult to start their own business since they typically had lesser income, low savings etc. This is why UK government introduced a new scheme called New Enterprise Allowance (NEA) which mainly focuses on the people who do not have jobs, and are aged above 18, and are interested to start new business. Interested people are sent to business mentors who are provided by UK's Public Employment Services, who examine the business plans the people have come up with and give their suggestions and guidance. If a business plan is approved, then entrepreneurs running it will be eligible for getting subsidy for the first 6 months. After six months, several people stop taking subsidy from government because they have managed to generate profits according to the Department for Work and Pension (DWP) survey done in 2013.

After conducting discussions with people who were with the NEA programme, we came to the conclusion that this programme completely supports areas like construction, gardening, hairdressing etc.

The next support which was given by the Government was building a start-up's loan company which was started in 2012, and whose sole purpose was to encourage self-employment and position start-ups as a viable career option. This programme was also introduced to increase the capabilities of youth; and reduce unemployment. Their schemes provide capital support to the start-ups which have potential. Here too, the business plans are reviewed and loans are provided which can be repaid in 5 years at 6 percent interest. The average amount which is given as a loan amount is £ 5,353. These loans are given by "business bank" and they have provided over £ 50 million as a loan till November 2013 and helped several people in starting their own business. These programmes not only provide financial support but also monitor the work quality. According to a survey done in 2013, UK government helped over 30,000 new start-ups in the form of start-up loan programme and NEA.

Coaching and Counselling

Young entrepreneurs often lack in the aspect of Social Capital which is crucial in business. So, the government helped them by mentoring them and helping them in building legitimacy and relationship with stakeholders which is the key to success. Several initiatives are taken UK to provide counselling and coaching support. They even offer financial support to young people to get coaching and counselling. Start-ups which are funded by the government have been more successful where they focus on proper coaching and counselling pertaining to business skilling, according to the Encumbrance Certificate (EC) survey in 2012.

Programmes for Women

In recent years, several policies and programmes have been launched which are focused on improving the business potential of women in UK. These programmes have had a major impact on women who were ready to pursue their career through start-ups and provided them a path of self-employment.

There are many initiatives taken by the government for female entrepreneurs:

* United Kingdom Female Entrepreneurship Ambassador (UKFEA)

This programme is a part of Europe network which helps females who are already established to inspire other women to start their own business, or provide them jobs in schools, as gardeners etc. According to the data by this network, 52 women have started their own start-ups through this programme, which subsequently led to employment for many others.

* Female Oriented Schemes

This programme gives assistance to women who are interested in running their own business by giving them training, suitable advice and also mentorship. They provide help to other women who face hurdles like lack of support lack of savings, have been unemployed for a long time, or come from minority groups. They also provide information and support to them on online platforms and give information about various tools which are useful for business.

There are many more schemes and programmes which have been launched in places like Scotland, Manchester and Wales which provide essential support to women who need to set up their own business.

Funding for the start-ups which are run by women have seen a major increase in the year 2008 because the British business banks have provided an investment amount of £ 25 million these start-ups. These funds were provided to encourage start-ups run by women and also prove to other women that they can also work in business in lead roles such as executives, advisors, investors.

Fostering Innovations

UK Government has started all these initiatives to ensure support to start-ups which have high potential and which have the capability to grow. Examples of these initiatives also include plans which have been introduced to allow women to get loans. Programmes are designed which can allow women to acquire equal investment.

The Enterprise Finance Guarantee (EFG) has been opened by business bank of UK. It provides a guaranteed loan program which women are eligible for when loans have been refused earlier by commercial banks because of the lack of security and other issues. Their programme was started in 2008 and it supports all age groups.

An impact study was done in 2013 about the business improvements in the EFG sector and it was found that 33 percent of growth was seen in EFG in the years 2009-2012 compared to other sectors like commercial loans and non-borrowers.

Programmes for Youth

Developing entrepreneurial mind sets and skills

In addition to programmes which only help in improving the financial status of people and develop the human capital, UK government also started programmes in 2010 aimed at encouraging young people for entrepreneurial activities in the regular education system. These initiatives are being taken to inculcate the skills and mindsets so that the young people of this generation are fully aware of self-employment which can then become a great career option and also provide them with technical skills, entrepreneurial knowledge and competencies which will be useful in the future to establish and lead successful business firms. The aim of this approach is that it can help the country by improving the economy by increasing work-ready mindset of young people. Economic capacity can also be increased.

Educational system has also introduced those subjects which are for the betterment of students since 2004. All the schools have incorporated "enterprise education" for an early understanding of business among the students.

Programmes for Minority Groups

Minority Groups have always been lagging in terms of self-employment and entrepreneurship. So the government has set targets of giving public funds to people who fall under this category. This is aimed at encouraging them. The government also had other aims to accomplish, such as dealing with issues of marginalisation and to improve the contribution of these people to the UK economy. In recent years, the government has tried to focus on issues which the people of these communities face like finance and educational support funds of many schemes.

At the same time various schemes for start-ups loans have given 6000 loans to the people in UK out of which 35 percent of loans were given to these minorities. In 2015 and 2017 studies of "small business surveys", it is stated that 30 percent of SME's had at least one minority group partner or a manager, and showcased robust financial status.

The Quality of Work Associated with Self-Employment

Several European reports have stated that the quality of work was affecting minority groups, young people, immigrants and women. Due to this, annual turnover of the business is affected. Such an issue needs to be dealt with and it needs to be made sure that it is resolved. People of these minority groups have started choosing their career in entrepreneurial side even through the business started by them has extremely low percent success rate.

Sustainability and Job Creation of Start Ups

Numerous questions have been raised on the business survival and job creation of start-ups for minority group people like young people, women and immigrants. The following data focuses on this issue. Enterprise Research Centre (ERC) have provided figures in 2017, and it shows that the business which had 3 years survival rate in the years 2013-2016 across the country was 70.3 percent, which is nearly 30 percent of start-ups which were started in 2013 and did not survive until 2016. The data provided by office for National Statistics (ONS) stated that there was only 54.6 percent of 5 years survival rate of business in the years between 2012 and 2017. These start-ups were started in 2012 and they were still working in 2017. The ERC declared that new companies will be dead after 10 years of their formation.

ERC showed evidence that 9 percent of the companies do not have over 5 employees during their formation. On a positive note, Department of Business, Innovation and Skills stated that start-ups have played a major role in providing a third of the 4.32 million jobs that were given on average per year between the years 2015 and 2017. Later on in 2017, the contribution of start-ups had risen to 35 percent.

A survey showed that gender plays an important role in start-ups, and the firms which are led by women had lesser level of performance. This was due to low human capital and less financial support. It is assumed that the start-ups which share these difficulties are mainly small scale business. These businesses are mostly led by young people who generally concentrate on compensation and success, rather than quality of work. The study states that the survival rate of start-ups lead by young people is significantly lesser that those start-ups lead by older, more experienced entrepreneurs. It is not the same case with everyone. Start-ups which lasted for more than 3 years and are led by people aged below 30 years have had double the growth rate compared to businesses run by people who are older. Ratio of this comparison is given as 206 percent vs 114 percent. We come to a conclusion after this research that encouraging and supporting start-ups which have high chances of success in the commercial market is a crucial way of generating job growth in the private sector. Also, government should design programmes which mainly focus on increasing the human capital of people who are young; otherwise they would end up with careers in either the labour market or other non-rewarding areas, which might affect quality of their lives.

CONCLUSION

The UK government has taken the responsibility to start initiatives and policies which mainly focus on employment which is done by those with an entrepreneurial background. They have created policies using different approaches. They are targeting groups like young people, women, and immigrants. These policies have also included services like financial support, counselling and coaching about the start-ups, and having a few experienced entrepreneurs to monitor the new ones and help them, give them support for business networking. Government is also trying to encourage entrepreneurial activities in educational institutions.

In UK, these programmes have been designed to help by designing:

- Policies which provide financial help and human support to already existing women entrepreneurs.
- Policies which are mainly designed to make young stu/dents of the country aware about the entrepreneurial activities.

These policies focus on various groups of people like unemployed people, women, and certain minority groups who have the innovation skills and potential to start their own start-ups.

The research done shows that there are positives and negatives effects of these policies which have been designed by the UK government. All the people who took help through these policies are majorly satisfied with the opportunities provided but some of the young people have failed to improve their careers through these policies as per some investigative reports.

Another aim was to create a positive attitude towards self-employment but even though people started opting this as a career, there has not been a very good success rate of the start-ups which were started with the help of the policies designed by the UK government. But the positive point was that due to the start-ups there was job creation and it contributed a lot to the overall job growth of UK.

The research also focuses on the quality of work self-employed people are delivering since it will be directly impact while encouraging others to choose self-employment as a career option. New start-ups which are led by young people, minority groups and women tend to face severe competition in the market and find it difficult to thrive.

*   *   *

My London Diary –
A Cross-Cultural Journey

AUTHOR BIO

K. Lalitha Niharika

Niharika is an MA clinical psychology 1ˢᵗ year student from Amity Institute of Psychology & Allied Sciences, Noida. Though she is from a science background, she decided on becoming a psychologist, as she felt the need of the society for psychological support. Identifying psychological causes behind many problems in the society such as ill health, job inefficiency and relationship issues Niharika aspires to make a contribution to the society and has chosen psychology as the best means to achieve her goal. Previously, before pursuing psychology, she completed her under-graduation and post-graduation in life sciences, and also worked as a junior research fellow for three years. Her research topic was evaluation of molecular basis of the anti-inflammatory and antioxidant activities of phytomedicines. She has also completed a PG diploma in forensic science and criminal justice, and feels the power of psychological tools cannot be understated. She writes a blog at:

https://thediscoveryofmind.wordpress.com/

My London Diary –
A Cross-Cultural Journey

K. Lalitha Niharika

Before Going to London

Though I had so many dreams to go abroad, it took a very long time for me to decide. I opted for the Study Abroad Programme very late. My mind was full of fears, doubts and questions. Is it worth to spend money to go abroad? Will I be able to learn anything? Am I going to miss any important courses of my semester? Will I be able to see all the good places? My family stays away from me and they were afraid to send me. To them, London was a whole new world. I met my family after receiving my visa and got an affectionate send-off. Finally I packed and sealed my doubts along with the luggage and started the journey.

Journey to London

Though I had travelled several times by air, the flight to London was a different experience. I felt as if I am travelling for the first time in my life. My co-passenger, who sat in the adjacent seat, helped me to arrange my bags. I thanked him and interacted with him. He was an Indian, born and brought up in London. He was so interesting that he deserves a paragraph in my London diary. We had a long conversation touching areas including psychology, philosophy, religion, family and so on. I was amazed to see that he had a little bit of knowledge in several areas though he introduced himself as a business man. Though he said he is a Londoner, he said he admired the ancient Vedic civilization of India. He described to me the comforts that are there in London. His family, when they came to India felt sad as they felt extremely disappointed with the poverty, illiteracy and corruption. He also told me it felt very complicated for them to live in India. Our conversation raised my curiosity. I was transported to London in my mind even before I reached. He acted as a bridge between India and London.

The Stay Club

It is the name of the accommodation allotted by Amity University. I entered the city with friends and travelled to The Stay Club in a classic Black Taxi. I felt dejected when the receptionist told me that I would not be able to stay with my friend, as we can occupy only the rooms allotted to us. I liked my room very much. Disappointment disappeared after I met my new roommate. My friend, our roommates and I decided to visit each other's room often. We had several get-togethers where we shared the food that we had brought from India. We also enjoyed cooking there.

The Vegetarian Food

Before going to London, all my friends and relatives scared me by saying that vegetarian food will not be available in London. Chapter 16 - My Choice of the book "The story of my experiments with truth" by M. K. Gandhiji also warned me to carry food. In that chapter, Gandhiji describes how miserable life was for him when he went to London. I took required things like pressure cooker, rice, and pulses to prepare my own food using the kitchen setup provided by The Stay Club.

Times have changed. Now the world has realized the importance of vegetarian and organic food. Though it is costlier, vegetarian food is available everywhere in London. I used to buy vegetables from Wembley market. It used to remind me of my town. Wembley is a place which provides everything that is required to live as per Indian culture. It has jewellery shops, Indian restaurants, Indian food items etc.

Amity University London Campus

Classes were conducted in Birkbeck University campus. I took an Oyster Travel Card and started travelling comfortably to campus and back. I attended classes and started thinking about research. I met my entire faculty and interacted with them. My teachers were Mr. Luke Minshall, Founder and Managing Director of Arimo consulting LTD, and Dr. Anthony 'Skip' Basiel, Freelance eLearning and New Media Consultant, Adobe International Education Leader (Alumnus). We were supervised by two faculties, who came from India - Dr. Anupama Rajesh, Amity University, Noida, Professor of Information Systems (Business Intelligence), Educational Technology and Ms. Sweta Tyagi. Dr. Anupama guided me and inspired me to write this diary. Amity University planned and took us on to two tours. One was to Cadbury Factory and the other was to Oxford University.

Oxford and Cambridge Universities

I was very fortunate that I visited Oxford and Cambridge University Museums. I could witness rocks which existed 35 billion years ago. I saw skeletons of dinosaurs, Egyptian mummies, many experimental models and unique species. I saw so many valuable ancient treasures belonging to various countries in archeological and biological museums. Being a biology student myself, I enjoyed seeing DNA double helical model, peppered moths that were used in experiments conducted by Majerus, chemicals and artefacts.

Architecture and Environment

London's architecture is marvellous. There is a pattern everywhere. All the houses look similar from outside. Streets are all brilliantly illuminated by the lights. Artists give background music to the beautiful tourist places and accept whatever the tourists give them as a token of appreciation. These artists were exceptionally talented.

I could see neither animals on the road nor flies in the air. Everything was in order, clean and in its place. Though the climate is very cold, all houses and campuses are very warm. It rained numerous times. Umbrellas are sold everywhere in all the shops.

Business and Shopping

No one sells tickets. No one guards ATM machines. Everything is automated. There are cheap markets like Primark, Tesco and Poundland where most of the things are sold very cheap. Camden town was a beautiful market.

Social Life

Couples were happy and intimate. Parents carried their infant babies in baby walkers so carefully. Children are so safe. Many people bring their dogs of different breeds to the parks. Parks are full with people and dogs on Sundays. There are several fun activities. People are so polite, calm and punctual. They apologize if they come in someone's way. All employees including bus drivers, shop keepers, vendors and receptionists are so polite. They never get frustrated. There are no street fights anywhere. People spend most of the time playing games in public places. They are so calm and peaceful. People would form groups and start chatting. I saw only two people who drank and behaved badly during my whole stay there. Disabled people got access to facilities. They have access to a normal life. They have entry facilities everywhere. Every individual is given the ownership and the responsibility to do his work.

Holy Places and Belief Systems

I visited several holy places including Westminster Abbey, King's College Chapel, Bath Cathedral, Salisbury Cathedral and Canterbury Cathedral. These places were calm and peaceful. I also practiced candle lighting and wrote my wish. Though I am an agnostic theist, I participated in these activities just to completely involve myself and fully absorb the experience of the environment. There are pseudoscientific practices as well such as Clairvoyance.

Seminars

I searched for free psychology seminars in Event bright. I found a few important and interesting seminars. I attended the seminars- (1) "Global Mental Health: Can talking therapies help?" (2) "Six differences in the needs of men and women in therapy" and (3) "2 Day Free Foundation NLP Training, Time Line Therapy & Hypnosis". I gained immense knowledge along with a NLP training certificate.

Tributes to Legendary People

I visited places like Freud museum, Kenwood Court and Karl Marx Grave to pay homage to the great people who once lived in London. A guide helped me understand significance of each and every object at Freud Museum. I felt amazed when I visited Sherlock museum. Though he never existed physically, he lives in minds of people. This is the reason I include him in my list of legendary people.

Treasures at Royal Palaces

I visited Lead Castle, Dover Castle, Hampton Palace, and Kensington Palace. All castles consisted of beautiful buildings surrounded by pleasant green gardens on all sides. There are beautiful water bodies in the gardens and they are main tourist attractions. Passage on a bridge surrounded by water is the unique feature of Lead Castle. Dover Castle is surrounded by beach with typical stones. Hampton Palace is surrounded by garden with trees and fountains. Kensington Palace has garden with arches made of Plants.

Tower of London consisted of several castles. It is filled with ancient armory. When I entered one of the buildings, I saw a few golden ornaments. When I entered inside, only one thing attracted me. It was shining brilliantly and distracting vision. It was almost forcing everyone to look at it. Curious, I went near it and saw that it was the 'Kohinoor Diamond'.

Night Life

I took a night bus tour and went for dinner several times. All the shops are closed in the evening by 5pm in most of the areas. Lights in the city are amazing. The city felt different in the night with all the glittering lights.

Examinations and Research

Students were asked to complete group projects in information technology and entrepreneurship. We presented individual research work in cross cultural study course. An important learning was team work. We made a group project on online therapy and my individual research was on mental health awareness and stigma.

I had an idea how to conduct research and publish a research paper before coming to London. After thoroughly reading the literature, and interacting with my faculty, I decided to narrow my research to pilot study by taking into account constraints like time, sources and requirements. I found that the mental health awareness is lower in India and is higher in London. Disparity could be explained in terms of stigma, pseudoscientific practices and cultural core beliefs.

I conducted a survey to estimate the mental health awareness. Survey was carried out on 89 people – 67 from India and 22 from London. Among them, 51.8% were females and 48.2% were males. They belong to a wide variety of religions and economic backgrounds. 18% of them studied psychology as an academic subject. Their age range is from 14 to 57 years. They were administered a questionnaire with ten questions. The survey measured the ability to recognize mental disorders, understanding causes, readiness to take self-help, belief in therapy, knowledge about mental health professionals, knowledge about mental health system.

Mean scores of participants from India and London are 5.5 and 8.4 out of 10 respectively. None of the subjects from London scored below 5.

I also carried out an observational study. Settings chosen for observational study were: (1) Mental health awareness programmes (2) Places where pseudoscientific method are practiced and (3) Conferences.

It was evident that programmes were being conducted to improve the mental awareness in London. A programme called Punk for mental health: Commercial Zone 2014 was auctioned to raise money for mental health research. It was conducted by London-based psychologist Dr. Joel Vos a.k.a. "the Punk Professor" at the Punk4MentalHealth festival 27 – 31 March 2017. It comprised of a series of events across London including live music and a reading from the DIY book, mental health talks and DIY presentations.

Pseudoscientific practices target mental health issues in India as well as in London. In India, astrology, exorcism, kundalini, pranic healings are popular. In London, clairvoyance, dianetics and NLP are very popular. However, Indian pseudoscientific practices have deep cultural roots.

Many conferences were conducted by British Psychological Society in London. In India, the conferences target the students, where as in London, they target common people. There was a psychologist reflective group which helps psychologists to cope up with the burnout. However, it could not attract many therapists and therefore got cancelled.

Return Journey

I got so adapted to London, that I felt very sad while leaving. Thinking and remembering about places that I have visited, the work that I accomplished and people whom I have met brought back a happy smile on my face when I was at the airport. Thought I went to London with doubts and questions in my mind, I came back invigorated and richer from the experience, motivated and fuller with self-confidence.

ACKNOWLEDGEMENTS

- I am extremely thankful to Dr. Anupama Rajesh for giving me an opportunity to write my experiences.
- I am thankful to Mr. Luke Minshall for his continuous guidance and supervision during SAP programme.
- I am thankful to Amity University for providing me an opportunity to travel abroad.
- I am thankful to all coordinators and teachers of SAP programme.

- I am thankful to my friends and family for their encouragement and support.
- I thank my friend Praneet Kaur for her company and support.
- I am thankful to all my friends and family for their encouragement and support.

*   *   *

Business with Pleasure

AUTHOR BIO

Suparna Arora

Suparna did her M.B.A from the University of Lucknow specializing in International Business after completing her Bachelor degree in Commerce and one year of M.Com in Applied Economics.

She worked for Marketec Systems and launched Organic teas with Bio dynamic cultivation in India in 1997 while also establishing the retail and corporate network.

For the same company she set up the marketing office in New Delhi for Jute products for the international market liaising with buying agents and buying houses, and organizing International fairs, she was also credited with getting the company one of their biggest orders from the Japanese segment.

She also worked for Pardesh Agencies Pvt. Ltd, a Buying house again a start-up and helped in building the supply network in India and marketing internationally mainly the United Kingdom and the European Market. She successfully brought Zara home, part of Inditex to India.

She moved to Canada and after getting her Investment license and worked as a financial advisor for the National Bank of Canada. She was very involved in training new hires in their role as Financial advisors.

At the moment she is voluntarily involved in a NGO project in USA.

Business with Pleasure

Suparna Arora

2001- My boss called me to his office and told me that I was flying to London in two weeks. I was working in a buying house which was a start-up in India by a friend. Let's call her Maggie. Maggie and I had known each other for many years. I had been working in the International Business division and contacted her for business. I never got any business from her but loved hanging around at her office cum home. She was of French origin and extremely creative.

One day I received a call from her. She mentioned that she had started a company with a friend who eventually became my boss. She had to urgently leave India and wanted me to handle her role in the business. The company was started to source Home and Lifestyle products from India for the International market. My role was to set up the business in India, as I had good understanding of the supply market. I also had been dealing with International Buyers.

My Boss was of Scottish origin, loved India with a passion, and couldn't imagine living anywhere except India.

We had bagged a very good buyer's account and my boss wanted me to see London and Paris to understand the International market, and get a good understanding of the Buyer side.

The first step was to get the Visa. I collected all the required paper-work and sponsor documents. Passing through lots of security checks and after waiting in a long queue, I finally got my number called for the interview with the Visa Officer. Just thirty minutes were left for the British High Commissions' Visa issuing office to close. The Visa Officer after asking detailed questions; asked me to present personal bank account details. As my company was sponsoring the trip and it was a Business trip I had not bothered to carry my personal statement. The officer told me that if I came back with the statement on the same day she would see me immediately, otherwise I had to go through the formalities all over again. Mobile phones were not allowed inside the High Commission. I had no idea where the car was parked as I had been dropped off at the gate by the office chauffeur. While walking to the gate I started going through my purse, not having any expectations I saw a paper which was a recent ATM receipt. My visa was immediately stamped.

Meetings and appointments booked, I landed at Heathrow Airport on a Friday night.

My boss didn't want me to stay by myself on my first trip so he had arranged for me to stay at a friend's place. They had recently renovated their attic and converted it in to a big bedroom with an attached bath. This is actual luxury in London. Mostly, older houses share bathrooms. There is usually one tiny bathroom to be shared by all members of the family. Though the water heating system is centrally regulated; which I learned during the trip.

I got the weekend to get a feel of the city; I realized I could get a mixed experience of work and leisure. So I tried making most of the opportunity. I decided to take the Hop-On and Hop-Off Bus and see the city. This is the best way one could see London. The buses are around frequently. When weather gets a little chilly, the lower level provides a break from the cold open air of the double decker bus.

The London "must see" bucket list included trips to the Tower Bridge, Westminster Palace, Change of Guards Ceremony at Buckingham Palace and the Big Ben. Immersed in history the city's buildings are unique and have grand architecture.

As time was a constraint I could not stop at many tourist stops. The museums were highly recommended but I decided to give them a miss; I wanted to visit Madame Tussauds. All the wax statues in Madame Tussauds are separated in different categories. There is the Hollywood section, Royal family section, and Religious leaders. Our Bollywood actors during those days were slowly being installed but now they have created an extensive section for them.

At Madame Tussauds, I was warned at the entrance that a certain area could be scary! I met a student visiting Madame Tussauds, she was travelling around Europe by herself, with no words exchanged between us we found ourselves taking the tour together. The funniest moment was her talking and asking for information at the information desk; not realizing they were wax mannequins. She didn't realize until I told her. Many a times I was also asking for direction or standing in line behind people who were very realistic mannequins.

At the end of first days' tour, when I reached my host's house I was welcomed to one of United Kingdom's traditional meal - Shepherd's Pie. It was delicious, and they shared the recipe with me which has been my prized possession from my London trip.

The advantage of staying at a local resident's home is, that there is a part of London only the locals know about. Green spaces, hidden markets and canals! London has everything.

London is a city with rich history and culture along with fine foods with sheer diversity. The pubs are the heart of London life. They are dotted all over the city. They are frequented by "after-work" crowd and best place to experience the brews.

Stratford-upon-Avon developed upon the banks of the River Avon is one of Britain's most popular towns for visitors, the birth place and land of William Shakespeare. Getting there from London about 100 miles away, takes approximately two hours thirty minutes or maybe a little less. I had always wanted to see Shakespeare's home town. Having studied in a Catholic school with Irish nuns, we had Shakespeare plays in our curriculum since Grade 7. Our teachers brought the plays to life by the way they read them to us. We were made to enact certain scenes while studying them, and basically learned to love Shakespeare.

The train journey was a wonderful experience, the train moved forward leaving behind the trappings of urbanity and welcoming the lush greenery. The train passed through beautiful meadows punctuated by villages and small towns. Shakespeare's house has been preserved intact on Henley Street. Shakespeare's acting career was spent with the Lord Chamberlain's Company, where he was considered a first rate actor. He returned to Stratford-upon-Avon in his later years where he died at the age of 52.

Monday morning was extremely unnerving and exciting. I had to travel on the Tube also known as The London Underground, changing two trains and meeting our most important clients all by myself, something my Boss so far always handled.

All I can say is, do not depend on the aging transportation system to get you to the meetings on time. The London Underground can be extremely unreliable, forcing the passengers to lengthy alternate routes. Londoners expect promptness, so make sure to have a time buffer when going for meetings.

Coming back to the appointment; the company which I was visiting, had started their growth with us. They started as a Mail Catalogue and had recently opened their first store at a prime location. They made impeccably stylish and beautifully designed products. They believed in style not fashion; and quality with attention to detail. They dealt in full range of lifestyle products.

The office was in an Industrial area; it was first time I saw a completely open concept office which are very common now. They had a sleep/ resting room for their employees. They also provided neck and back massages to them! This was again a completely new concept to me. Technology companies all over the world are famous for now taking extra care of their employees, making sure that they stay in office, "later the better".

I was taken around the office. Seeing the actual buying procedure followed by the company: from designing, sampling, final selection and placing orders. This actually helped me to understand timelines, quality standards and the buyer's mindset. Logistics was another important area for me. This particular buyer as it was a Mail catalogue and now had a store. Packing, labeling and shipping in the correct pallet was a top priority. Meeting the buyer develops and improves relationships and the understanding of the needs helps to increase the business. Communication helped me to work on a line which the buyer was not even aware that India could do. The advantage we had over China; for this market was that we were open to designs, sampling and could do small quantity orders. Yes we spoke the same language, comfortably!

I learned a lot from this visit. A retail buyer focuses on product; they research trends, and are responsible for selecting the products that will appear in store or on mail catalogues. The merchandisers ensure financial and commercial viability of the product selected. They also ensure that stock flows to the business where it will sell the most. The buyer and the merchandiser work together to deliver the selected product range to the customer; at the right place at the right time, and most importantly at the right price.

After an exhausting day of work the company staff wanted to take me out for dinner. They decided to take me out to a famous 'Fish and Chips' restaurant. There is nothing more British than fish and chips. Generally they are eaten freshly cooked wrapped in newspaper and eaten outdoors on a cold wintry day. It is considered a national dish. There was a time that fish and chips had become an essential diet to the common man. I was not taken to the small take away shops but to an expensive fish and chips restaurant, where I tried the beer battered fish and chips.

The next day, I had an appointment with a Fabric buyer who had a small store but was expanding very fast. She was considering importing fabric from other parts of the world. She was located in a beautiful town. This town was full of blooming gardens, tree lined streets and fresh country air. The town was extremely picturesque. All the people on the streets seemed very laid back and polite. Older people seemed to have all the time to talk whenever I stopped to ask for directions. So very different from the hustle bustle of London life; it was very enjoyable to sit by the roadside quaint tea shop and sip hot English tea. There were fruit shops on the road side. I spotted the fruit raspberry which had been referred many times for colour and I had always wanted to taste it. I immediately bought it. The fruit was beautifully wrapped in a small paper box. I didn't realize that this particular fruit was very sensitive to heat and by morning due to the room heating had started to get mouldy.

Mobile phones were there but small companies like ours did not provide them to their employees for International travel, at least not back then. Things did change in a year or two with the way technology has advanced. No one could have thought that smart phones would completely change business communication. At that time internet was not easily available. At the end of the day I used go to the nearest Internet café to check my email.

My office assistant forwarded me an email for an important appointment which got missed due to the lack of communication and time difference. Something which would not happen in today's world of communication.

It was 9:00 pm and the sun had not set yet. It took me a day to get used to having dinner in full day light. Now settled in the United States I eat my dinner at 6:00 pm!!

The trip to London was almost over. There had been many exciting and anxious moments in a new country. There was something about London, probably the diversity which had made me feel at home instantly. I had to go further to Paris via the Eurostar. It's one of the quickest routes between the two countries. Flying is a quick way but going to the airport checking in hours earlier, makes train travel an easier and faster way of travelling between the two countries. The very thought that it speeds underwater via the Channel Tunnel is exciting but I noticed nothing as the view outside the window was of absolute darkness. The Eurostar train arrived right in the heart of Paris, at Gare du Nord station. Another Country and several other experiences to pen down!

*   *   *

Brexit- From the Eye of a Londoner

AUTHOR BIO

Leena Chand

Leena is a Therapist by profession and is settled in United Kingdom after marriage. She is born and brought up in New Delhi, India. Growing up in a multi-cultural city like New Delhi helped her adjust well to the multi-ethnic culture of London in particular; and United Kingdom in general. Her quest to explore new things and a constant desire to challenger her own abilities guided her journey from healthcare profession to Management. She studied International Business at Indian Institute of Foreign Trade, India, from where she broadened her management concepts. She has also worked in Banking Industry in the past but her heart lies in healthcare.

She enjoys various pursuits and writing is one of them. When not working she spends most of the time with her daughter. She also has a creative bone and embarks on various creative papercraft projects. She enjoys dual responsibilities of a healthcare profession and a mother. With a supportive husband she always finds time for activities she is interested in.

Brexit- From the Eye of a Londoner

Leena Chand

A word of caution for the readers - If you are expecting this article to enlighten your insight into Brexit from a macro economical perspective then please stop reading now and get on with your other important chores (may be its time to wash your laundry). This article is only about how I as a Londoner have observed Brexit so you may not come across fancy management jargons like Trade Agreements, Passporting etc. But if you have anyways decided to carry on reading then may be grab a cup of tea.

Dynamics of Brexit

Who am I first? I am just another Londoner who works to pay the bills and quite wishfully enjoys doing it. And it was business as usual until 23rd June 2016. This is the day which shocked lot of people around the world. Yes, Britain decided to leave Europe after its referendum held for the second time. What was interested to see was the turnout of the voters who voted to leave. The turnout was high at 72%, with more people turning out to vote than in 2015 general election. Over 30 million people voted. *(http://www.bbc.co.uk/news/uk-politics-36616028)* Mostly younger people like me voted to remain. Londoners voted to remain. So quite rightly so to say I was shocked to see the results. London is very multi ethnic so it might have had impact on voting as most of the areas who voted to remain has more English population *(http://www.bbc.co.uk/news/uk-politics-36616028)*. I am mentioning all this so as to make readers understand dynamics of Brexit. I believe it would be wrong to say that the underlying sentiment for leave were based on race but rather according to my understanding it is more about dissatisfaction rising amongst the Britons who have seen the days where they didn't had to wait for months for NHS appointment for a knee surgery for example. Britain has a growing ageing population as according to the office of National Statistics. In 2015 Britain's population consisted of 63% between ages 16 to 64. There is large number of 68 years olds due to the spike in the birth-rate after the end of World War II. Life expectancy over the last few decades has been steadily increasing which can be owed to improving healthcare and lifestyles more so for population aged 65 years and above.

(https://www.ons.gov.uk/peoplepopulationandcommunity/populationandmigration/populationestimates/articles/overviewoftheukpopulation/mar2017)

All of the above statistics imply that there will be even more pressure on healthcare in the coming years. Not something any British citizen looks forward to and hence Britons who are in favour of "Leave Campaign" want to curb free movement of people into the United Kingdom to improve healthcare access, and this was indeed one of the major points of the Leave Campaign where they showed or rather predicted how NHS waiting list could improve post Brexit.

It is definitely a joyous and proud matter for any country to mention that its population's life expectancy is improving and the nation boasts about its improving healthcare system but this also reflects that in the coming years there will be less working population to support pensioners. In 2016, there were an estimated 308 people of a pensionable age for every 1,000 people of a working age. By 2037, this is projected to increase to 365 people. This increase means that there will be fewer people of working age to support a larger population over State Pension age. While a larger population increases the size and productive capacity of the workforce, it also increases pressure and demand for services such as education, healthcare and housing.

(https://www.ons.gov.uk/peoplepopulationandcommunity/populationandmigration/ populationestimates/articles/overviewoftheukpopulation/mar2017)

Not to forget the discontent of Britons over EU nationals' encroaching shares on UK's benefits and social Housing. The DWP analysis says European Uunion migrants on "in-work" benefits cost the taxpayer £530m in 2013. That represents a modest 1.6% of the year's total tax credit bill.

(https://www.theguardian.com/uk-news/datablog/2015/nov/10/eu-migrants-on-benefits-separating-the-statistics-from-the-spin)

However, to inform the readers, just as European Union nationals can claim benefits in United Kingdom; Britons can claim Benefits of other European countries as well. At least 30,000 British nationals are claiming unemployment benefit in countries around the EU. Research by the Guardian has found, based on responses from 23 of the 27 other EU countries, about 2.5% of Britons in other EU countries are claiming unemployment benefits – the same level as roughly 65,000 EU nationals claiming jobseeker's allowance in the UK. The picture is quite different for the poorer east European countries which have joined the EU over the past decade, with hardly any Britons drawing unemployment benefits in those countries.

(https://www.theguardian.com/uk-news/2015/jan/19/-sp-thousands-britons-claim-benefits-eu)

The fear of transferring more control to Brussels, were one of dominant factor for Euro sceptics in Parliament to draw Britain into second referendum. A lot has changed in the dynamics of European Union since first referendum held in UK in 1975 with new countries been added from East Europe. After EU enlargement in 2004 the UK experienced a far greater influx of East Europeans than had been anticipated. *(http://www.bbc.co.uk/news/world-europe-25134521)*

Healthcare, benefits and growing migrants from East European countries were quite dominant points in "Leave Campaign".

My Perspective

Now that we have had a glance at Brexit dynamics, let's revert back to our original topic. How do I see its impact? Well my world has not changed upside down after Brexit. I still work in a very multi ethnic environment with great harmony. I still have an Italian as my best friend. I eat Danish in my breakfast, drive German to work, sleeps on Swedish self-assembled bed, enjoy Italian feast with friends on Friday night and my daughter's favourite bread loaf is French.

I do wonder though will it still be that easy for me to go on holidays to Spain as it used to be earlier. Earlier, I could just plan my trip today, pack my bag and leave tomorrow and worth mentioning that sometimes the cost of flight to European countries are cheaper than flying to Scotland, but what now after Brexit? I would surely need more planning, book my annual leave well in advance, get visa and then fly. Not that I would mind doing so as this has its own fun but it would certainly need some time to get used to this kind of holiday planning.

What about the holiday home I was planning to buy in Tenerife? That would surely need to go on hold for now. There is certainly an impact seen on real estate market in parts of Europe post Brexit. Britons accounted for 14.5 per cent of purchases of Spanish homes by foreigners in the first quarter, according to Spain's property registry. That's the lowest proportion since the registry began compiling data in 2006.In 2016, UK buyers made up 19 per cent of home purchases by non-Spaniards. That compares with 38 per cent in 2008 when British appetite for buying Spanish holiday homes was at its peak. Britons bought about 2,175 homes in Spain in the first quarter of 2017, down from about 2,800 in 2016, according to calculations based on data from the registry.

(http://www.independent.co.uk/news/business/news/brexit-spain-holiday-home-buy-afford-eu-european-union-a7750586.html)

But it definitely made me think about those Britons who have already bought houses in Europe. Well if someone has a holiday home only then may be not a massive difference apart from change in taxation on rental income and inheritance tax   *(http://www.solicitorsinspain.com/articles/how-will-brexit-affect-british-property-owners-spain)* and yes, I have heard of visa waivers but that all depends on when eventually the process of separation begins. But more uncertainty is hovering on those who have settled there permanently. It will have an impact on how they get access to healthcare and benefits in that country. However, negotiations are continuing to protect rights for both EU nationals moved to UK and Britons in EU before Brexit as much as possible. What will exactly be the outcome only time will tell!

Talking of the real estate prices in London well I have not seen much fluctuation in property prices in London as there is always shortage of housing in London and more so for social housing but, as discussed above, Brexit might impact real estate market of places in EU where the majority buyers are Expats/Britons.

I believe it is too early to understand the impact of Brexit on overall economy of Britain but yes, some impact I saw quite quickly was of David Cameroon resigning from the post of Prime Minister. I did not want to see him leave, as did many others. On the flip side, it marked another interesting event which was Britain getting its second female prime minister

By becoming Britain's second female Prime Minister, Theresa May has made the country just the sixth in Europe (and 17th in the world) to have had more than one female leaders. *(https://www.washingtonpost.com/news/monkey-cage/wp/2016/07/16/so-the-u-k-has-its-second-female-prime-minister-what-policies-put-more-women-in-power/?utm_term=.b91793da7591)*

It is fascinating to see how in a day one decision can bring so many changes in nation and to its people. Unfortunately, some changes were more worrisome socially then economically. I am talking about surge in hate crime post Brexit. Many of Police Stations in England and Wales saw record levels of hate crimes in the first full three months following the EU Referendum. According to new analysis, more than 14,000 hate crimes were recorded between July and September 2016. In October 2016 the Home Office published provisional figures which suggested the number of hate crimes in July 2016 had been 41% higher than 12 months earlier. (http://www.bbc.co.uk/news/uk-38976087) But in the midst of this political upheaval Britain only came out strong and showed that it has and will always stand for justice and abide by the law.

Another negative impact could be its effect on funding of research in the field of healthcare. Hospitals like Great Ormond street has expressed concerns that the loss of European funding for medical research could cost the lives of some vulnerable children. Since 2010, Great Ormond street hospital received £25 million from European Union to fund research for developing new treatments. This approximates to its 10% of budget for research. The Great Ormond street hospital also mentioned that it fears losing its EU staff and long-standing EU partnerships. *(http://www.bbc. co.uk/news/uk-england-london-36863872)*

What Next?

Article 50 has been invoked and Britain is officially on its way out of the European Union after 44 years as a member. It's a long union and we may say we have left Europe, but have we really? Well not really yet because the time-frame allowed in Article 50 is two years so there is still time for complete divorce. (http://www.bbc. co.uk/news/uk-politics-39143978). As quite interestingly depicted in Ancestry DNA advertisements, that average British person's DNA is 60% European so we may be leaving Europe but Europe will never leave us.

* * *

REFERENCES

http://www.bbc.co.uk/news/uk-politics-36616028

https://www.ons.gov.uk/peoplepopulationandcommunity/populationandmigration/populationestimates/articles/overviewoftheukpopulation/mar2017

https://www.theguardian.com/uk-news/datablog/2015/nov/10/eu-migrants-on-benefits-separating-the-statistics-from-the-spin

https://www.theguardian.com/uk-news/2015/jan/19/-sp-thousands-britons-claim-benefits-eu

http://www.bbc.co.uk/news/world-europe-25134521

http://www.independent.co.uk/news/business/news/brexit-spain-holiday-home-buy-afford-eu-european-union-a7750586.html

https://www.washingtonpost.com/news/monkey-cage/wp/2016/07/16/so-the-u-k-has-its-second-female-prime-minister-what-policies-put-more-women-in-power/?utm_term=.b91793da7591

http://www.bbc.co.uk/news/uk-38976087

http://www.bbc.co.uk/news/uk-politics-39143978

My London Diary

AUTHOR BIO

Aryan Kumar

Aryan is a diligent student striving to achieve his goals. He is currently pursuing Bachelor of Business Administration from Amity School of Business, Noida. He has completed his schooling from Amity International School and scored a perfect 10 CGPA in class 10th and a very respectable 91% in class 12th. He was the subject topper in Accountancy and Informatics Practices.

Aryan has always been an all-rounder with enthusiastic participation in sports and extracurricular activities. He has competed in various swimming, tennis and IT events and excelled in all facets. He is an extrovert who likes to interact with people and learn from their experiences.

My London Diary

Aryan Kumar

London, the heart of England, and the place almost every one wishes to visit at least once. There is something about this place which attracts people. Is it a combination of culture, beauty, people, and hospitality or is it something else? Everyone has their own reasons. Currently I am in my last teenage year which is 19 and I will be 20 by the time this book is published. Like any other teenager, I dream to travel the world and to fulfil the feeling of wanderlust, I have travelled to several places in India and abroad. In India I have covered Tamil Nadu, Karnataka, Kerala, Maharashtra and I am eagerly waiting to visit Hyderabad. I want to repeat my trip to Goa but this time with my friends. Internationally I have visited Paris, Dubai, Singapore, Moscow and obviously the heart of England and the place which will stay in my heart forever - London, home to the great river Thames.

London is situated in south east Britain. London is the most populous city of England and one of the most important financial centres of the world. London is home to more than 3 million people out of whom around 40% are foreign born; including nationals from India, United States, Russia, Australia, other European countries and countless others. More than 300 languages are spoken in London. The most dominant religion there is Christianity followed by Hinduism, Islam, Buddhism, and Judaism etc. Interestingly the city has the highest number of billionaires of the world. The number is a staggering 72.

The city is considered to be the fashion capital of the world. Some people go to London especially for shopping. It is one of the four most fashionable cities in the world. The people of London and their fashion sense have a huge impact on the global fashion trends. London is like an iceberg - it has more to it than you think. There are many facts I learned while exploring this beautiful place. I recorded numerous facts to preserve my memory of London. Some of them which I would like to share are:

- The famous House of Parliament is the largest palace of the country.
- Interestingly, it is illegal to die in the House of Parliament.
- Big Ben is a bell, not a Clock Tower.
- The weirdest pub name in London is "I am the only Running Footman" in Mayfair.
- There is a train station on Thames that has its entrances on the both sides of the river.

- The Aldgate Station is home to a massive pit where approximately 100 bodies were buried.
- Contrary to its name, more than half of the Tube Network runs above the ground in London.
- The "Black Cab" drivers in London have to master all the routes and need to know all the landmarks and streets in order to pass the test to become a cabdriver.
- Harrods's sold cocaine till 1916.
- London's GDP is significantly more than many European countries.

There are countless more facts to this delightful place and listing them all would not be an easy task. London is like the ocean, the more you explore it, the more secrets are uncovered.

The Travel

In the summer of 2015, my family decided to go for a vacation but this time to a place exotic and classy. We have a family tradition to go on a vacation every year. We either take a domestic vacation or an international one. In the summer of 2015, I suggested that we should take a trip to the United States, mainly covering the West Coast including Los Angeles, San Diego, San Francisco and many more places. Later on before finalizing anything, our plan got delayed. As my vacations were about to get over and we did not have enough time to apply for a United States visa, my father suggested that we should tour Europe and The Great Britain. The travel plan initially was to tour the major European countries and Britain. Initially, that seemed like a viable option, but once we brainstormed the itinerary, we came to a conclusion that this would probably not be a good idea as we would have to skip several important and prestigious attractions. We finally decided to cover the whole of Europe part by part. For the trip we narrowed down to visit to London and Paris, two of the most iconic and most visited cities in the world. Our preparations for the trip started by applying for the necessary travel documents; making stay arrangements and informing relatives and friends in the UK of our plans. A very funny moment which I remember happening before the trip was when my mother came back from office one day and found my father packing all his clothes for the trip. She took away his bag and completely emptied it. She said that we all would take empty bags with us and will do all the necessary shopping in London. We would take only one or two sets of clothes for the journey and the rest will be bought from London only. This was a fantastic idea and was fun at the same time to go to foreign lands with empty bags and do all our shopping over there.

Finally the day arrived, the day of the travel. Our flight was at 4:00 am in the morning and we had to leave the house by 11:00 pm the previous night. After doing a final check of the luggage we were carrying and locking the house; we left the house at 11:00 pm sharp and reached the airport within no time. The thing with my family is that we like to reach the airports early so that we can shop from duty-free shops and have headroom for being late, so it is a win-win situation! We had an Indigo flight to Moscow first and then we had a connecting flight to London after a four hour layover at Moscow! I had not eaten my dinner because of the packing rush at home, so I ate at the airport lounge. I and my father bought some snacks from the duty-free shops like chocolates, beverages and other eatables. We were certain that we would have pot-bellies by the end of the trip. Subsequently, we boarded the flight, slept peacefully and reached Moscow. We realized that we had missed the in-flight beverages because we were sleeping but we didn't really care that much. Moscow, already visited by us earlier, was a familiar place especially the airport. We had to spend four hours in the Moscow Airport so we basically toured the whole airport, explored every small outlet over there, did some shopping for some native Russian items and had brunch. One interesting thing I noticed was that the Russian Mcdonalds is my favourite so far out of all the Mcdonalds I've seen in other countries.

After touring the whole airport, we rested a bit and boarded the connecting flight to Heathrow airport. After spending reasonable amount of time in the flight we finally reached London. A remarkable thing with London is that once you are in London you start to behave in the most British way ever i.e. - being polite, talking respectfully, being courteous etc. I don't know why this happens but I really like it. We completed the immigration formalities at the airport, took a cab and went to the hotel which was near Central London. We were staying at The Marriot which is considered to be one of the best hotel chains there. We had our evening snacks at the hotel and went out for a walk in casual attire around the area. The day was well spent. We ate good food, the weather was great, the hotel was nice and the people were extremely helpful. I sensed that this would be a start to a perfect vacation. From the next day till the end of our London trip we visited some of the most amazing places, tried the local cuisine, interacted with some of the most generous locals and learn a lot about Britain. The most memorable places we visited were:

The London Eye

The ticket for London Eye is quite expensive and the line to get aboard was long, but once you enter the capsule and reach the topmost point; you get the best view of London. Honestly, it felt that I could see most of London from the top. There is this beautiful view you get from the top of the river Thames as well. If you are familiar with London, then you can also spot The Big Ben and Harrods. The London Eye is supposedly the tallest Ferris wheel in Europe and one of the tallest in the world. It was inaugurated in 1999 and consists of 32 pods, each of which can hold up to 25 people.

The Big Ben

A remarkable thing I learnt when I visited this great tower is that the name "Big Ben" refers to the bell that hangs in the tower. Otherwise its name is the Clock Tower of London. Honestly the tower is good to look at, nothing extraordinary. The most interesting thing about the bell is its mechanism and the way it works. The Big Ben, which is the biggest bell out of the four in the tower, rings every hour and rings once for every hour at that time. The other four bells ring every 15 minutes. The sound of these bells is melodious and it reminds you of classic British movies of the 80's and 90's. The clock does not run on electricity, rather it works by winding up the weights it is attached to. Electricity is only used to power the lights so the clock can be visible at night.

Buckingham Palace

Being in London, we also visited Buckingham Palace. Since childhood I had dreamt of visiting a proper English palace where the King and the Queen would reside. This idea came because of all the cartoon films I had seen in my childhood. I learnt that Buckingham Palace is the place where Her Majesty and her Royal Associates carry out their duties as the Head of the State. An interesting fact is that over 50,000 people visit the palace as the queen's guests at banquets, lunches, dinners, receptions etc. every year. In 2002, to honour the Queen for her golden jubilee, more than one million people gathered in front of the palace. Imagine the crowd cheering and the thrill! The most famous part of the palace is the royal balcony where Her Majesty the Queen herself on several major occasions appears and greets the crowd.

Harrods

One of the most beautiful attractions of London would be "Harrods". Harrods is actually a luxury departmental store which is one of the main tourist attractions of London. It is spread over five acres of ground, consisting of seven floors with a total area of around one Million square feet! This marvel took four years to build. Harrods had the very first moving staircase in London. Harrods is covered with thousands of lights (around 12000) as was told by a very friendly employee I befriended there. The whole building stands out at night and looks absolutely beautiful at night when those lights are turned on. The employee told me that the motto of Harrods is "All Things for All People, Everywhere" and they take this motto very seriously. In the 20ᵗʰ century, they even had a python guarding a very expensive set of sandals; they sold alligators and even elephants! This was incredible to hear. I bought myself some cool gadgets and peripherals from there. It was an incredible experience.

The Culture

The overall experience was pleasant and positive. I learnt an unbelievable number of things about United Kingdom. Although there were some negative aspects to the trip, I mostly enjoyed the experience. I would like to throw some light on the British culture. The very first thing that comes to your mind when you think about a Briton is that they are very co-operative and friendly. They have an extremely formal way of talking and have been nurtured to treat everyone with respect. I feel that about 90% of the Briton's are indeed like this. They are very helpful and have a pleasant personality. They prefer individualism over group work. Yes that's true. The thing with them is that they seek privacy from unknown people and do not trust anyone or everything. They do not open up to people very easily and are reserved till you get to know them properly. As they are very reserved, they do not like to boast in any form. This came as a surprise to me as I thought British people are quite proud of their country and themselves. They would seek out opportunity to vaunt but surprisingly this isn't the case. They prefer to keep quiet about their achievements and tell people about their failures.

I had also noticed that Brits are very proud of their motherland, their diversity, their cultural and their heritage. They do not appreciate it when someone talks negatively about their country. This actually makes sense; this type of feeling should be there in the hearts of everyone for their country.

For the first time in my life, I was conscious of the time. We had this sort of a fixed schedule every day for our travel. So I constantly had to monitor my timings for everything. Actually this was because of the time consciousness of the British, they are extremely punctual, and do not like to be late at all. They are very careful of their time as well as others. They would neither be later nor early. I remember an instance where our relatives had hosted a dinner and invited us and some of their colleagues over to their house for a casual dinner. We were advised by our relatives to be punctual. I found this pretty odd initially but later accepted this as a solution to avoid any embarrassments.

The Britons take their work seriously and schedule their activities accordingly. Labour laws are strict in London. They work within fixed timings and often do not do overtime or leave late.

To discuss another interesting aspect: food; well most of the food is pretty bland in flavour at least for the Indian palate who are used to spices and variety of flavours in their cuisine which Indians also anticipate in other cuisines. English diet includes various meats, gravies, sauces, puddings etc. Traditional English breakfast consists of a sunny-side-up fried egg, toasted bread, butter and fried bacon give a healthy start to the day. They also sometimes take cereals with milk. I learned that the Brits love roasted beef. They consider it as their national culinary pride. They also love pasties, fish and chips, usually accompanied with beer. The Brits usually choose Cod for their fish preparation.

The British have their own variety of cheese available. They also like sandwiches and roasted chicken. Indian cuisine is famous over there. More and more people prefer Indian cuisine whenever they have to go out and eat. Indian food is extremely expensive even from a regular take-away or a dine-in place. Actually my family preferred to have Indian food over the traditionally available British cuisine at times. As an Indian, the Indian food we had there can be termed as merely satisfactory. Whenever we ordered Indian cuisine, we would usually order a non-vegetarian gravy based dish for me and my mother and another gravy based vegetable for my father, an entrée dish and some Chapattis or "Naans". Indian food made in Britain is towards the sweeter side and lacks flavours. I personally don't like the recipes they use and how they cooked the food. I believe a cuisine is best experienced from the place where it originated.

Our hotel was in central London. Central London is a hub of corporate offices, eating joints, pubs and shopping complexes. Every evening, I used to have fish and chips from different eating places. I found fish and chips to be the ultimate comfort food. My father relished freshly brewed beer, and tasted fresh brewed beer from as many pubs as possible. Another thing we learned is that no one should visit a London pub between 4 pm and 7 pm in the evening on weekdays as it would be packed with people coming straight from the office with their colleagues. We made this mistake once and had to wait for over an hour for our order.

Apart from food, I have to say that British people have a very good sense of style and dress. Most of the residents I saw over there were extremely well-dressed. This is mostly because of how inexpensive some apparel stores are in London. I was surprised that the same brands in India costed almost double the price. I bought myself two pairs of shoes, some great leather jackets, shirts, t-shirts and some pretty comfortable pair of jeans. I also bought myself a gaming console from a renowned retail brand.

London is a fantastic place. I really enjoyed my stay over there with my family, and look forward to visit the place with my friends in the future. The only thing I didn't like about the place was the number of tourists one sees at every major or minor hallmark over there, but then – the city's so exquisite that everyone wants to visit. Hence, we really cannot blame the popularity of London, can we?

*   *   *

ABOUT THE AUTHORS

Prof. (Dr.) Gurinder Singh

Group Vice Chancellor, Amity Universities

Prof. (Dr.) Gurinder Singh, Group Vice Chancellor - Amity Universities, Director General, Amity Group of Institutions and Vice Chairman, Global Foundation for Learning Excellence & Director General Amity International Business School, has an extensive experience of more than 21 years in Institutional Building, Teaching, Consultancy, Research & Industry.

A renowned scholar & academician in the area of International Business, he holds a prestigious Doctorate in the area along with a Post Graduate degree from Indian Institute of Foreign Trade where he illustriously topped with 7 merits.

He holds the distinction of being the youngest Founder Pro Vice Chancellor of Amity University for two terms, the Founder Director General of Amity International Business School and the Founder CEO of Association of International Business School, London. He has been instrumental in establishing various Amity campuses abroad including at London, USA, Singapore, Mauritius & other parts of the world.

To understand the dynamics of Industry, Dr. Singh went on a sabbatical to Industry for one and half years and spearheaded the indigenous and international strategic operations of a renowned Industrial group with a business strength of INR 200 billion in the capacity of Chief Executive Officer.

He has spoken at various international forums which includes prestigious Million Dollar Round Table Conference, at Harvard Business School, Thunderbird Business School, NYU, University of Leeds, Loughbrough Business School, Coventry Business School, Rennes Business School, Essex University, UK, University of Berkeley, California State University, USA, NUS, Singapore, and many more.

He has received more than 25 International and National awards and has graced a host of talk shows on various TV Channels.

He is a mesmerizing orator and has the rare ability of touching the human soul.

He is internationally recognized as a known Professor in the area of Management and is known in the field of academics as an institution builder, a writer, professor, distinguished academician, a top class trainer, International Business Expert & the Champion of the Hearts of Students.

Prof. (Dr.) Sanjeev Bansal

Dean - Faculty of Management Studies & Director, Amity Business School, Amity University Uttar Pradesh

Prof. (Dr.) Sanjeev Bansal is Dean FMS & Director of Amity Business School, Amity University Uttar Pradesh. Under his leadership ABS has scaled heights and has been ranked in the top ten Business Schools of India in four consecutive years in succession. An admired academician, he is Ph. D. and D. Litt., his doctoral work is an exemplary study in the area of Decision Sciences from Delhi. In an acclaimed career span of about 28 years in teaching, research and consultancy, he has been invited to be a part of several prestigious academic / professional bodies and in his advisory capacity, has steered them to success.

He is an avid researcher and has more than 150 research papers in prestigious journals to his credit. He has authored 27 books and has guided 17 research scholars to produce works of immense educational impact.

Apart from his areas of specialization, he also likes to explore and research the vistas of spirituality, management and quality of work life. During his distinguished career he has had many accomplishments and is hailed as an institution builder, a loved teacher and an ardent researcher.

Prof. (Dr.) Anupama Rajesh

Professor
Amity Business School, Amity University Uttar Pradesh, India

Prof. (Dr.) Anupama Rajesh is Professor at Amity Business School, Amity University, India. Her qualifications include Ph.D. in the area of Technology in Education, M.Phil. (IT), M.Phil. (Mgmt.), M.Ed., M.Sc. (IT), PGDCA, PGDBA. She has also been trained for Case Writing at INSEAD Paris. She has a teaching experience of about 20 years including international assignments which include a teaching stint in London and Singapore and training of Italian and French delegates and students. She has written more than 40 research papers and case studies for prestigious international journals and has eight books and several book chapters to her credit. She is reviewer of renowned Sage and Emerald journals. Her research interests are Business Intelligence, Educational Technology, Marketing Analytics etc. while her teaching interests are Business Intelligence, E-Commerce, IT enabled processes and so on.

She is an avid trainer and has trained Union Bank of India, NHPC, ILFS, TATA Motors, Bhutan Power Company employees as well as Commonwealth Games Volunteers and army personnel. She is a Master Trainer from Microsoft, Infosys Partner for Business Intelligence and Academic Partner for SAP ERM Sim.

She has recently won the ADMA Research Award and has also been awarded several Outstanding Paper Awards at prestigious conferences at institutes such as IIM Ahmedabad. She also has a MOOC to her credit.

Prateek Mangal

Director, SSR Management Consultants Pvt. Ltd.

Prateek works as the Director – Client Services, for SSR Management Consultants Pvt. Ltd. and is also a founding partner in an entrepreneurial venture – Shilp Metals Pvt. Ltd. An MBA from Indian Institute of Foreign Trade - Kolkata, and International University in Geneva, Switzerland; he is also a Diploma holder in Cyber Law from Asian School of Cyber Laws, Pune and has taken several courses on Big Data and Blockchain. He is also pursuing a doctorate degree with research focus on Big Data and Sustainable Development.

Prateek started his corporate journey with Triton Management Services and served the FMCG giant in Africa and India. He has eight years of experience in FMCG and Manufacturing Industry and is widely travelled across Asia, Africa and Europe and is an expert of International Trade.

Prateek has co-authored and edited a casebook titled "Compendium: Management Cases from Emerging Markets". He has authored several Book Chapters, Case Studies, and has presented and published research papers on key FMCG and manufacturing issues. His chapter on 'Marketing Analytics' has been published in the book "Stratégie: Business Intelligence & Analytics". He is also a prominent Social Worker and runs an NGO 'Neelabh Foundation' to finance studies of underprivileged children in Uttar Pradesh, India.

Nirav Sahni

Nirav, a 2018 graduate of McGill University (undergraduate business school) is an author of several management publications. His first book titled *'Compendium: Management Cases from Emerging Markets'* was published in 2016. Additionally in 2017, he co-authored a Deloitte thought leadership publication on the TMT sector. His research paper on FDI in India won the 2016 Renvoi International Case Competition and was subsequently published in a book titled the same. Nirav also holds to his name a case study on the co-operative sector published by the Case Centre, UK.

While at McGill, Nirav served on the Dean's advisory council for freshman engagement, was appointed a Teaching Assistant for the Entrepreneurship and Innovation course and ran a radio podcast show with Prof. Karl Moore (Top 50 Management thinkers of the World) called 'The CEO Series' having interviewed leaders that include- Justin Trudeau (Canadian Prime Minister), Muhammad Yunus (Nobel Prize Winner), Narayana Murthy (Infosys Chairman) and George Daley (Dean of Harvard). In 2017, he completed a 6 month project with McKinsey in their Montreal office and was recalled the subsequent year as mentor for the same program. For corporate experience, Nirav has worked at Deloitte for 3 consecutive summers across their strategy consulting, corporate finance and analytics teams. Prior to McGill, Nirav took courses in Financial Statistics and Economics at Harvard University and was ranked amongst the top 5% of his class and recommended by his professors. An avid learner with a keen interest in emerging markets, he has attended, been invited to and organized conferences at Harvard Business School and Columbia Business School and was also offered admission to IIT Delhi as a visiting student.